The Skyscraper in American Art, 1890-1931

The Skyscraper in American Art, 1890-1931

by
Merrill Schleier

A DA CAPO PAPERBACK

Library of Congress Cataloging in Publication Data

Schleier, Merrill.
  The skyscraper in American art, 1890-1931 / by Merrill Schleier.
      p.   cm. — (A Da Capo paperback)
  A revision of the author's thesis (Ph.D.) — University of
California, 1983.
  Reprint. Originally published: Ann Arbor, Mich.: UMI Research
Press, 1986.
  Includes bibliographical references.
  ISBN 0-306-80385-2
  1. Skyscrapers in art. 2. Arts, American. 3. Arts, Modern — 19th
century — United States. 4. Arts, Modern — 20th century — United
States. I. Title.
[NX650.S58S34   1990]   89-25608
704.9′44′097309041 — dc20   CIP

This Da Capo Press paperback edition of *The Skyscraper in
American Art, 1890-1931* is an unabridged republication of
the edition published in Ann Arbor, Michigan in 1986. It is
reprinted by arrangement with the UMI Research Press.

Published by Da Capo Press, Inc.
A Subsidiary of Plenum Publishing Corporation
233 Spring Street, New York, N.Y. 10013

Contents

Figures

Acknowledgments

The realization of this study would not have been possible without the generous support of the Smithsonian Institution. They not only provided the necessary finances to pursue my research, but created an atmosphere of intellectual growth and exchange. Throughout my tenure at the National Museum of American Art from 1979 to 1980, my mentors, the late Dr. Joshua Taylor and Dr. Judith Zilczer of the Hirshhorn Museum, provided valuable guidance and stimulated an interdisciplinary approach to the subject. Further appreciation is extended to Dr. Lois Fink, curator of research at the National Museum, who provided a forum for both intellectual discourse and comradeship among the research fellows.

The art history faculty at the University of California, Berkeley, nominated me for a Kress Fellowship to initiate the project. A subsequent Humanities Graduate Research Grant from the university facilitated the continuation of my research. My thanks to the late Mary Davis of the Kress Foundation for her belief in the pursuit of scholarship.

Appreciation is also extended to Pomona College and the American Council of Learned Societies for granting me a Graves Award. The generous stipend allowed me to finance the preparation of the manuscript and obtain the necessary photographic reproductions. I would also like to thank the University of the Pacific for giving me a Scholarly Activities Grant. Due to their joint assistance, I will be able to continue my interest in urban and industrial imagery, focusing on the period after the Depression.

My mentors at Berkeley, Dr. H. B. Chipp and Dr. Peter Selz, contributed long hours to evaluating the material presented in this study. Without their continued assistance and encouragement and their astute criticism, this book would not have been possible.

Dr. Dickran Tashjian of the University of California, Irvine, reviewed the manuscript tirelessly and thoroughly, offering suggestions concerning organization. Many of the ideas put forth in the final section were inspired by him. Homage is also paid to Dr. Wanda Corn, who evaluated the manuscript in its initial stages, and whose pioneer scholarship in American art and culture served as a model for this study.

For their assistance and professionalism, I am indebted to the staffs of the Archives of American Art in Washington, D.C., the Beinecke Rare Book and Manuscript Collection at Yale, the International Museum of Photography at the George Eastman House in Rochester, New York, the Museum of Modern Art Library, New York, and the libraries at the National Museum of American Art.

Last but not least, special acknowledgment is due to my husband, Glenn Lapp. His astute criticism, tireless devotion, and emotional support helped make this book a reality.

Introduction

Skyscrapers not only changed the city's topography, but they multiplied during a period when America's perception of itself was being questioned. The advent of the tall building, assertive symbol of technology and business acumen, reflected cultural changes that were taking place. Its mere presence prompted debates concerning material advancement to the detriment of human priorities, the relationship of business to spirituality, the expansion of cities at the expense of the land, and the position of American art and architecture in relation to European examples. Simply, the skyscraper was an anathema to observers such as William James, who sought to preserve traditional culture and ways of life, and as the pinnacle of ingenuity and progress to nationalists and modernists. Skyscraper images often embody these tensions.

It is important to separate depictions of skyscrapers from general representations of technology and urbanism. Scholars have previously treated them as a homogeneous unit, analyzing visualizations of bridges, the machine, and the tall building interchangeably.[1] The skyscraper's inimitable character inspired a particular iconography all its own. For example, the skyscraper's loftiness prompted visual interpretations which chronicle the architecture's outdistancing of churches in the celestial sphere. Others pay homage to height by conveying the soaring and seemingly infinite potential of American ingenuity.

Many of these general studies categorize the artistic response, especially in the 1920s, as largely favorable; Joshua Taylor saw them as "images of urban optimism" and Martin Friedman spoke of the "proud symbols of technological splendor."[2] Although the pictorial interpretations of Hugh Ferriss and Charles Sheeler are unequivocally favorable, most artists responded in ambivalent terms. The first skyscraperists tried to hide the tall building's so-called mundane, purely commercial character by either incorporating it into the natural landscape or employing evocative veils of pigment. Painters and photographers often relied on eighteenth-century theories of the picturesque, disseminated in popular periodicals such as

Scribner's and *Century* beginning in the 1890s. This equivocal position was more pronounced in skyscraper imagery of the 1920s, when debates concerning skyscrapers' effects on the city dweller emerged with renewed vigor. Bolstered by the consistently harsh commentaries of Lewis Mumford throughout the decade, artists often rendered the artificial city as hopelessly devoid of anything living, filled with jagged-edged skyscrapers impinging on the available space.

A consideration of intellectual and cultural history, literature, and popular criticism of America is essential for assessing skyscraper imagery. Past analyses have concentrated too closely on style and formal analysis.[3] While it is important to acknowledge the skyscraper renderers' debts to cubism, futurism, and dada, this approach omits the contributions of others. Only by assessing artists' responses to the skyscraper with those of their contemporaries, do patterns of thought and consistent attitudes begin to emerge. This methodology is particularly useful for the early years of the century, when both imagery and commentary concerning the skyscraper were scattered and infrequent.

Often narrow stylistic analyses lead to an evaluation of American art in the context of European developments without a consideration of native attitudes toward the city.[4] For example, Alfred Stieglitz's photographs, writings, and gallery practices tell us more about the reactions of painters John Marin and Max Weber to the skyscraper than do the superficial resemblance of their works to those of Italian futurist Umberto Boccioni or French orphist Robert Delaunay.

Skyscraper imagery is also inspired by the actual appearance of the American city, an area which has received scant attention in the scholarship to date.[5] An analysis of artists' repeated depictions of the Woolworth Building, 1920s setbacks, and the contrast of skyscrapers and churches provides insight into the ways the architecture itself dictated the visual response.

Despite the paucity of information on depictions of the skyscraper, two general works on urbanism were useful to this study. Wanda Corn's pioneer article "New New York" (1973), which concerns paintings and photographs of Manhattan's modern marvels from 1900 until 1910, integrates the art with both popular commentary and literature.[6] She concludes that early artistic chroniclers were uncomfortable with the rapid pace of growth, sprawling overhead "els," rising office buildings, and dynamic electric lighting, employing "sublime, picturesque and exotic" vocabularies for their images.

While Corn concentrated on the early years of the century, Joshua Taylor evaluated the years after World War I.[7] He examined American artists' responses to the city in view of international developments, from futurism to the Bauhaus, providing information on forgotten luminaries such as the architect and renderer Hugh Ferriss. Taylor's belief that the city was a symbol of man's exhilaration served as a springboard for many of the ideas presented in this book.

A firm foundation in architectural history is an important component of this study. Carl Condit's thorough scholarship on the skyscraper, particularly as it developed in Chicago, was a necessary prerequisite. For an account of the skyscraper in New York, Arnold Lehman's doctoral dissertation was equally crucial.[8] Finally, Stanley Peter Andersen's unpublished research on the architectural community's response to the skyscraper provided a perspective on the polemical discussions concerning the tall building's viability. Especially valuable was Andersen's discussion on the tensions between Ferriss and staunch antiurbanist Lewis Mumford. Andersen provided the groundwork for my own analysis of Ferriss's and Mumford's impact on skyscraper imagery.[9]

1

The Critical Response
to the Skyscraper, 1890–1917

By the 1890s, skyscrapers became an integral part of New York's and Chicago's topography. A confluence of financial, technological, and social forces prompted their development. The nation experienced a building boom in response to the economic prosperity and the desire to rebuild that followed the Civil War. Land costs soared astronomically as the competition for centralized institutions in the business districts increased. Since it was financially prohibitive to expand laterally, the only viable option was to extend vertically.

Natural disaster played a part in the need for safe, efficient architecture. In October 1871, a fire ripped through the heart of Chicago's financial district. Since most buildings were wood framed, almost half of the total property was destroyed. Even the cast iron members of larger buildings melted under the extreme temperature.

It is difficult to determine whether necessity was the mother of invention in Chicago's Loop district or Manhattan's southern tip; but not long after the fire, a number of technological advances coalesced. Perhaps the most important was the weight-bearing steel skeleton frame which permitted buildings to soar limitlessly. The passenger elevator, reinforced concrete for caisson foundations, firecladding for steel components and, of course, height characterized the skyscraper.

Although there is some disagreement, most architectural historians concur in the opinion that William LeBaron Jenney's Home Insurance Building (1884) of Chicago was the first skyscraper.[1] By the 1890s, the midwestern city could boast of a number of buildings featuring various aspects of the new technology. Holabird's and Roche's Monadnock Building (1893), Louis Sullivan's Gage Building (1898), and Carson Pirie Scott Store (1899) are among the most illustrious extant examples.

New York's more stringent fire codes, which prohibited the use of structural steel, were finally changed in 1892, paving the way for the proliferation of tall buildings on Manhattan Island. One can still recreate the enthusiasm artists felt before R. H. Robertson's Park Row Building (1889), Daniel Burnham's Flatiron Building (1903), and Cass Gilbert's Woolworth Tower (1913).

Shortly after the appearance of the skyscraper in New York and Chicago, its aesthetic viability became a hotly debated issue. Conservatives like Henry James and the painter William Merritt Chase sought to preserve the traditional and the European-derived aesthetic. Culture was to be protected, at all costs, from the crassness of business and commercial interests. Regarding the skyscraper as a usurper of time-honored values, the product of base materialism, and an aesthetic anathema, James and other traditionalists advocated its abolition.

In accord with James were the realist writers William Dean Howells and Henry Blake Fuller, who may be categorized as "ambivalent urbanites." Despite the fact that they often employed towered cities as backdrops for the exploits of their characters, their indictments of New York and Chicago respectively were harsh and uncompromising.[2]

Blake's *The Cliff Dwellers* (1893), perhaps the first novel to treat the skyscraper at length, pictured Chicago as a raw, brutal environment, where people clamored frantically for material success.[3] The Clifton, an eighteen-story office building replete with multiple elevators and glittering windows, served as the setting for the physical and metaphorical strivings of the office employees. Yet beneath its modern veneer, people were reduced to an almost primitive state. Physically frail and morally bankrupt, they failed miserably in relation to family, friends, and community. Fuller, and his fellow Chicago realists Will Payne and Frank Norris, viewed the new skyscraper city as an unhealthy place, where congestion and pollution dominated. Conditions were perceived as so perilous that the activity surrounding the skyscraper was likened to war and hell. These subjects were taken up by artists in succeeding decades.

While a negative view was dominant until around 1910, there were those that praised the new architecture as the first truly American creative endeavor. By the late 1890s, Progressives such as the artist Robert Henri, the architect Louis Sullivan, and the educator John Dewey attempted to revamp their respective fields by insisting they reflect the present native experience rather than relying on antiquated European prototypes. As a result of their nationalistic pronouncements, these observers created a favorable climate for the acceptance of the skyscraper.

Concurrently, journalists and art critics began to call for the depiction of the tall building in *Scribner's*, *Century*, *The Craftsman*, and *Camera Notes*. By the 1890s, general magazines were instrumental in keeping the public abreast of topical issues. Previously, most popular periodicals were sold for thirty-five cents and appealed to the rich and aristocratic. Once the price was reduced, editors began to include a broad range of timely subjects. An observer noted that *Century*, whose editor was the trained newspaperman Richard Watson Gilder, "deals with matters of contemporary human interest" and keeps "in touch with the people." E. L. Burlingame, editor of *Scribner's*, asserted that he was concerned with the "great working life and practical achievements of the country."[4] From its inception in 1896, *Scribner's* "Field of Art" column promoted the skyscraper.

A close examination of many of these statements of encouragement reveals that attitudes were still influenced to a large extent by the negative commentators. Viewing the skyscraper as inherently mundane and ugly, they suggested that it was possible for artists to infuse their depictions with emotion and poetry. Creative personalities responding to this advice often adopted a picturesque vocabulary, suppressing the tall buildings' industrial character in favor of a skyscraper image which accorded with conservative notions of taste.

It was not until the turn of the century that skyscrapers were finally accepted as subjects suitable for the fine arts. The lack of recognition occurred, in part, because of the dominant perception that skyscrapers were a product of commercial interests, thus wholly incongruent with elevated artistic matters. From approximately the Centennial Exposition of 1876 until the outbreak of World War I, the dominant aesthetic thought was firmly rooted in Old World values and conservatism.[5] Employing religious terminology, cultured intellectuals such as the Harvard art historian Charles Eliot Norton asserted that art should be the embodiment of abstract ideals, an expression of the country's "faith" and "loftiness" of spirit.[6] The self-appointed wards of high culture, including William James, Edith Wharton, and George Santayana, advocated the preservation of tradition borrowed from a wide variety of European sources. Rather than regarding these adaptations as eclectic in a negative sense, these traditionalists believed that since fledgling America lacked a viable cultural past, drawing from the entire gamut of western civilization afforded one the opportunity to absorb only its high points.[7]

In order to imbue their subjects with a high moral tone, artists often rendered human figures as symbolic virtues and landscapes as representations of God's work. The depiction of the here and now was rejected in favor of the absolute or the ethereal. As the architectural historian Richard Guy Wilson observed recently, even in those works that did not seek to communicate a sense of the ideal, such as genre and historical subjects, "the influence of the idea" could be detected in "art's removal from the world of mundane realities."[8] One need only recall the cloistered, exotic interiors of Sargent, the contemplative female protagonists of Dewing's insular, indeter-

minant ambiances, and the other-worldly character of Inness's late landscapes to appreciate how far art was divorced from current actualities.

The most important argument leveled at the tall building by traditionalists and realists alike was that its commercial character was physically and
ideologically antithetical to aesthetic concerns. The rupture between elevated artistic matters and the crudity of business, a common literary theme
of the period, was explored in Frank Norris's *The Pit* of 1902.[9] At the onset
of the novel, which explores the machinations of Chicago's financial district, the major female protagonist is pursued by two gentlemen of contrasting dispositions. One is a sensitive, aesthetic type who occupies his time
"gently in the calm, still atmosphere of art . . . painting, reading or . . .
developing his stained glass"; the other, an aggressive capitalist and specula-
tor, procures his fortune in the midst of the city's burgeoning skyscrapers.
Won over by the forceful spirit of the latter, she discovers to her chagrin
that their married life together is secondary to his stock market dealings.
Often alone and neglected, she realizes the incongruity between business
and high culture. "The clatter of millions of dollars, and the tramping and
wild shouting of thousands of men . . . invaded the very sanctuary of art,
and cut athwart the music of Italy and the cadence of polite conversation."[10]

The most articulate spokesman of this view was Henry James, an
expatriate who immersed himself in European tradition. In the acclaimed
The American Scene, written in 1904–1905, James surveyed the changes
that had transpired during his thirty-year absence.[11] Discounting tall office
buildings, he maintained that they were "giants of the mere market," hence
implying that despite their physical dimensions, they were opposed to lofty
ideals. Comparing the skyscraper built for economic expediency to Giotto's
bell tower in Florence, he pointed to their inherent differences. Unlike the
American tower erected for pure material gain, "beauty has been the object
of its creator's idea" in Giotto's endeavor, suggesting that architecture must
be the product of an elevated conception in order to possess aesthetic credibility.[12]

This rupture between the so-called fine arts and commercial interests is
nowhere more obvious than in the simultaneous erection of the utilitarian,
curtain-walled buildings of the Chicago School and the World's Columbian
Exposition of 1893. Despite the pioneering of a new and experimental mode
of building, the official notion of architecture was firmly rooted in *beaux-
arts* notions of taste. After visiting Chicago, Howells commented on the
dramatic contrast between the rapid urban expansion and the great white
city of the exposition. Preferring the utopian simplicity and harmonious
balance of the fair, he attacked Chicago as a "Newer York, an ultimate
Manhattan, the realized ideal of that largeness, loudness and fastness,
which New York has persuaded the Americans is metropolitan."[13]

The rupture between business and art was also evident in the tastes of the nation's leading art patrons. Many of the "American Medici," as they have been recently termed, secured their fortunes in industry, yet were ironically unwilling to accept an art based on their American milieu.[14] Amassing a huge fortune from railroads and real estate, the Vanderbilts erected seventeen houses filled with assorted treasures from Europe. Frank Copperwood, the major protagonist of Theodore Dreiser's *The Titan* also engaged in seemingly incongruous pursuits. Despite his rugged, individualistic, and not always ethical manner of doing business in Chicago's developing rapid transit system, Copperwood also collected art. Instead of purchasing the work of the American realists who were depicting the metropolitan scene, his aesthetic tastes were wholly European in orientation. Paintings by Luini, Pinturricho, Van Beers, Bastien-Lepage, and Gerome comprised his collection.[15]

Expectedly, one of the most popular art displays of the World's Columbian Exposition was entitled "Foreign Masterpieces Owned by Americans." Whether this popularity resulted from a sense of cultural inferiority on the part of collectors or from the investment potential of recognized European artists, there was definite resistance to both American artists and native subjects.

In addition to the widespread notion that monetary and aesthetic matters were mutually exclusive, a sizable number of commentators considered the tall building physically ugly. Since art was supposedly concerned with the depiction of the beautiful and the orderly, keynotes of a classical aesthetic, this attitude precluded a consideration of the skyscraper as a suitable subject for artistic endeavor. Writing in *Harper's Weekly*, an early observer lamented that tall office buildings "would be calculated first to occasion surprise" in the "well-ordered and stable mind," and second to fill the "artistic and aspirant soul with utter disgust." Fuller elaborated on this disparaging view. Employing terms derived from the natural landscape, he painted a picture of wanton chaos and irregularity. At the top of one of "these great capitains," one would find "the rugged and erratic plateau of the Badlands . . . in all its hideousness . . . a wild tractful of sudden falls, unexpected rises, precipitous dislocations. The high and low are met together. The big and the little alternate in a rapid and illogical succession."[16]

This image of urban chaos was to attain an increasing number of adherents. Howells detested the hodge-podge of tall buildings in Manhattan and Chicago. In *Letters of an Altrurian Traveller*, a fictional account of the reaction of a Martian to the United States in 1893, Howells complained of the "long stretch of one of their tiresome perspectives (that of the New Yorker) which is architecturally like nothing so much as a horse's jaw bone,

with the teeth broken or dislodged at intervals . . . a chaos come again."
James's popular characterization of the New York skyline as a "pin-cushion
in profile" summed up the attitude of a generation of detractors.[17]

Those who considered the skyscraper physically objectionable were no
doubt comparing the new steel-framed structure to European prototypes or
more traditional buildings. Not only were groups of skyscrapers criticized
for their lack of homogeneity, but also single buildings were thought to be
distorted. An anonymous art critic, writing in *Scientific American*,
observed that "their exaggerated vertical proportions" rendered "it impossible to judge these buildings by ordinary canons" of beauty. James referred
to the skyscraper as a "fifty-floored conspiracy against the very idea of
ancient graces."[18]

Those that wished to maintain a genteel conception of the city viewed
the skyscraper as a usurper of its more traditional architectural monuments.
Commercial interests were blamed for encroaching upon the delicate
flowers of civilization. The eclectic academic artist William Merritt Chase
deplored the current situation in Manhattan: "It is most discouraging to
find one bit after another of the old architectural artistic productions wiped
out of existence . . . The skyscraping monsters have smothered quite out of
existence as objects of beauty many of the mighty landmarks of this city . . .
old Trinity Church down Broadway, Dr. Parkhurst's church in Madison
Square and many others too numerous to mention."[19]

It was James who explored most extensively this view of the skyscraper
as undermining, both physically and philosophically, the very foundations
of culture and tradition. In *The American Scene*, he blamed tall buildings
for overshadowing and replacing the revered older structures of the past as
well as for extinguishing the sense of refined community so reminiscent of
his boyhood in New York. Of the older edifices supposedly victimized by
the skyscraper, he singled out the once preeminent Trinity Church, now
"mercilessly robbed" of its "visibility." Clearly, this particular building was
selected because of its past status as the tallest building in Manhattan, "the
pride of the town and the feature of Broadway." Because of the encroach-
ment of the massive skyscrapers on the financial district, it had been
reduced to a "poor, ineffectual thing," James lamented.[20]

James's characterization of Trinity Church as a building deprived of its
status not only referred to its physical dimensions, but also to the replace-
ment of sacred spiritual values by the forces of economic growth. Recalling
an intense religious and aesthetic experience in one of Manhattan's
churches, James claimed that his thoughts were wrenched from its jewel-
like windows to the sinister forces of materialism epitomized by the skyscraper. He believed that office buildings threatened both important public
monuments and the ideals and aspirations embedded in their external

forms. As the muckraker Lincoln Steffens observed in a discussion of the overshadowing of Trinity Church, "the enterprise of business" had "surpassed the aspiration of religion."[21] In an illustration accompanying his article, appropriately titled *Higher than the Head of the Cross*, a church spire was juxtaposed with the loftier Park Row Building, a format that was adopted by later renderers of the skyscraper.

The new office building was also blamed for the destruction of respected, older neighborhoods and communities, the very fabric of American social life. Howells complained: "Business and poverty are everywhere slowly or swiftly eating their way into the haunts of respectability, and destroying its pleasant homes. They already have the whole of the old town to themselves. In large spaces of it no one dwells but the janitors." Likewise, James was horrified to revisit the streets of his boyhood, the refined enclave of Washington Square. To his dismay, the site of his birthplace had been replaced with a "high square impersonal structure," which caused him to feel amputated from half his history. Even the Ashcan artist Jerome Myers bemoaned the disappearance of the old, colorful neighborhoods which he found more vital than the bland industrial milieu. He was sorry to see the destruction of the tenements in favor of the "beautiful and sanitary New York" because picturesque types were seen less often.[22]

Like their genteel contemporaries, the muckrakers and realists inveighed against the changes wrought by the skyscraper. But whereas James and Howells stressed the destruction of tradition, these observers evaluated the detrimental effects on the health of the urban inhabitant. One of the consequences of rapid urban and industrial expansion was the noxious fumes which pervaded the atmosphere of Chicago. Fuller regarded the western metropolis as an airless country in which "the medium of sight, sound, light and life becomes largely carbonaceous," a place where buildings loom up "through swathing mists of coal smoke." In the novel *The Money Captain* of 1896, Chicago realist Will Payne referred to the "enormous blotch of smoke" which hung perpetually over Chicago's horizon. "At first glance the neighborhood had the effect of a thicket of huge buildings. Towering cornices rose everywhere, and the air about them was murky," he noted.[23] A cartoon which appeared in *Life* magazine of 1898 expressed concern that allowing these conditions to remain unchecked would result in a city inundated with pollution. The future metropolis of 1910 was pictured as a city of limitless height and smoke, all sources of natural light and air obfuscated.[24]

The increased proliferation of titanic buildings seemed to render human life inconsequential as well. Contemporaries noted that the gargantuan scale of the buildings literally dwarfed the people in their midst. The popular journalist Edgar Saltus surveyed the swarm of humanity from above, observing pessimistically that "the ants are beings — primitive but human hurrying grotesquely over the most expensive spot on earth. They hurry because everybody hurries . . . in the hammers of the ceaseless skyscrapers . . . in the ambient neurosis." James also spoke of the dehumanizing effects of the skyscraper, which engendered both congestion and anonymity. In his view, people were reduced to "the consummate monotonousness of the pushing male crowd, moving in its dense mass . . . a welter of objects in which relief, detachment, dignity, meaning, perished utterly."[25]

Tall buildings were also perceived as the physical manifestation of antihumanitarian impulses. Conceived as a way to maximize profits in view of rising land values in the nation's metropolitan centers, skyscrapers were viewed by many as symbols of capitalism incarnate. In an article appropriately titled "The City of Mammon," written in response to his trip to the United States, the Russian writer Maxim Gorky inveighed against the Manhattan skyscraper for its negation of the true notions of democracy espoused by Jefferson and Whitman in favor of the lust for money. This pursuit of the "yellow devil gold" resulted in a huge city of stone, iron, and glass which enslaved the masses. The American poet Amy Lowell observed the inequities perpetrated by the few against the many revealed by the skyscraper.

> Above, one tower tops the rest
> And hold aloft man's constant quest:
> Time! Joyless emblem of greed
> Of millions, robbers of the best
> Which earth can give, the vulgar creed
> Has seared upon the night its
> flaming ruthless screed.[26]

The clamor for wealth in the business district and the dehumanizing quality of life among skyscrapers prompted more than one observer to compare this frenetic activity to the violence of war. Fuller likened "all this downtown racket" to "the music of a battle hymn." Norris presented perhaps the most troubling account when he referred to the obnoxious male voices which "filled the air with the noise of battle," maintaining that this was a "drama in deadly earnest — drama and tragedy and death, and the jar of mortal fighting."[27]

Tall buildings represented such a threatening menace that detractors compared them to consuming ogres and the urban environment to a living hell. Saltus began his aforementioned article on the following negative note: " 'What do you know of New York?' said one wanderer to another. 'Only what I have read in Dante,' was the bleak reply." Fuller expressed similar sentiments, referring to the Chicago environs as a "basso inferno" and likening the people of Chicago to the wayfaring stranger who asked Virgil about Dante: "Chi è costui, che senza morte, va per lo regno della morte gente?" Gorky presented the most disparaging view of metropolitan living of the time. In his opinion, residing in New York was synonymous with entrapment in the bowels of the nether world. "It belches forth clouds of smoke. . . . When you enter it you feel you have fallen into a stomach of brick and iron which swallows up millions of people. . . . It is the first time I have seen such a huge phantasmagoria of stone, iron and glass, this product of the sick and wasted imagination of Mercury and Pluto."[28]

In addition to its association with the work of the devil, the skyscraper was also associated with the wrath of God. The incongruity of the New York skyline and the magnitude of borrowings from architectural styles of the past prompted contemporaries to liken the skyscraper to the tower of Babel. More importantly, it was linked with the biblical structure because of its presumptuous attempt to "storm heaven," a sphere reserved previously for religious architecture.[29] Implicit in the comparison was a word of caution: continuation of this folly could result in the destruction of the skyscraper.

Contemporary with the negative view of the skyscraper, a minority of commentators applauded its existence. But by 1911, an apologist noted that "to sneer at skyscraping New York is less in vogue nowadays than it was some years ago."[30] The initial acceptance of the tall building both architecturally and artistically resulted, in part, from the reformist spirit which characterized the Progressive Era in the early years of the century. Reevaluating the previous belief in the superiority of European art and culture, Americans began to look to their own heritage and surroundings for inspiration. A reassessment of American culture was taking place in a number of forums. In *School and Society* of 1899, John Dewey rejected the traditional notion of education based on rote memorization of the classics. Instead, he encouraged an educational system based on practical experience. Only a "sense of reality acquired with first hand contact with actualities" would foster ingenuity and imagination.[31]

Like Dewey, the Ashcan artist and educator Robert Henri believed that a similar approach should be applied to the teaching of art. In *The Art Spirit*, Henri articulated his opposition to the academic teaching methods in the art institutions of the country, settings which he felt fostered mediocrity. Referring to the artist as a "sketch hunter," he encouraged his pupils to derive their subjects from their immediate surroundings instead of copying the old masters. Art should not be separated from life, he insisted.[32]

Despite the Ashcan artists' preference for both the picturesque and the vignettes of daily life, as opposed to the erection of a new metropolis, they engendered a climate of acceptance for skyscraper subjects. Even more significant was their rejection of traditional notions of beauty and propriety in favor of the so-called mundane and abhorrent. Defending the tall building against such charges of ugliness, Henri maintained that the skyscraper was indeed beautiful, "typical of all that America" meant.[33]

The synthesis of art and life also found expression in the writings of Louis Sullivan, the early proponent and architect of the skyscraper. The major impetus for the writing of his *Kindergarten Chats* of 1901 was to "liberate the mind" from the "serfdom to tradition." Distinguishing between the "historic feudal" and the "advancing democratic" minds, Sullivan called for a living art derived from one's own time. He encouraged architects to adopt only those forms which reflected "the function of the building" and the native experience, rather than a slavish copying of European prototypes.[34]

To be of one's own time and reflect one's own milieu, an overriding concern at the turn of the century, expressed the growing sense of nationalism that characterized American arts and letters. Echoing Walt Whitman, who insisted on the necessity of a class of native authors, Henri called upon artists to employ American motifs. In an effort to express an intrinsically local sensibility, artists sought subjects that could best convey their aims. In this context, the skyscraper was praised as the true expression of American creative genius and a symbol of nationalism. Mary Fanton Roberts, editor of the periodical *The Craftsman* and a strong proponent of this concept, observed: "The skyscraper is the first absolutely genuine expression of an original American architecture. In this tall eccentric tower we have begun to feel our way toward national building—buildings that suit our needs, our comfort, our landscape, without regard to any nation or civilization."[35]

In their attempts to embrace the skyscraper as a symbol of nationalism, critics bestowed upon it features attributed to an American "personality" or spirit. According to Sadakichi Hartmann, who wrote frequently in *Camera Work*, just as the United States was only in existence for a short period of time, supposedly unencumbered by centuries of stultifying tradition, the tall building was also in possession of the "forceful vitality of youth, adolescent in its tentative desire for beauty." Norris, who otherwise inveighed against the city of Chicago in *The Pit*, categorized the new metropolis as the physical manifestation of an American sensibility. "Here, of all her cities, throbbed the true life—the true power and spirit of America; gigantic, crude with the crudity of youth . . . sane and healthy and vigorous . . . infinite in its desire," he claimed.[36]

Not only perceived as pubescent in spirit, the skyscraper was also imbued with the properties of sexual awakening and activity, obviously a result of its phallic shape. "Surging," "restless," "vigorous," "assertive," and "primal" were qualities applied to the building by a wide variety of commentators. Henri described its peculiar morphology as "indicative of our virile young lustiness."[37]

Anthropomorphizing the tall building seemed to represent a desire to make it comprehensible. Observers even began to liken the erect, vertical structure to a man. Louis Sullivan praised H. H. Richardson's commercial Marshall Field Store, an important precursor to the skyscraper, as "a real man, a manly man," which sings the song of procreant power. According to the architect, every building was the image of the man you do not see. This notion was so widespread that one of the foremost philosophers of the period, George Santayana, differentiated between refined and pragmatic architecture, assigning them gender characteristics.

> One-half of the American mind, that not occupied intensely in practical affairs, has remained . . . slightly becalmed; it has floated gently in the backwater, while, alongside, in invention and industry . . . the other half of the mind was leaping down a sort of Niagara Rapids. This division may be found symbolized in American architecture: a neat reproduction of the colonial mansion . . . stands beside the skyscraper . . . the one is the sphere of the American man, the other . . . of the American woman.[38]

Apologists for the tall building also attempted to counter charges that it was encroaching upon the city's revered, older buildings by comparing skyscrapers to monuments of the past. In response to disparaging remarks concerning Daniel Burnham's Flatiron Building (1903), Alfred Stieglitz asserted that it was as important to America as the Parthenon was to Greece. Another commentator went so far as to categorize Ernest Flagg's Singer Building (1908) as an example of civic architecture. "This forty-seven story structure rises above the surrounding skyscrapers as a great shaft in memory of some hero or military triumph. To one coming up the bay or across the river, it appears as a monument rather than a business structure."[39]

In response to the cultural nationalists who were stressing the importance of the American experience, critics in popular periodicals urged painters to render the skyscraper. These magazine writers were close to the pulse of the present because of the requirement to chronicle the contemporary scene. Perhaps the earliest words of encouragement appeared in *Scribner's* "Field of Art" column of 1896, where it was argued that the much-abused skyscrapers could provide excellent "painter's motifs."[40]

Partisans of both Chicago and New York literally implored artists and writers to formulate a new aesthetic based on urban life. In "The Artistic Side of Chicago" (1899), the author observed untapped artistic material in the rapid city building, citing a number of artists and writers who were portraying the burgeoning new metropolis. Despite these fledgling attempts, however, he claimed that the true chroniclers of Chicago still had not emerged. "The city awaits her artistic creator. She may think she exists in literature, but it is only in a form at once evanescent and tentative. No one has yet risen to rescue her from oblivion and give her immortality through art . . . The city seems to cry out to the workers with pencil and pen." In a "Plea for the Picturesqueness of New York" of 1900, Sadakichi Hartmann also strongly encouraged artists to depict both urban subjects and the skyscraper.[41]

European commentators of the American scene were cited often so as to lend skyscraper depictions additional credibility. Presumably, these foreigners had seen the best of both worlds and were in a better position to pronounce judgment. Excerpts from Paul Adam's *Vues d'Amerique* of 1906 were included in the American periodical *Current Literature*. Addressing the issue of young girls practicing copying, Adam advised that "they would do well . . . to transfer to their watercolor pads these colossal, tower-like structures and the buildings that cluster in their shadow . . . I firmly believe that the Americans have discovered a new type of architecture which their coming art will raise to a high degree of excellence."[42]

Despite the praise of the skyscraper by nationalists and the increased encouragement to render it, artists and their apologists still viewed the new architecture as inherently ugly or mundane. Numerous articles ostensibly in favor of the tall buildings reveal an underlying ambivalence inspired, in part, by the dominant views of James and Howells. The first artists to render the skyscraper were often credited with the creative ability to transform the commonplace structures into works of aesthetic merit, capable of evoking poetic associations. Usually this meant the depiction of the skyscraper in accord with traditional notions of taste. The early skyscraperist Colin Campbell Cooper was praised for his ability to subvert the true character of the buildings by concentrating on dramatic weather effects. A reviewer noted that "crude as these buildings are today, the drift of the sunlight on them, the glorious and often merciful veils of mist . . . help us to the relation toward them of instinctive joy."[43] Likewise, Maude Oliver of the conservative *International Studio* praised Chicago artist Albert Fleury for deriving "his inspiration in the city's apparent ugliness, and who, through the medium of an exceptionally sensitive touch, has happily recorded beauties and poetry."[44]

Roland Rood, a frequent contributor to *Camera Work*, echoed the equivocal viewpoint when he pronounced "our skyscrapers ugly and our factory districts dreary deserts" but encouraged the artist to imbue these industrial scenes with "his or her personality." Justifying his position with the employment of pseudoscientific theories of evolutionary development,

Rood explained that the reluctance to accept the aesthetic merits of the skyscraper came from the imprint of antiquated notions of beauty on our brain in a "particular molecular form." Nevertheless, he was hopeful that as our brains developed, we would lose this link with our prehistoric past and "in the distant future come to look upon buildings in the shape of banks and stock exchanges . . . as being poetical, and even skyscrapers may be the ideal architecture." Cautioning the artist not to confuse his "inherited race associations" with personal likes and dislikes, Rood concluded on an optimistic note. The true artist could disobey these laws of nature and "succeed in the almost impossible feat of combining . . . thoughts with railroad yards, locomotives and skyscrapers."[45]

Further evidence of the art community's ambivalence to the skyscraper is revealed in the prevailing attitude concerning the depiction of individual office buildings. Despite the so-called unaesthetic appearance of the lone edifice, some felt that the mass or aggregate of buildings could evoke pleasure. The popular journalist and satirist Jesse Lynch Williams asserted that skyscrapers were "vulgar" and "impertinent" as separate units, but as a group they were aesthetically agreeable. As late as 1913, the American impressionist Childe Hassam summed up this position: "If taken individually a skyscraper is not so much a marvel of art as a wildly formed architectural freak. . . . It is when taken in groups with their zig zag outlines towering against the sky and melting tenderly in the distance that the skyscrapers are truly beautiful."[46]

Many artists believed that the proper appreciation of skyscrapers meant viewing them not only *en masse*, but also from the proper vantage point. An anonymous critic, writing in *Scribner's* of 1896, maintained that skyscrapers were impressive enough when observed from the town, but that this was "nothing compared to their beauty when seen from a point a mile beyond the houses." Hassam noted that standing too close to a skyscraper would be like "sticking your nose in the canvas of an oil painting." Rather, it was necessary "to stand off at a proper angle to get the right light on the subject."[47] Employed to counter the charges of the detractors who were supposedly not viewing the tall building correctly, this argument was ambivalent itself.

The debate concerning the skyscraper's viability and aesthetic merit prompted the artistic acceptance of the theme in the early years of the century. Yet the initial depictions often reflected the tensions of these polemical discussions. The tall building was viewed simultaneously as a symbol of national pride and as a mundane, commercial structure that required an infusion of poetry and a picturesque vocabulary to counter its prosaic character.

2

Tradition and Innovation, 1890–1917

The first images of skyscrapers appeared in popular illustrated magazines accompanying articles on the new urban America. In the 1890s, *Harper's*, *Century*, and *Scribner's* included views of the skyline and port, skyscrapers in construction, nocturnal views celebrating electricity, and the flurry of people around tall buildings.[1] These early skyscraper subjects reveal that in *fin de siècle* America, the popular illustrator was able to take more risks than his academic counterpart.[2] Despite the use of innovative subject matter, however, the illustrator was still bound by the notion that art must be tasteful. These pioneer depictions of urban America were cast in the vocabulary of the picturesque, the tonal, and the evocative, serving as important visual precursors to painters and photographers of subsequent decades. Countering the often disparaging content of the articles they meant to augment, these popular images set the stage for the acceptance of the tall building as a suitable subject for the fine arts.

Once the skyscraper was tacitly accepted by such established American artists as Childe Hassam, Colin Campbell Cooper, and Birge Harrison, consistent themes and "ways of seeing" the building emerged in the early years of the century.[3] Subjects included the transmutation of the historical city in favor of the modern metropolis, seen in the juxtaposition of church and skyscraper. These contrasts of old and new, which resulted from skyscraper construction, were among the most dramatic urban spectacles. The proliferation of steel scaffolds also engendered a fascination with the marvels of modern technology. Artists such as Joseph Pennell and Alfred Stieglitz, who recorded the coexistence of old and new buildings, were inspired by these manifestations of industrial progress. Change was the keynote theme of the day.

Artists explored, often inadvertently, the impact of the skyscraper on the people of the city. The numerous images of Wall Street, often rendered from high above a lofty skyscraper, conveyed the inconsequentiality of the people in the street below. Yet the interaction of people and skyscraper was far from uniformly negative. Construction workers were lauded as the new

American folk heroes, belying the notion that tall buildings squelched the spirit of the individual.

Artists interested in rendering what was quintessentially American about skyscrapers often selected specific areas of the city. Wall Street was depicted for both its congestion and status as the financial hub of the nation. Individual office buildings were also seized upon for their peculiar characteristics, reinforcing their effectiveness as objects of advertising.

The Traditional Building and the Skyscraper

The transformation of the city from a community of genteel brownstones, quaint monuments from the American Revolution, and pavilion-like *beaux arts* structures to a rising metropolis was widely commented upon at the turn of the century. Books bearing titles such as *New York Old and New* (1909), by Rufus Rockwell, attest to an awareness of a historic and modern Manhattan.[4]

While urban detractors such as Howells and James bemoaned the destruction of the city's venerable historical monuments, John C. Van Dyke welcomed the appearance of the new commercial office buildings. Self-styled lecturer in modern art, critic, and popularizer, Van Dyke rejected conventional methodological approaches to art history, preferring the freshness and spontaneity of his subjective impressions. This resulted in his predisposition to contemporary urban America, despite his frequent descriptions of it as an integral part of the natural landscape. In his book, *The New New York* (1909), as the title suggests, Van Dyke championed the rising city. In the introduction, he stated categorically that the new city, rather than the old, would be pictured. Critical of the prevalent skyscraper phobia, he maintained that people simply hung onto the past as a force of habit. New York should not be preserved as a "historical museum in the large"; rather, it should continue to develop its commercial potential, he argued. Recognizing those who "rise up with indignant protest that there are other things in New York than trade and commerce," he challenged the traditionalists by maintaining that "the skyscraper of commerce looms above the university and the art gallery on the horizon line of the city." The skyscraper not only was preeminent in height, but also "filled the most conspicuous place in the interest and affections of the city's people."[5]

Even the revered Trinity Church was not spared from Van Dyke's theories of economic determinism. Of the church once attended by George Washington, he noted somewhat apologetically: "Alas, fair Trinity! With all its beauty it is only a survival. Its usefulness as a church is gone and it lags superfluous on the scene."[6] To critics like James, he replied that economic expansion was a necessary prerequisite to the very luxuries and monuments they sought to preserve.

The view that European-derived architecture was not relevant to the industrial urban centers of America was echoed by art critics evaluating the new skyscraper depictions. Regarding the work of Colin Campbell Cooper, one critic noted that the artist was previously a painter of Old World buildings, but that these subjects were no longer applicable to the American milieu: "As students and artists we admire and study these wonderful buildings, but we have no share in the spirit that produced them, or we would be building them today. . . . We may have love and reverence for these but our problem in life is so far different that we can not work it out on the old lines."[7]

In accord with their literary counterparts, artists could not fail to observe the dramatic opposition of the old and the new so evident in Manhattan. One popular journalist accurately described the painter's excitement before the antithetical aspects of New York, remarking that "at present there are still enough of the old buildings left to enjoy the astonishing contrasts as he turns any corner of Broadway." One of the greatest "finds" for the artist, the author asserted, was the "incongruity of old and new types" of architecture.[8]

Pennell had already noted these startling contrasts as early as 1905. In *The Four-Story House* (fig. 1), he was intrigued by the interaction of the relatively unassuming buildings of the past with the enormous turn-of-the-century towers, concentrating on the disparity in heights. Pennell's illustrations for Van Dyke's *The New New York* further support the artist's acceptance of modernity. In *Singer Building — Early Evening* (fig. 2), Manhattan's loftiest skyscraper of 1908 is seen illuminating the nocturnal sky, dwarfing the slender pinnacle of Trinity Church. Unlike his friend James, Pennell sympathized with the march of progress and pointed to the absurdity of the tiny edifice in the downtown section of Manhattan. The artist's publisher, Frederick Keppel, provided insight into Pennell's urban preferences. "He cares as little as ever for the recognized 'showpieces,' — just as little as Whistler himself — and says of our Old City Hall, and the Grace Church . . . that they are all very well in their way but the same things . . . may be seen in almost any other civilized capital; but the towering piles of the New York 'skyscrapers' have impressed Mr. Pennell very strongly."[9]

Despite Van Dyke's suggestions for the artistic subject matter to accompany *The New New York*, many of Pennell's images are independent in conception.[10] Whereas the writer was pessimistic about the feasibility of the old and new to coexist, Pennell often pictured them in total harmony. Van Dyke had categorized the Old City Hall as "too delicate, too lovely, too feminine for contact with those great structures of steel and granite"; Pennell rendered the civic monument in accord with the adjacent steel-framed World Building (1889–90) by George B. Post (fig. 3). The similarity of the baroque cupolas indicates that the New York skyscraper was often stylistically like its architectural predecessors. In an article entitled "Picturesque New York" of 1892, Pennell's colleague the architectural critic M. G. Van Rensselaer explained the artist's position: "Even you, young artist, born on the Pacific slope and now fresh from Parisian boulevards, can see that your New York is picturesque. But I wish that I could show you mine, which is not mine of my infancy, or mine of today, but the two together, delightfully, inextricably, mysteriously, perpetually mixed."[11]

One of the most dramatic juxtapositions of the ancient and the modern in downtown New York was that of St. Paul's Church and the adjacent Park Row Building (1899) by R. H. Robertson and the St. Paul's Building (1899) by George B. Post.[12] Probably what fascinated skyscraperists was St. Paul's legacy as the oldest extant religious edifice in New York. Completed in 1764 by James McBean, it provided the quintessential contrast of old and new.

The photographer Alvin Langdon Coburn, a close associate of Alfred Stieglitz and a frequent contributor to *Camera Work*, was among the first to record this subject. In 1905, he rendered the buildings in evocative silhouette, a method he adopted from the careful study of Japanese prints, and presented them as relatively equal in size and dimension (fig. 4). In view of the actual towering of the two skyscrapers over the diminutive colonial edifice, it is telling that the photographer selected such a viewpoint. Recently inspired by the religious monuments of Europe, at this point in his career Coburn seemed unwilling to admit the prominence of the skyscraper.

The modernist painter John Marin explored New York's incongruities with the most consistency. Beginning in 1911 and continuing throughout 1914, he rendered both Trinity and St. Paul's Churches in relation to New York's skyscrapers. In one watercolor, the painter presented a view similar to Coburn's (fig. 5).[13] Although it displayed a synthesis of *fauvist* brushwork and the embroidered strokes of Bonnard and Vuillard, the image's static quality seems more akin to a photograph. Like Coburn, Marin presented the religious monument as taller than the business structures.

By 1912, Marin presented St. Paul's as towering dramatically above all the buildings in the immediate area; and by 1914, it assumed a position of domination over the entire skyline (fig. 6). The church is shown as erect and immovable, while the surrounding buildings shift and topple. Rendered as if viewed through a wide-angle camera lens further reinforced the preeminence of the church. One is reminded of Marin's often quoted description of Manhattan's changing topography as "the warring of the great and the small," for which he found ample evidence in New York.[14]

The contrast of churches and skyscrapers reflected not only changes in the city's topography, but also a confrontation of spiritual and materialist values. Like James, many commentators of the time decried the destruction of religion in favor of capitalism and gain. Hoping for a return to piety, one physician categorized the clamor for wealth a disease called "newyorkitis," while the Christian socialist Walter Rauschenbusch indicted the capitalist system as antireligious.[15] At the beginning of the twentieth century, America was still very much a Christian nation and the new business ethic was seen as markedly opposed to its moralistic principles. It is no accident that Cass Gilbert's Woolworth Building (1913) was fashioned in the guise of a Gothic cathedral. Nicknamed the "cathedral of commerce," it seemed to reconcile the rift between business and religion. No doubt, the numerous renditions of church and skyscraper reflect the tensions and shifts in cultural values. This conflict surfaced again during the war years in the writings of Van Wyck Brooks and Waldo Frank, who blamed commercialism for the nation's lack of spirituality.

While the aforementioned images represent a keen awareness of the relationship between the historical past and the transformations wrought by the present, the juxtaposition of church and skyscraper indirectly indicates the artistic dialogue with European culture. Pennell likened New York's Grace Church and Old City Hall to the architecture of Europe, and Stieglitz viewed the skyscraper in relation to traditional buildings. Frederick Evans's photographs of Ely Cathedral were purposely illustrated with Stieglitz's photographs of the recently completed Flatiron Building in *Camera Work*. An editorial comment in the periodical demonstrates Stieglitz's self-conscious attempt to point out the differences between European and American architecture. "In contrast to the antiquity of the architectural subjects of Mr. Evans, we reproduce the extreme modernity of the 'Flatiron,' " he asserted.[16]

It is significant that Pennell, Coburn, and Marin had been enthusiastic admirers of the venerated monuments of Europe prior to the adoption of the skyscraper. By the early 1880s, Pennell had already etched the architecture of London and Tuscany, remaining a tireless chronicler of historical buildings throughout his career. Shortly after the turn of the century, Coburn explored the differences between various international centers. In his photographic essay "Contrasts," he juxtaposed scenes from New York, Paris, London, Venice, and Liverpool in an effort to capture "the spirit of representative cities."[17] Prior to Marin's final return to the United States in 1910, he produced highly detailed etchings of the cathedrals of Europe. It seems plausible that these renderers of the skyscraper possessed a heightened awareness of the differences between Europe and America as a result of having been seasoned abroad.

Another indication of the American artists' dialogue with the parent culture was the constant likening of the skyscraper to European buildings or cities. Attempting to establish the superiority of New York's wonders, Pennell encouraged the tourist to pay heed to "the color more shimmering than Venice, by night more magical than London. . . . Piling up higher and higher right before you is New York, and what does it remind you of? San Gimignano of the Beautiful Towers away off in Tuscany. . . . You land in streets that are Florence glorified. You emerge in squares more noble than Seville."[18] *October Haze* (fig. 7) by Childe Hassam visually conjures up associations with medieval cities or of traversing the waterways of Venice at sunset. Selecting a distant vantage point and concentrating on the scintillating autumnal reflections he removed the city from the present.

This inability to accept the skyscraper resulted in the widespread likening of it to buildings of the Near and Far East. Van Dyke exclaimed that the same architecture "that thoughtless people jeer at, catches light as readily as a Moslem minaret." In an effort to prove New York's superiority, he claimed that the series of skyscrapers in Manhattan "make up walls more massive than those of Stamboul." "Even if the city lacked the silvery domes of Constantinople," Van Dyke rationalized, "it is not without its tall towers flying flags against the blue."[19]

The likening of the modern marvels to more traditional buildings was symptomatic of a desire to situate America within a historical context. The inability to draw upon things American as well as the desire to outdo Europe in grandeur suggests a feeling of cultural inferiority on the part of American artists and intellectuals. This lack of confidence in cultural matters is manifested in the attitude that life in the United States was generally mediocre and prosaic. Earlier, Nathaniel Hawthorne summed up this position in his preface to *The Marble Faun* of 1860. "No author, without a trial, can conceive of the difficulty of writing a romance about a country where there is no shadow, no antiquity, no mystery, no picturesque and gloomy wrong, nor anything but commonplace prosperity," he claimed.[20] To answer the charge that skyscrapers were mundane, utilitarian structures, it became necessary to point out their similarity with the palaces, towers, and churches of Europe and the East.

Construction

New York as a city in a perpetual state of transformation has been noted throughout its history. As early as 1840, the English traveller Philip Hone observed the city's "annual metamorphosis." "The spirit of pulling down and building up is abroad. The whole of New York is rebuilt once in ten years." Up until America's involvement in the World War I, numerous commentators remarked on the impermanence of the city's architecture. After returning from a vacation, Howells noted that an "architectural geyser" had shot up where formerly a "meek little ten story edifice cowered."[21]

The constant tearing down of buildings and the erection of skyscrapers in the major cities of the United States provided an omnipresence of steel scaffolds and massive excavation sites. To a generation grappling with the formulation of an authentic American art, the steel skeleton provided an excellent solution, for it stood as an inherently native feat of engineering. The skyscraper was literally made possible by the invention of the steel frame. In depicting the virtual support of future buildings, artists were reflecting what was peculiarly American about American architecture.

Functional and utilitarian, the skeleton frame illustrated an aspect of the American sensibility already noted on the occasion of the 1851 International Exposition in London. As Sigfried Giedion observed, visitors to the show were particularly impressed by the "simplicity" and "technical correctness" of American industry. As a result, the functional superiority of the skyscraper was recognized almost immediately. Responding to critics who accused it of squelching the life of the individual, Mary Fanton Roberts of *The Craftsman* praised the tall building as the best possible solution in a congested urban area. "This light towering building was not designed in the first place for beauty nor to satisfy any aesthetic cravings of citizens of the metropolis. It was built to meet the demands of a rapidly increasing population in a restricted area. The one thought that ruled the erection of the tall, steel-framed building was strength, simplicity and the maximum of light and space."[22] The dadaists Duchamp and Picabia would later assert that America's true contribution to art was its industry and engineering.

The technology involved in skyscraper building was also a source of fascination and wonder. Newspapers and magazines abounded in lengthy, often technical descriptions of various building projects. Popular periodical articles are surprising for their thoroughness concerning all aspects of construction. "A shaft was sunk 90 feet below the level of Broadway," it was reported. Next, "rock caissons were lowered and anchorage and reinforcement rods were placed." Finally, on top of "this base the steel framework was raised, so braced and anchored as to distribute the strain and weight."[23]

Drilling into the "earth's vitals," as the initial stage of skyscraper building was described, became a veritable sidewalk show in the early years of the century. Detailed chronicles on the scope of construction attest to the public's amazement concerning what was required to build a skyscraper. Mildred Stapley, a popular journalist, reflected the prevailing enthusiasm for the city's numerous excavation sites: "This matter of foundations — these mysterious, invisible feats of engineering which insure the safety of the fortieth story tenant — have not they also the power to stir the imagination?

Do the crowds of office workers who pass their noon respite in watching the caissons slowly sinking into the depths of the earth—do these noon audiences go away unstirred?"[24]

Art critics were not immune to the spectacle which prompted urban dwellers to marvel at excavation sites. As early as 1900, Stieglitz's colleague Sadakichi Hartmann pointed to their power to stimulate the artistic imagination. "Wherever some large building is being constructed the photographer should appear," he urged. Yet it was still a disappointment that he "never had the pleasure" of seeing "a good picture of an excavation or an iron skeleton framework."[25]

Several years later, Pennell fulfilled his expectations. In an etching entitled *A Hole in the Ground* of 1904 (fig. 8), a deep depression in the earth is juxtaposed with adjacent vertical office buildings. The artist maintained that "the tearing down of an old structure for the building of a new one" often provided "unexpected vistas."[26]

Following advice to paint his own milieu from his mentor Robert Henri, George Bellows recorded the excavation for the enormous Pennsylvania Station (fig. 9).[27] In a quick flurry of strokes, he conveyed the gritty atmosphere of New York in subtle browns and off-whites.[28] Like Pennell, Bellows stressed the startling contrast of the cavity's depth and the loftiness of skyscrapers, pointing to the expansion of space both downward and upward. Yet Ashcan artists ultimately preferred the activity of the worker whose efforts made the march of technology possible. The metropolitan dweller reigned supreme over the skyscraper among Bellows and his colleagues.

Skyscraper builders were acknowledged for their courage in the face of overwhelming obstacles and danger, a theme later developed by the photographer Lewis Hine. Christened "cowboys of the skies," they were hailed as "rough pioneers . . . of the steel pushing each year their frontier line up toward the clouds."[29] The rugged individualism of these men could be employed to counter the charge that skyscrapers resulted in the exploitation of the masses.

The courage and prowess of the construction worker was acknowledged early in the popular Chicago press. In the story "A Young Man in Upper Life," a reference to the new experiences available to skyscraper inhabitants, the realist George Ade explored the distractions suffered by a young office worker. Usually motivated, Mr. Ponsby could not concentrate because of the construction of a tall office building directly outside his window. What alarmed him the most was "the solitary column showing itself above the ledge, and perched on top of this column a man." The man would often keep his balance by "hooking his toes behind the column and hugging it with his knees."[30]

Pennell explored all aspects of the theme. He developed a philosophy known as the "wonder of work" which included "building, digging, constructing," and "demolishing."[31] Before the advent of the skyscraper, Pennell had been fascinated with subjects pertaining to industrial development and the fabrication of buildings. As a youth, he drew the old mills in Germantown and etched the scaffolds on Philadelphia's public buildings. In 1881, Pennell executed a wash drawing of the Bethlehem Steel works to accompany an article in *Century* magazine.[32]

Pennell traced his notion of the "wonder of work" to artistic renditions of the past, including Rembrandt's "true mechanical renderings" of the mills and dykes of Holland, Claude's "commercial harbours," Turner's "Steam, Rain, Speed" [*sic*], Whistler's recognition of the aesthetic possibilities of "the poor buildings" and the warehouses of London, and the depictions of rural labor by Courbet, Millet, and Legros.[33] By citing these old masters, Pennell was attempting to lend the industrial themes of America historical credibility. Ultimately, Pennell's theories on labor involved the current technological progress in this country. Rather than relying on retrogressive images of work, the artist advised that "it is to America we must turn, to White's etchings of Brooklyn Bridge, Cooper's skyscrapers, Alden Weir's New York at Night, Bellow's docks, Childe Hassam's high buildings, Thornton Oakley's coal breakers — to these one must look for the modern renderings of work."[34]

In addition to the general labor subjects available to the artist, an essential component of Pennell's philosophy was the erection of skyscrapers. He described New York as "the city that has been built since I grew up . . . built by men I know, built for people I know." His interest in buildings in progress was corroborated by his wife, Elizabeth Robins Pennell, who claimed that the artist would stay over in New York many weeks to study "already built or in the building," its "monsters of many moods." She reported that he constantly cancelled appointments, "so impatient was he to get back to his inexhaustible skyscrapers." "I'll try to look into lunch tomorrow — but the mill is grinding — and when it does so, I don't like to stop the machinery," Pennell wrote to one of his colleagues. The mill grinding was an obvious reference to the incessant clattering of steel in Manhattan, a process which he likened to his own creativity.[35]

Despite Pennell's recognition of the multiple aspects of skyscraper construction, workers were all but absent from his images. Rather, he concentrated on the limitless soaring of the steel scaffolds. Skies are often darkened suggestively to enhance the drama of the derricks suspended crosswise in the air (fig. 10). Although he included the entire process of building in his conception of the "wonder of work," the skyscraper images bespeak of a fascination with progress. Pennell seemed to confirm this view. "What I have all my life been trying to show in my work is just this, that there is something in engineering work — the great work of our age," he reported.[36]

The steel skeleton as an image of modernity was also photographed by Stieglitz. In *Old and New New York* of 1910 (fig. 11), a rising scaffold is contrasted with the somber brownstones of a past era. The older structures are symbolically cast in darkness while the lithe metal frame seems to herald the dawn. Stieglitz's fascination with advancements in architecture is in keeping with his battle for the acceptance of the semimechanical process of photography.

Not all renderers of the emergent city saw the massive construction effort in positive terms. The journalist F. Hopkinson Smith launched an aggressive attack on the physical destruction of his beloved old New York. In *Charcoals of New and Old New York* (1912), written and illustrated by Smith, the erection of the skyscraper was viewed as a destructive process.

> So in go the testing drills, way down. . . . Then the blasting begins. . . . Now the caissons are sunk — big round as ship's funnels and many times as long. Down they go, slowly . . . the brown ground hogs digging like moles in the foul air. A swarm of titans rush in. Up go the derricks, — the cranes swing, — half a score of engines vomit steam and smoke. Then . . . a gigantic skeleton of steel . . . punctured with a thousand browless eyes.[37]

Hassam rendered a rather disparaging view of a skyscraper's construction. In *The Hovel and the Skyscraper* of 1904 (fig. 12), a rising steel frame is seen amidst a group of nondescript tenements, reminiscent of the subjects chosen by Pennell, Coburn, and Marin. Considering the artist's preference for the more refined aspects of Manhattan, perhaps he was alluding to the absurdity of the increased expansion of business in view of squalid housing conditions. In addition, the rapid increase in "business and poverty," as Howells previously commented, was seriously lowering the quality of life in the nation's urban centers.[38]

The Skyline

Manhattan's distinction as an island, coupled with the proliferation of tall buildings on its southern tip, provided an unobstructed view of its emergent skyline. From James's pejorative characterization of the aggregate of buildings as a "pin-cushion in profile" to those who rhapsodized about its picturesque variety and uneven contour, the developing New York skyline was widely noted.

The irregular silhouette of the city's numerous skyscrapers did not develop until the mid 1890s because of New York's restrictive building codes limiting the use of structural steel. But by 1892, the picturesque potential of the "skyline" was commented on. Photographs of downtown Manhattan from the bay began to appear in popular periodicals two years later, indicating the rapid changes that had transpired. Lincoln Steffens observed that "the sky-line of New York is changing so rapidly that the American traveller who goes abroad can recognize with more certainty the profiles of foreign cities he approaches than that of his own metropolis."[39]

So as to assess the profound changes which characterized the decade, in 1897 *Harper's Weekly* published comparative drawings of the skylines of 1881 and the present.[40] Whereas Trinity Church still dominated the horizon in the former decade, by the 1890s a multitude of new buildings attained preeminence, including the St. Paul's, the American Surety, and the Standard Buildings. A chart of comparative heights, published in 1908, corroborated the rapid upward growth of the city in the last five decades (fig. 13).[41]

The awesome height of the numerous buildings engendered laudatory commentaries on the aesthetic merits of the skyline. What captivated both natives and tourists alike was the approach to New York by sea. The art critic M. G. Van Rensselaer observed that "the most picturesque of all sights that New York offers is . . . when seen at night by a boat on the water." The "abrupt, extraordinary contrasts of the skyline are then subdued to a gigantic mystery." Pennell described the journey enthusiastically, proclaiming the superiority of New York: "As the steamer moves up the bay on one side the Great Goddess greets you, a composition in color and form, with only the city beyond, finer in the world than ever existed, finer than Claude ever imagined or Turner ever dreamed. . . . Piling up higher and higher."[42]

The New York skyline was perceived as among the most breathtaking of man-made wonders. "Words are inadequate to describe this apparition," exclaimed Paul Bourget. Accompanying an etching of the panorama of tall buildings entitled *Cortlandt Street Ferry* (fig. 14), Pennell described the scene in almost rhapsodic terms: "The towering splendor of New York is one of the marvels of the world. The mind can only grope afterwards to express its proportions."[43] In order to enhance their grandeur and unreality, the artist situated the buildings among swirling, cataclysmic cloud formations, suggesting that their dramatic breadth was equal to the power of nature.

The foreign traveller to these shores was also awed by the approach to Manhattan Island. An article in the sympathetic periodical *The Craftsman*, probably authored by Mary Fanton Roberts, articulated the visitor's response to the fantastical city by the sea.

> To see the American skyscraper is the desideratum of all foreigners. And when for the first time the European visits this country he receives his most lasting impression as the ship bearing him swings from the harbor and makes its way along the riverfront of New

York. . . . He is astounded by this strip of country appearing o'nights a veritable
fairy-land, — a fairy-land people with argus eyed giants, the so-called skyscraper.[44]

In keeping with the desire to remove the tall buildings from commonplace realities, commentators could not resist comparing the skyline to
European cities by the sea. Pennell boasted that the New York skyline by
day was superior to that of Venice and more magical than that of London at
night.[45] Viewing the approach to Manhattan, contemporaries were probably
reminded of the aquatic views of London and Venice by Whistler. The
journalist and illustrator F. Hopkinson Smith pictured the American skyscrapers as if on route to the Italian city at dusk (fig. 15). The tallest
skyscraper on the horizon was, in fact, Le Brun and Sons' Metropolitan
Tower (1909), which was based on the Venetian campanile!

Not only was the panorama of skyscrapers by the sea the source of
imaginary and exotic musings, but it was also seen as inextricably linked
with the city's commercial activities. Since the seventeenth century and the
chartering of the Dutch West India Company, New York had assumed the
character of a busy center of trade. By the 1860s, the port handled more of
the nation's imports and exports than any other city. With the appearance
of skyward buildings at the end of the nineteenth century, observers associated them with the ferries and ships docked in the harbor. Jesse Lynch
Williams noted that "behind a foreground of tall masts with their square
rigging and mystery (symbols of the world's commerce, if you wish), looms
up a wondrous bit of the towering white city of 1900, a cluster of modern
high buildings."[46] Accompanying the text, the Philadelphia artist Henry
McCarter pictured the lofty, geometric web of ships' masts superimposed on
tall office buildings. In 1907, a similar photographic image by Alvin
Langdon Coburn was published in *Camera Work* (fig. 16). In view of the
conflict between religion and materialism, perhaps the three cruciform patterns are meant to suggest that commerce and business epitomize the faith
of the future.

In addition to the static juxtaposition of lofty masts and architecture,
waterfront skyscrapers were rendered in the context of the hustle-bustle of
port activity. In Stieglitz's *The City of Ambition* of 1910 (fig. 17), steaming,
chugging ferries are seen travelling from the harbor, flanked by the city's
looming skyscrapers.

An awareness of the emergent New York skyline was inevitably linked
with the impressive span of the Brooklyn Bridge. Completed in 1883 by the
Roeblings, the bridge embodied principles later found in tall buildings.
Both were technical feats of engineering, employing and exploiting the
potential of structural steel. The bridge and the skyscraper seemed to reinforce and expand the view of New York City as a major metropolis. In

many respects, the bridge made it feasible to transport large masses of people to a centralized area in Manhattan, which may have indirectly prompted the desire to build upward. Moreover, the ingenuity necessary to erect both technical wonders expanded traditional notions of horizontal and vertical space.

From a purely visual standpoint, the aggregate of skyscrapers from Brooklyn Heights included the vast, curvilinear sweep of the Roeblings's steel suspension structure. Artists interested in celebrating the progress of New York often employed the span of the bridge to crown the aspiring, vertical buildings. In a painting by Leon Kroll, the triumvirate of transportation, business, and commerce is used to characterize New York (fig. 18). A watercolor by John Marin celebrates the dual symbols of technological achievement merged into a single entity, stressing the equivalent loftiness of the bridge's towers and of the skyscraper's pinnacles.

The Financial District

The largest concentration of skyscrapers in New York was located on the southern tip of Manhattan Island, in an area known as the financial or Wall Street district. With its shift from the seat of government to a center of banking at the beginning of the nineteenth century, Wall Street represented the heartbeat of the nation's pecuniary interests. By 1832, it was regarded as "the street which contains most of the floating capital of the city" and "the mart for bankers, brokers, underwriters, and stock-jobbers." "Speculation of every shape, character, color and dimension" were planned and executed here.[47]

The final consolidation of the New York Stock Exchange and the introduction of the first ticker machines in the 1860s resulted in the district's prominence in the volume of business handled. Congestion and the necessity of centralization forced land values upward, in turn prompting the erection of loftier buildings. By the turn of the century, Wall Street was inextricably linked with the proliferation and domination of tall buildings. Those critical of the business community's practices even heaped insults on its architecture, representative of the questionable dealings which it housed.

In contrast to the harsh critics of capitalism, however, the positive acceptance of New York as the financial center of the United States prompted numerous images of Wall Street. The theme of Van Dyke's *The New New York* reflected this optimistic view of business, pointing to the skyscraper as the economic and architectural keynote of the future. Commenting on the pecuniary orientation of the city, Jesse Lynch Williams praised the "wonderful bit of the towering white city of the new century" as "symbols of modern capital."[48] Wall Street and the business transacted there were viewed as peculiarly American. Van Rensselaer noted that both the buildings and the district's activity reflected a native sensibility. H. G. Wells preferred the dynamic activity of Wall Street, which he found "all American and local," to the nostalgic views of Fifth Avenue.[49]

For contemporary artists and writers interested in exploring native architecture, it was logical to proceed to the financial district. Perhaps more than any other single location, the skyscraper's impact on, and interaction with, the throngs of humanity could be explored there. Observers began to comment on the accelerated movement of crowds among the skyscrapers. Pennell referred to the Stock Exchange as "the scene of strange business tumult and excitement" but noted that in the "curb market" there was no less animation. In accord with Pennell, Van Dyke observed that the majority of activity took place in the street. "Most of the business on Wall Street is transacted on the sidewalk. The phrase 'in the street' has been taken too literally, as meaning that operators in the stock market carry on business involving millions in an unconventional shirt sleeve manner while leaning against a lamp post."[50]

In the tradition of the illustrators of urban tour guides, who selected the most significant sights and spectacles of a city, many of the early skyscraperists were drawn to Wall Street. Pennell, Hassam, Cooper, and Coburn selected identical viewpoints from which to render the monetary center. From the corner of Broad and Wall Streets, the compact, classical Stock Exchange building both symbolically and physically caused the momentum of the crowds around the tall buildings. In a painting by Hassam, the building is illuminated to stress its incalculable impact as a financial institution (fig. 19).

The centralization of skyscrapers in the downtown region not only inspired the rapid activity of the countless throngs, but also pointed to the disparate size relationship between the titan buildings and the people who filled the streets. H. G. Wells described the Wall Street area in terms of a "cliff of material achievement above a black froth of people," while another author maintained that the office buildings reduce human beings to Lilliputians and black ants.[51]

Wall Street was often rendered from above, so as to stress the dramatic inconsistency in size, prohibiting the viewer from mingling freely on the sidewalks and curbs. As in the urban scenes of French impressionist Pissarro, who recorded the cluster of humanity from lofty heights, people were reduced to indeterminant dabs.[52] Unlike the rather sparsely populated Parisian boulevards rendered by Pissarro, the chroniclers of lower New York conveyed the density and anonymity of the masses which resulted from urban congestion.

Nature and the Picturesque

Despite the novelty of the skyscraper theme, many of the initial renderers of tall buildings sought an artistic vocabulary which accorded with accepted notions of taste. In order to conform to the prevailing conservatism of the American art establishment of which they were a part, a detailed depiction of the skyscraper was discouraged. Either a subjective response to the external world or the ability to reflect its symbolic significance was preferred. As Birge Harrison, theoretician on landscape painting and frequent skyscraper renderer, recommended: "Of course one must paint what one sees, but one must see with the mind as well as with the eye. The true vision means not only the power to see and to recognize beauty, but the power to see it stripped of all its vulgarities and inessentials."[53]

Hassam provided explicit instructions for rendering the urban landscape correctly. Comparing the portrait of a city to that of a person, he believed that it was necessary to "catch not only the superficial resemblance but the inner self," not to aim for versimilitude but to "strive to portray the soul of the city with the same care as the soul of a sitter." Hassam's skyscraper images were appropriately praised by a reviewer for their success in depriving the buildings of their "rawness and afflictive realism." The "poetic vision" of Cooper was similarly applauded, especially his transformation of the "prosaic structures" by "inclusion and elimination."[54]

The so-called factual character of business architecture was suppressed in a variety of ways. The buildings were often cast in atmospheric veils or mists, transporting the viewer to an other-worldly realm. This process of subtle suggestion is seen in the skyscraper renditions of Harrison, who immersed the renowned Flatiron Building in ephemeral climatic and temporal conditions.[55] As a result, the loftiness and particularities of the building are reduced to an amorphous glow (fig. 20). A passage from Van Dyke's *The New New York*, which is remarkably similar in content to Harrison's painting, points to the uniformity of this view of the skyscraper. "How very beautiful the high ridge of skyscrapers look shrouded in that silver-gray mist, their tops half disappearing in the upper blend of rain and clouds. . . . What mysterious appearances these high buildings take upon themselves with their masses of light and dark floating in the heavy atmosphere of rain." Even James allowed for the "parts and pieces melting together rather richly now of 'downtown.' "[56] The French expatriate Albert Fleury, among the first to paint the skyscrapers of Chicago, situated Burnham and Root's Masonic Temple in a mixture of blustery snow and industrial smoke (fig. 21). Stieglitz attempted to convey the solidity and lightness of the Flatiron Building by immersing the monolithic structure in the evanescence of a winter blizzard (fig. 22).

As Wanda Corn has pointed out, the preference for tone in *fin de siècle* America was heir to the nineteenth century's "search for the beautiful and the sublime in nature" and represented a discomfort with the rate of urbanization.[57] The distaste for the momentary realism of the native Hudson River School and the French impressionists led artists to forge a synthesis between objective reality and "subjective sentiment," as George Inness so aptly phrased it.[58] The sources for this mode of representation are varied, including a strong link to the moody romanticism of the Barbizon masters, the loose, painterly style of Whistler, the late works of George Inness, and the evocative, unreality of European symbolist painting.[59]

In addition to the exploration of weather conditions, urban artists were sensitive to the changing appearance of skyscrapers at different times of day. Unlike the work of the French impressionists, the fleeting aspects of nature were explored for their suggestiveness or drama. The most popular time of day to render the skyscraper was in the evening, when the darkened envelope blurred the harsh realities of daylight and lent the scene an air of mystery. The nocturne also provided a vehicle to explore the luminous reflections created by then new electric lighting.

The casting of natural scenery in darkness enjoyed a tradition in American landscape painting. Although inspired, in part, by their connection with the Barbizon painters, native artists could refer to the writings of Edgar Allen Poe for poetic inspiration.

> At midnight, in the month
> of June, I stand beneath the
> mystic moon
> An opiate vapor, dew, dim
> Exhales from out her golden rim
> . . . .
> Wrapping the fog about its breast
> The ruin molders into rest.[60]

The nocturne enjoyed a renewed appeal due to the popularity of Whistler. Despite his move to Europe in the 1850s, the American press covered the 1878 Whistler-Ruskin trials extensively. Whistler's death in 1903 and Pennell's undertaking of a major biography on the artist rekindled this interest. Urban photographer Edward Steichen spoke of the impact of Whistler on the developing American artist. Steichen recalled that when he began painting nocturnes in Milwaukee, the city did not have a gallery to speak of. He could not recall any specific influences except those gleaned from popular periodicals. Yet Whistler's work attracted him, especially the nocturnal subjects.[61]

The paintings and photographs of Steichen clearly demonstrate the transfer of *fin de siècle* notions of landscape painting to the depiction of the new skyscraper. His early endeavors in both media display an obsession with nature by moonlight. In a letter to Stieglitz, he rhapsodized "We had a moon night before last — the like of which I have never seen before — the whole landscape was still bathed in a warm twilight glow — the color simply marvelous in its dark light — and into this rose a large disc of brilliant golden orange in a warm purplish sky."[62] Steichen's first skyscraper photographs were of the Flatiron Building at night, illuminated by both lunar and electric light reflecting off the wet asphalt (fig. 23). In order to simulate the rich tones of the natural scenery he admired, his prints were touched with yellow, blue, and green pigment.[63]

Skyscrapers at night provided artists with the opportunity to explore the jewel-like effects of electric lighting. Not only did the street lamps and advertisements glow with this marvel of modern science, but office buildings at night were often illuminated both within and without.[64] By the 1890s, observers commented upon the effects created by the radiant buildings. Jesse Lynch Williams exclaimed: "it is already quite dark, but the city is still at work and the towering office buildings are lighted — are brilliant indeed with many perfect rows of light dots."[65] In accord with Williams's description, painters such as Julian Alden Weir presented nocturnal images of the numerous skyscrapers, focusing on the scintillating effects created by the intermittent dabs of electricity. And F. Hopkinson Smith described the multitude of ways electricity affected the new architecture: "When the shadows soften the hard lines and the great mass loses its details, and skyscrapers melt into a purple grey . . . when the glow worms light their tapers in countless windows, when the towers and steeples flash greetings to each other . . . when the streets run molten gold and the sky is decked with millions of jewels."[66]

Stieglitz and his colleagues were particularly enamoured with the mysterious potential of the nocturne and the wonder of electricity at night. In one of the first photographs taken at night employing artificial lighting, Stieglitz demonstrated his ability to expand the boundaries of the medium. Not only an experiment in the feasibility of evening photography, *Icy Night, New York* of 1897 (fig. 24) is both an eerie, somber view of the city and a record of its rapid conversion to electricity.

Following his mentor's example, Coburn rendered a silhouette of Ernest Flagg's Singer Building (1908) at twilight, bedizened in glittering evening costume (fig. 25). It was "the most exquisite of all New York's daily effects," proclaimed H. G. Wells.[67] Since the Singer was the first skyscraper to possess internal and external lighting, the building could be rendered more lucidly in darkness.

This is not to suggest that skyscrapers were perceived solely in murky mists and veils; rather, artists were also stimulated by the exploration of the spectacle of light and color. Prophecizing on the future of American art, Harrison encouraged artists to paint "the glimmering iridescent effects that happen only under the great blue arch of the sky, the glory of the noonday sunlight, the pale beauty of dawn" and "the golden glow of sunset." Van Dyke situated the skyscraper in similar colored ambiances. Observing the Flatiron on a July afternoon, he perceived it "float in a rosy atmosphere . . . the high sky above it showing a pallid blue suffused with pink." Of the high tower of the Times Building, he saw it "run from a red glow at sunset through pink mauve and lilac." Sadakichi Hartmann's poem "To the Flatiron" pictured the building in a variety of luminous effects.

> On Roof and Street, on park and pier
> The spring-tide sun shines *soft and white*,
> Where the "Flatiron," gaunt austere,
> Lifts its huge tiers in *limpid light*.
>
> From the city's stir and madd'ning roar
> Your monstrous shape soars in massive flight;
> And 'mid the breezes the ocean bore
> Your windows flare in the *sunset light*.
>
> . . . .
> Well may you smile over Gotham's vast domain
> As dawn greets your pillars with *roseate flame*.[68]

This concern for light's varied properties was inspired by the French impressionists. Yet unlike Monet and Renoir, who wished to convey the transient aspects of nature, Americans explored the expressive and subjective properties of color and light in a language that may be termed proto-abstract.[69]

The rendering of skyscrapers in various seasons and times of day suggested that tall buildings were viewed as an integral part of the natural scenery. From the onset, skyscrapers were likened to lofty mountains and the spaces between them to canyons or plateaus. In Fuller's novel *The Cliff Dwellers* numerous analogies are drawn with the natural topography: "These great canons — conduits, in fact, for the leaping volume of an ever-increasing prosperity. . . . Each of these canons is closed in by a long frontage of towering cliffs."[70]

A number of commentators noted the similarity between the aggregate of skyscrapers and specific lofty mountain ranges. Van Dyke compared the Manhattan skyline to the "wall of the Alps," while another observer evoked the following lines from Tennyson.

> I climbed the roofs at break of day:
> Sun-smitten alps before me lay,
> I stood among the silent statues,
> And statued pinnacles, mute as they.[71]

Pennell often entitled his skyscraper renditions canyons or cliffs, conveying the steep precipices created by the titan structures. In *Cliffs of West Street* of 1912 (fig. 26), the backs of buildings were viewed from the Hudson River, revealing a variegated silhouette of anonymous monoliths, their undifferentiated surfaces suggesting mountains.[72]

The New York skyline was often the source of natural analogy. Aside from their obvious associations with cliffs, tall buildings were likened to emergent plant life, perhaps to reinforce their ever-rising, changing character. James called them "this loose nosegay of architectural flowers," while Hassam praised the light of New York as garlanding "the skyscrapers with rosy tints that suggest the flowers of spring."[73]

The likening of cityscapes to features of the land was symptomatic of a desire to accommodate the new urban topography to accepted notions of landscape painting, a rich tradition in nineteenth-century American art. In addition, the fusion of architecture and natural scenery was an important concept associated with the picturesque as originated by the eighteenth-century English theoreticians William Gilpin and Uvedale Price. Developed to justify the untamed appearance of the English countryside in contrast to an ordered, classical conception of nature, the picturesque provided a whole new vocabulary of aesthetic appreciation for scenes previously considered unworthy. At the end of the nineteenth century in America, artists seized upon the precepts of the picturesque to justify their employment of the skyscraper. To those that criticized the tall building for its so-called crudity, lack of proportion, chaotic, uneven appearance, and ugliness, apologists could respond as their eighteenth-century precursors had.

In his *Essay on the Picturesque* of 1798, Uvedale Price described a once smooth and symmetrical building which was now rough and uneven due to its abandonment to the vicissitudes of time. This building was not ugly as formerly thought but picturesque, Price maintained. Earlier, William Gilpin had differentiated between the smoothness and neatness associated with the beautiful and the roughness and irregularity associated with the picturesque. Price concurred: "The most picturesque . . . buildings are old castles for they in general consist of towers of different heights, and of various outworks and projections, particularly where the abruptness and irregularity of the ground, has in a manner forced the architect to adopt the same irregularity in the shapes and heights of his buildings." Castles were extremely picturesque, owing to the erection of the various parts at different times.[74]

Similar rationalizations were employed in defense of the new office building. Perhaps the earliest connection of the skyscraper with eighteenth-century aesthetic theory occurred in M. G. Van Rensselaer's 1892 seminal article, "Picturesque New York," which defined the picturesque aesthetic that was to dominate American industrial imagery for the next two decades. A well-respected art and architectural critic, Van Rensselaer was favorably disposed to lofty architecture and commercial building. She not only wrote on English cathedrals, but hers was also the first definitive biography on the Chicago architect Henry Hobson Richardson, appearing in 1888. In her works, widely published in the popular magazines of the day, she adapted her views of European architecture to the new office building.[75]

Acknowledging Uvedale Price as an authority on the picturesque, she expounded on its characteristic features, including "harmonious and alien elements," "sharp and telling contrasts," "variety," atmosphere, the nocturne, and "the beauties of light and shadow." Although New York was considered prosaic compared to Paris and Nuremberg, the sensitive observer could discover a multitude of sites in Manhattan. The "entertaining panorama of ruddy architectural irregularities spotted by the more aggressive tall white or yellow irregularities of recent years" were among the scenes recommended by Van Rensselaer.[76]

Concurrent with the inception of its "Field of Art" column in 1896, *Scribner's* began a campaign for the artistic acceptance of the skyscraper. In three separate articles, painters were encouraged to explore the "picturesque quality of the much abused office buildings." Although unsigned, this series was probably authored by the architect and critic Russell Sturgis, an early champion of Chicago's skyscrapers. Following Sturgis's exhortation, the journalist John Corbin observed in *Scribner's*: "Hideous it assuredly is to the rhythm — loving eyes of an architect, and all its details are incongruous — the front of a Grecian temple surmounting a rocket. . . . *Yet the eye that delights in varieties* of light and shadow, *in the surprises of perspective and in the picturesque juxtaposition of masses, will find endless subjects of interest.*"[77]

Responding to the early discoverers of the picturesque in urban America, artists began to describe and render the scenery of New York and Chicago in similar terms. In *Landscape Painting* of 1909, Harrison asserted that there was "a strange picturesqueness in some of our modern steel mills" and "our skyscrapers have an unusual beauty all their own."[78] For Harrison, the picturesque aspects of the city were represented in uncommon viewpoints and the exploration of various atmospheric effects.

Many artists of the time associated the picturesque with the tonal. In an exhibition entitled Picturesque Chicago, Fleury rendered the city in a variety of hazy and indistinct weather conditions. Alfred Stieglitz's *Picturesque New York* of 1897, a collection of photographs of Manhattan and other European cities, explored weather conditions and light.[79]

Although this interest in tonal effects had formal precedents in nineteenth-century painting, Uvedale Price had stressed the effects of light and shade. According to Christopher Hussey, the most respected modern writer on the subject, since the seventeenth century, "overall tonal unity and accentuated chiaroscuro" and painterly values were keynotes of the picturesque. Indeed, Price's praise of an eighteenth-century contemporary painter's work may have been uttered at the beginning of our own century: "The peculiar beauty . . . which arises from the even surface, and the silver purity of tint in that farthest building — from the soft haze of the atmosphere, and the aerial perspective produced by the union of these circumstances . . . makes the architecture retire from the eye, and melt into the distance."[80]

Pennell claimed that he studied the skyscraper for its "grandeur, picturesqueness," and "mystery of pathos," suggesting a more emotional interpretation which incorporated features of the sublime.[81] An examination of Pennell's skyscraper images reveals a number of adaptations of the picturesque, including the fusion of architecture with the natural scenery and the exploration of tonal effects. But the artist was particularly fascinated with the irregularity and variety of unequal building heights.

It is difficult to determine if American artists and intellectuals, aside from Van Rensselaer, had actually read Gilpin and Price.[82] However, their employment of equivalent terminology indicates a comprehensive knowledge of the general concepts associated with the eighteenth-century theoreticians. While an identification of picturesque features in their art is often problematic, many contemporaries felt that merely adopting the skyscraper pictorially represented an acceptance of its principles. It was left to Stieglitz and the photographers affiliated with the "291" gallery to recognize the skyscraper as commercial architecture, instead of as an integral part of the natural landscape.

3

Alfred Stieglitz, Modernism in America, and a New View of the Skyscraper, 1890–1917

Stieglitz and the City

It is necessary to consider Stieglitz separately for his pioneer contribution to the positive attitude concerning urban imagery at the turn of the century. Although he was an integral part of the intellectual climate that viewed the skyscraper in equivocal terms, his overriding belief in progress and experiment, his photographs of metropolitan New York, and the lively dialogue on various aspects of urban living expressed in *Camera Work* inspired a receptive attitude toward the tall building. He stimulated the photo-secessionists, those who broke away from the conservative New York Camera Club in an effort to promote photography as a fine art, to consider the city as a viable theme. He also contributed to the inspiration of American modernist painters affiliated with the "291" gallery, who communicated many of the views first disseminated by Stieglitz.

Stieglitz's preference for urban subjects was motivated by a number of progressive beliefs similar to those that led to the creation of "291." His confidence in the march of progress was the cornerstone of his activities, from his championing of photography as an aesthetic medium to his introduction of modern art to a largely provincial American public. He stated: "The progress of the ages has been rhythmic and not continuous, although always forward. In all phases of human activity the tendency of the masses has been invariably toward ultraconservatism. Progress has been accomplished by reason of the fanatical enthusiasm of the revolutionist."[1]

Stieglitz's belief in progress also extended to science and technology. While studying at the Berlin Polytechnic in 1884, he expanded the medium's limits by photographing a still dynamo illuminated by sixteen power electric bulbs. After his return to New York, he was the first to photograph the city employing artificial lighting. Even the "291" gallery was conceived of as a "laboratory of experiment," so strong were his convictions concerning the innovations of technology.[2] The October 1911 issue of *Camera Work* corroborated this view: in addition to three skyscraper images, it included depictions of a railroad, a dirigible, and an airplane.

Despite his reservations concerning the United States, many of Stieglitz's efforts reveal a nationalist pride. During his student days abroad, he defended products of American technology against derisive attacks from his European colleagues. Moreover, he criticized native photography as too conventional and dependent on outworn formulas, encouraging early artists of the camera "to push ahead with that American will power which is so greatly admired by the whole civilized world."[3] His subsequent support of the American painters Marin, Hartley, O'Keeffe, and Dove attest to his belief in his own country.

The photo-secessionists were also opposed in principle to the staged studio images and hackneyed efforts of a sizable number of American photographers. Stieglitz criticized the "conventionality of the subjects chosen," including "the same types of country roads, of wood interiors, the everlasting waterfall, village scenes . . . piazzas etc." Gertrude Kasebier, a colleague at "291," voiced a similar opinion: "Who has educated the public to a false standard of photography? Who sanctions the painted background, the paper maché accessories, the high backed chair, the potted palm. There is one prominent photographer who never need sign his productions for the sake of identification. The same Turkish cushion, and muslin rose appear in all his photographs of society women."[4]

Stieglitz became the epitome of Henri's "sketch hunter," scouring the streets of New York for subject matter, a method which reinforced his rejection of hackneyed subjects. The critic Charles Caffin stressed that Stieglitz worked chiefly in the open air, allowing his models to pose for themselves. Likening him to the impressionists, Caffin asserted that the photographer sought the "effects of vivid actuality."[5] In accord with Henri, Dewey, and Sullivan, Stieglitz rejected theoretically the rampant eclecticism of the period in favor of contemporary realities.

However, Stieglitz's initial response to New York was colored with ambivalence. Upon his return from the stimulating atmosphere of Berlin with its varied cultural offerings, he found *fin de siècle* New York hopelessly boring; his "yearning for Europe was constant." This sense of detachment prompted feelings of profound depression. He recalled that "it was strange to experience such unhappiness in my homeland among my own people, to feel no point of contact with anyone or anything. The streets were filthy. For months despite being twenty-six years old and living with my parents, I cried every night, not from self pity, but from a sense of overpowering loneliness."[6] Ironically, the photographer's mood of despair drew him closer to the source of his anguish. Wandering through the city with his camera, he imbued his subjects with his sense of isolation. Often, he focused on the seemingly inconsequential aspects of life—a long rag-picker or a driver watering his horses on a bleak winter day. Dull, murky tones were employed to reflect his feelings of despondency.

Although he held an abstract belief in progress and the importance of technology, these ideas were at odds with his sympathies toward the common man and his distrust of materialism.[7] In *Spring Showers* of 1900 (fig. 27), perhaps his first photograph to display the skyscraper, a tiny human figure is dwarfed by the enormity of an office building. Buffeted by the overwhelming power of the elements, the sweeper performs his obsolete task in view of the seemingly omnipotent forces of nature and urbanization.

Like his contemporaries, Stieglitz considered the urban milieu to be inherently mundane and unaesthetic. He believed it was the artist's responsibility to infuse his productions with subjective sentiment. Referring to his own work, he noted although "metropolitan scenes" were "homely in themselves," they had been "presented in such a way as to impart them a permanent value because of the poetic conception of the subjects." He corroborated this view in a *Camera Work* editorial describing his *The Hand of Man*, a photographic view of a railroad yard, as "an attempt to treat pictorially as subject which enters so much into our daily lives that we are apt to lose sight of the pictorial possibilities of the commonplace."[8]

Imbuing the prints with his personality was also symptomatic of his desire to dispel the myth that photography was a purely mechanical process, a mere handmaiden of art according to Baudelaire.[9] Stieglitz fought indefatigably to demonstrate that it was as subjective as painting. His urban views of the 1890s reflect his intention to record "the evolution of an inward principle." In an interview with Theodore Dreiser which occurred on the roof of a skyscraper, the writer reported the following: "Dark clouds had clustered around the sun, gray tones were creeping over the plateaus of roofs; the roar of the city surged up tense, somber and pitiless. 'If we could but picture that mood,' said Mr. Stieglitz, waving his hand over the city."[10]

Despite his numerous misgivings concerning urbanization, he conceived of a series of one hundred views of New York in 1893. Four years later, he published *Picturesque Bits of New York and Other Studies*, which featured preliminary interpretations of Manhattan, including *Winter-Fifth Avenue* and his experiments employing artificial lighting.[11] The desire to record the varied aspects of the city continued intermittently throughout his career. As late as 1932, Stieglitz exhibited ninety-six urban photographs at his gallery, An American Place. These spanned his career from the 1890s until 1932. In an introductory statement, he spoke of wanting to "establish the continuity and underlying idea of the work as a whole."[12]

By the end of 1903 and the publication of his photograph of the Flatiron Building in *Camera Work*, he assumed a more positive attitude toward the skyscraper. Having observed it during the course of construction, he saw the Flatiron anew during a violent snowstorm. Employing atmospheric effects, he sought to convey the "lightness of the structure combined with solidity."[13] He spoke with awe concerning the whole process of fabrication, commenting specifically on the steel and the workers as they ascended the enormous scaffolds. His interest in construction and his intent to convey the building's relative weightlessness indicated a recognition of the contributions of modern technology.

Although Stieglitz acknowledged the technical advances embodied in the skyscraper, the building is still interpreted in the language of the picturesque. Partially obscured by snowy gusts, it is incorporated in the natural landscape. Moreover, the placement of a tree parallel to the picture plane, so as to suggest depth, displays his understanding of Japanese principles of design.[14] This use of picturesque features and non-Western methods of composition serves to remove the image from its contemporary American setting. Thus, in 1903, his progressive attitudes concerning the skyscraper do not coincide with the images themselves.

By 1910, Stieglitz demonstrated a willingness to accept the skyscraper on its own terms. The tall building is no longer rendered in the language of nineteenth-century landscape painting, but celebrated as a symbol of American business prosperity. The titles of, and the messages implicit in, these later endeavors convey his new positive attitude. *The City of Ambition* communicates New York's material expansion and commercial orientations, while *Old and New New York* applauds the erection of a lofty steel scaffold (figs. 11 and 17).

His correspondence in the years prior to the war reinforce his positive regard for the city. Replying to a letter from Marsden Hartley in 1914, he sought to counter the painter's disparaging remarks: "You speak of New York as an unspeakable place. It is truly that. But it is fascinating. It is like some giant machine, soulless and without a trace of heart." The following year, he wrote to Sadakichi Hartmann concerning his current preference for urban living: "To live in the country I hope doesn't necessarily mean that one becomes an intellectual hayseed. . . . So why live in the country? That is what a real skyscraper still does for me."[15]

The dissolution of the "291" gallery, the entry of the United States in World War I, and the beginning of his involvement with Georgia O'Keeffe in 1917 prompted Stieglitz's unprecedented antipathy toward New York. From his resort at Lake George, he wrote to the photographer Paul Strand: "New York seems very far away and I assure you I don't miss any part of it — if I never saw it again I don't think I would hear it call." A month later, he reiterated his distaste for the "noise and dirt and city hum drum — the newspapers, the extras — Wall Street."[16]

The promotion of Stieglitz's ideas occurred in a variety of forums. The periodicals he edited and published, the works he exhibited in his galleries, and the numerous discussions he facilitated insured the dissemination of his views on technological progress and the viability of the skyscraper. In many ways, his major magazine, *Camera Work*, served as a mouthpiece for his continued dialogue with the urban milieu.

The Periodicals

Stieglitz's role as editor of *The American Amateur Photographer* (1893–1896), *Camera Notes* (1897–1902), and *Camera Work* (1903–1917) aided in the artistic recognition of the skyscraper. In the earlier magazines, the subject was briefly alluded to. *Camera Work*, on the other hand, featured numerous urban photographs as well as lively dialogue on various aspects of the metropolis.

The first mention of the possibilities of photographing the skyscraper occurred in an article entitled "Architectural Photography" in *The American Amateur Photographer* of 1893. Although he was concerned predominantly with technical matters, such as the proper selection of lenses, cameras, and vantage points in the rendition of various types of buildings, the author recognized the challenges involved in skyscraper photography. Referring to a skyscraper currently under construction, he stated:

> Mr. F. H. Kimball will require a man of some resource to photograph the Manhattan Life Building on lower Broadway. . . .It is to rise twenty stories, the highest habitable building on Manhattan island. . . . In the case of an isolated building . . . I would advise a view to be taken from a point across the street. In the case of high buildings, such as are under construction, that would be impractical.

The author's desire to assign architectural photography to the chronicler is evidenced by his criticism of that " 'fuzziness,' which his associates considered artistic," but which he found ill-suited to architectural photography's documentary purpose.[17]

Whereas *The American Amateur Photographer* suggested the aesthetic possibilities of urban photography, *Camera Notes* supported its cause. In "A Plea for the Picturesqueness of New York" of 1901, Hartmann encouraged photographers to render the numerous aspects of their urban milieu. In the course of its publication, *Camera Notes* included various industrial and metropolitan scenes to augment Hartmann's advice. In 1900, Stieglitz's famed *Winter-Fifth Avenue* of 1893 and Clarence White's *Telegraph Poles* were reproduced. In the first number of the following year, Prescott Adamson's *Midst Steam and Smoke*, a view of a factory in snow, was offered. The next issue featured a catalogue of the members exhibition of the New York Camera Club which listed Ed Heim's *The Edge of New York* and D. H. Godwillie's *Bulls and Bears of Wall Street* as well as Charles H. Loeber's view of the Brooklyn Bridge. In January of 1902, Stieglitz's *Spring Showers* of 1900 appeared, perhaps the first of his published skyscraper views.[18]

The urban photographs of the United States included in *Camera Work* are too numerous to mention.[19] From the appearance of the Flatiron Building in 1903 to Paul Strand's interpretations of Manhattan in the last issue of 1917, views of the city were included regularly. More importantly, a lively debate concerning the impact of urbanism and the viability of skyscraper subjects was offered in its pages.

The October 1903 issue of *Camera Work* included Stieglitz's *Flatiron — Winter*, Hartmann's "The 'Flat-Iron' Building — An Esthetical Dissertation," and his poem, "To the 'Flat-Iron.' " While this issue of the periodical represented ostensibly a celebration of the skyscraper, a closer examination reveals that Stieglitz and his colleagues still held misgivings. Hartmann praised both the building's picturesque quality and its utilitarian properties. Yet he criticized "the pernicious habit of industry, yelling and writhing before the juggernaut of commerce." An excerpt from his poem underlines this ambivalant position.

From the city's stir and *madd'ning roar*
Your *monstrous* shape soars in massive flight.[20]

Joseph Keiley's article "Landscape A Reverie" provided a more dismal appraisal of metropolitan living. The author complained about congestion, the hustle-bustle, noise, and pollution: "Morning and evening ferry-boat, street car, elevated train are packed to suffocation. . . . Time for reflection there is none — it is always hurry, hurry. . . . We hear but the roar and the rattle of the city whose din is never still. We breath air heavy with overuse, surcharged with noxious gases."[21] As an antidote to this oppressive existence, Keiley recommended an escape to the country.

Perhaps the most detailed exploration of the aesthetic merit of the skyscraper and other urban sites to appear in *Camera Work* occurred in the previously discussed "The Origin of Poetical Feeling" by Roland Rood. The author presented a detailed analysis of our so-called aesthetic predilections, encouraging a reevaluation of these tastes. This position had been prefigured, in part, by Hartmann, who questioned the relative connotations of beauty which were dependent on the particular *Zeitgeist*.[22]

By 1911, Stieglitz and his colleagues no longer found it necessary to criticize or justify the city. The October issue of *Camera Work* presented the skyscraper in unequivocally positive terms and served as a celebration of New York City and technological progress. It included four skyscraper images of the previous year by Stieglitz, *Spring Showers* of 1900, a host of urban photographs from the 1890s, and depictions of a dirigible and an airplane. Relying on a "straight" or unmanipulated approach to the medium, the skyscraper was finally divorced from its previous associations with the picturesque. This may have reflected Stieglitz's desire to explore the mechanical potential of camera art, a direction which accorded with his current enthusiasm for industrial development. Moreover, Stieglitz wished to differentiate the "straight" method from the abstract directions of modern painting, as evidenced by the inclusion of a Picasso drawing in the same issue.

An article by Alvin Langdon Coburn reinforced Stieglitz's optimism. In "The Relation of Time to Art," Coburn linked the technical modernity of photography to the skyscraper, suggesting that the camera was particularly suited to the rendition of office buildings. "Photography born of this age of steel seems to have naturally adapted itself to the unusual requirements of an art that must live in skyscrapers, and it is because she has become so much at home in these gigantic structures that the Americans undoubtedly are the recognized leaders in the world movement of pictorial photography."[23] The camera's ability to capture momentary impressions was appropriate for depicting New York's rapid pace, Coburn asserted.

The last two issues of *Camera Work* introduced the urban photographs of Paul Strand and the reemergence of a more ambivalent view of the tall building. Although a few of the images suggest a fascination with the abstract patterns of the city, others express the alienation and loss of identity experienced by the urban dweller. These images seem to sum up Stieglitz's own equivocal feelings toward the city at the time. Although he was optimistic concerning the strides made by modern science, he felt that the city squelched the individuality of the metropolitan inhabitant.

Alvin Langdon Coburn

Stieglitz's persistent dialogue with the city had important ramifications for the photo-secessionists and the American modernists affiliated with his gallery. As a result of his pioneer efforts in urban photography, the skyscraper assumed a prominent role in many of their endeavors. The reoccurrence of specific buildings and sites in their paintings and photographs attest to the group's coherence and the members' influence upon one another.

Coburn was the most important urban photographer associated with the "291" circle, aside from Stieglitz.[24] In February 1906, Coburn had his first skyscraper images published in the *Metropolitan Magazine*, a London-based periodical. In addition to *St. Paul's Church and the Park Row Building* (fig. 4), picturing the contrast of religious and commercial architecture, the magazine included a nocturnal view of the Flatiron Building in silhouette.[25]

In 1907, Coburn began to relinquish the attitudes associated with the picturesque. In *Portsmouth U.S.A.* (fig. 28), an image of the lofty Park Row Building surrounded by industrial smoke, and in *New York* (fig. 16), he defined the skyscraper in terms of business and commerce. Coburn's avoidance of any devices to manipulate the photograph conveys his desire to interpret the skyscraper on its own terms, three years before Stieglitz's own "straight" images of the tall building. Coburn's explanation of the photograph reinforced his desire to divorce the skyscraper from retrogressive associations. "If I have made the observer feel the dignity of the architecture with its straight lines and practically unornamented and with only the proportions to give it charm . . . I am satisfied," he maintained.[26]

Coburn was so enamoured with Manhattan's rapid upward growth that in 1909 he conceived of a book on the subject. Entitled *New York*, it seemed a realization of Stieglitz's desire to record various aspects of the city. Perhaps acknowledging his debt to Stieglitz in this regard, Coburn wrote to inform him of the project. "Of course there is no end to the things there are to do. There is New York for example. I have the material for a set of plates that I very much want to do."[27]

The following year, Coburn's photographic essay on the metropolis was published simultaneously in New York and London. Featuring a foreword by H. G. Wells, Coburn explored comprehensively the skyscraper theme. Wells's introductory remarks enhanced the spirit of optimism which characterized the imagery.

> I WILL confess an unqualified admiration for the skyscraper—given the New York air to reveal it clearly to its summit against the sky. The Flat-Iron I visited again and again . . . that I might see it at every phase in the bright round of New York day and night . . . the most exquisite of all New York's daily cycle of effects, Mr. Coburn has given a picture of the Singer tower at twilight, in which I verily believe . . . has caught some of the exhilaration in the air.[28]

The photographs are a frank display of Coburn's enthusiasm for the sky-scraper. Almost half of the twenty images are of tall office buildings, such as *The Singer Building—Twilight* (fig. 25), *The Singer Building—Noon*, *The Park Row Building*, *The Flatiron*, *The Metropolitan Tower*, *The Skyline*, *The Battery*, *The Waterfront* (fig. 16), and *The Stock Exchange*. The remainder of the photographs depict the building of tunnels, the city from above, nocturnal views celebrating electricity, and suspension bridges. While a few of these works are still misty, tonalist endeavors, the majority continue the direction set forth in his photographs of 1907.[29] Presented in crisp, objective terms, the skyscraper is rendered independently rather than as an integral part of the natural landscape. Coburn's selection of four well-known office buildings continued Stieglitz's earlier selection of the lone Flatiron. The images of specific skyscraper sites display Coburn's intention to interpret the skyscraper as a symbol of business and commerce.

Stieglitz's admiration for Coburn's skyscraper views is seen in his inclusion of a photograph entitled *New York* (1907) in *Camera Work*. Yet is it ironic that Stieglitz failed to reproduce any of the images from Coburn's book, *New York*, aside from a picturesque, nocturnal view of the Singer as an advertisement for the new publication. Instead, the "New York" issue of *Camera Work* included an article by Coburn on the suitability of the camera for the rendition of the skyscraper.[30] It appears that Stieglitz wished to claim credit for the fresh approach to the depiction of the skyscraper pioneered by Coburn four years earlier.

Coburn's exhibition, entitled New York from Its Pinnacles (1913), at London's Goupil Gallery displayed his continued interest in the skyscraper. The show featured *The Woolworth Building*, *The Municipal Building*, and *The House of a Thousand Windows* (fig. 42), all views of specific buildings. *Trinity Church from Above* and *The Octopus* (fig. 29) explored the appearance of the city from distant heights. Coburn explained: "These five pictures were made from the towers of New York's highest buildings. How romantic, how exhilarating it is in these altitudes, few of the denizens of the city realize, they crawl about in abyss content upon their own small concerns, or perhaps they rise to the extent of pointing with pride to 'the tallest building in the world' the Singer."[31]

The Octopus and *The House of a Thousand Windows*, which Coburn described as a "cubist fantasy," were particularly important in his development of abstract photography. In surveying the city from above, Coburn became attuned to the camera's ability to record a multitude of detached, undifferentiated shapes. Coburn's colleague at "291," the painter Max Weber, urged this expansion of photography's boundaries. In the photographic periodical *Platinum Print*, Weber asserted that "photography is a flat space art, as is drawing, painting or printing. The page or the canvas is empty, but pregnant with birth as space, waiting for the touch of the inspired mind. There is a universe of light and colored form in matter."[32] Coburn acknowledged Weber for instituting a group of exercises with the intention of being "as abstract as it is possible with the camera," while the latter was a teacher at The Clarence White School of Photography in 1916.[33]

Coburn's abstractions of the city and his subsequent development of vorto-
graphy were inspired by the theories of modern art articulated by Weber.

Coburn was the most persistent photographer of the skyscraper at the
turn of the century. By 1907, he developed a more objective approach to the
rendition of the tall building, removing it from its previous associations
with the picturesque. Perhaps more than any other photographer in the
Stieglitz group, his skyscraper views influenced the attitudes of the American modernists recently returned from Europe. In addition, he was among
the first to explore the abstract possibilities of camera art in the rendition of
the American city.

The Celebration of the Individual Skyscraper:
The Flatiron, Singer, and Woolworth Buildings

The selection of specific skyscrapers comprised a significant component of
the Stieglitz circle's artistic inspiration. The repeated appearance of the
Flatiron, Singer, and Woolworth Buildings in their work suggests that only
those buildings with distinctive, often dramatic characteristics were
selected.[34] New York skyscrapers, in particular, were often designed to serve
as advertisements for either entrepreneurs or corporations. Those features
designed to catalyze the public's enthusiasm often aided in the acceptance of
the skyscraper as a suitable subject for the fine arts.

Daniel Burnham's Fuller or Flatiron Building (1903), on the corner of
Twenty-Third Street and Broadway, contributed to the artistic recognition
of the skyscraper. Perhaps more than any other single building at the time,
it enjoyed the overwhelming attention of the public and the popular press.
Its loftiness and unobstructed presence on Madison Square, long recognized
as a picturesque site before the erection of the tall building, made the
Flatiron seem more formidable than those that were crowded together on
the southern tip of Manhattan Island. Its most distinctive feature, which
earned it the nickname "Flatiron," was its eccentric shape—a shape which
led one critic to refer to the building as a "stingey piece of pie."[35] Stieglitz
likened it to a "ship's prow in motion," while Mary Fanton Roberts saw it as
a "gigantic galleon sailing majestically in a shadowy harbor."[36]

Its triangular form was also considered the cause of the notorious
windstorms which often churned up around it. These swirling gales provided much titillating amusement for the voyeurs of the city (fig. 30). In a
fictional account, *The Real New York* (1904), the antics around the Flatiron
forced one character to "tuck her chin into her breast to keep her hat from
joining the others." Her "skirts, though she clung to them with both hands,
snapped and swirled about her like a flag in a tempest."[37] But the windstorms around the Flatiron engendered not just amusing publicity. *New*

York Times headlines from 1903 until 1906 read: "Sues Flatiron Owner—Clothier Says Winds Deflected by Big Building Wrought Havoc," "Wind Causes Boy's Death—Blows Him Under an Automobile Near Flatiron," and "High Wind Upset Women and Horse . . . Accident at Park."[38]

Stieglitz was inspired to render the Flatiron during a massive snowstorm when the winds would be the strongest. His affection for the building persisted throughout his life, causing him to complain in 1919 about a great victory arch which threatened to overshadow it. "The poor Flatiron, gosh! how it must suffer," he lamented. Several years later, he entertained the notion of having his ashes scattered from its pinnacle![39]

Stieglitz's enthusiasm for the Flatiron, the exposure accorded to it in *Camera Work*, and its singular shape and reputation inspired members of the "291" circle. Coburn, Steichen, and Marin rendered the building in similar terms. Following Stieglitz's depiction, the earliest seems to be by Coburn. In a letter to Stieglitz written from abroad, Steichen referred to Coburn's new photograph as disappointing. "The Flatiron I consider good if you want to show it to someone who knows it," Steichen contended. "But in London it is simply a black mass—meaningless and badly composed."[40] Despite Steichen's negative evaluation, Coburn borrowed from Stieglitz's initial endeavor by stressing the building's triangular shape and soaring quality. In another version of the Flatiron from his *New York* series, Coburn's wintery image of the building from Madison Square is almost identical to that of Stieglitz.

In response to Coburn's "black mass," Steichen photographed the Flatiron in 1905. In Steichen's multiple renditions, the lone building looms out from the dark sky (fig. 23). A branch is placed parallel to the picture plane, reminiscent of Stieglitz's use of Japanese principles of composition.

Upon his return to New York in 1909, on the occasion of the exhibition of his paintings at "291," Marin executed a watercolor of Burnham's popular building, suggesting a direct link between urban painting and photography in America (fig. 31).[41] The work owes much to his photo-secessionist colleagues in the static quality of the image and the positioning of the tree in the foreground. Rather than evaluating the formal elements of the painting in the context of Italian futurism and French orphism, both of which had not been developed at this early date, it is important to view Marin's early skyscraper views in the context of the ideas and stylistic preferences at "291."[42]

Ernest Flagg's Singer tower (1908) soon replaced the Flatiron as New York's most popular skyscraper. Nicknamed the Singerhorn, an obvious reference to the Swiss alps, it was the tallest building in Manhattan, reputed to have exceeded the biblical tower of Babel in height. Its most exciting feature was the new observatory. For a nominal fee, one could ascend to its summit to view the sprawling metropolis below. According to an article in the *New York Times*, published on the eventful day of its opening, several hundred square miles of New York and its environs could be surveyed. Express elevators catapulted to the tower in one minute, prompting one woman to liken the experience to an airship ride.[43]

The association of the Singer with airships and dirigibles was a common one and conjured up dreams of the future. Harry M. Pettit's cover for Moses King's contemporary *Dream of New York* included the Singer in a prophetic architectural fantasy (fig. 32). In the midst of mammoth structures and flying machines stood Flagg's tower, dwarfed by imaginary super skyscrapers. These interpretations of Manhattan's loftiest tower may have been prompted by the architect's announcement in the popular press that he was planning a thousand foot tower at Broad Street and Exchange Place.[44]

Like the Flatiron, the Singer captured the imaginations of the members of the "291" circle. In addition to his early renderings of the Flatiron in 1904–1905, Coburn was the first of the group to photograph the Singer in 1909 (fig. 25). His visual essay, *New York*, included two separate views of the building, the only skyscraper to be selected for special study. Coburn continued to hold the Singer in high regard. In 1910, he sent Max Weber a photograph of the building and a note encouraging him to continue his skyscraper views.[45] Three years later, on the occasion of his show, New York from Its Pinnacles, Coburn referred to the Singer as an inspiration for many of his photographs of the city from above. He reported that "only the birds and a foreign tourist or two penetrate to the top of the Singer tower where some of these vistas were exposed."[46]

In 1909, John Marin began to render the Singer. Certainly, the widespread publicity surrounding the building served as a source of inspiration. Yet a comparison of Marin's early rendition of the tower with Coburn's *The Singer Building — Twilight* further establishes the link between urban photography and painting (figs. 25 and 33). In both subject and compositional format, Marin's architectural portraits owe more to his photo-secessionist colleagues than to European modernism.

Marin's adoption of the Singer was more than just an initial fascination. In 1910, he completed at least seven watercolors in which the Singer figured prominently.[47] The most revealing is *Downtown from River*, in which the rounded tower rises from a mass of anonymous geometric planes (fig. 34). Irradiant lines emanating from the building's pinnacle bestow upon it the status of a religious icon. In view of the current tensions between church and skyscraper, perhaps the artist wished to portray the tall building as the cathedral of the future.

The same year, Stieglitz photographed the Singer tower views which were subsequently published in *Camera Work* as *The City of Ambition* (fig.

17) and *The City from Across the River*. His awareness of the identity of the edifice is borne out by the title *Singer Building from the Hudson River* (1910) in the 1932 exhibition of his New York photographs at his gallery, An American Place. The inclusion of images of both a dirigible and an airplane in the same issue of *Camera Work* suggest that he associated the Singer with the dawn of a new era of urban travel.

The last major building to absorb the collective efforts of the members of the "291" circle was Cass Gilbert's Woolworth Building of 1913. Considered the apex of skyscraper design, it was proclaimed by the prominent architectural critic Montgomery Schuyler to be "the culminating triumph of commercial architecture."[48] Three years before the completion of the building, a massive publicity campaign was launched on its behalf. No less than fourteen articles appeared in the *New York Times* chronicling its progress and development. Many of the reports stressed its unprecedented dimensions. A typical article, entitled "55-Story Building in Lower Broadway," enumerated its major features.

> It will cost $12,000,000 and will cover the block from Park Place to Barclay Street Three Stories Underground—Twenty Five Stories in the Tower—Height 750 Feet—Highest Structure in the World.[49]

Perhaps more than its immense proportions, it symbolized the rise from rags to riches of Frank W. Woolworth. A commemorative volume was published shortly after the building's completion which praised the dime store magnate. "Apart from the Woolworth Building as a marvelous memorial to American creative genius its opening ceremonies merited observance on a national scale, if only for the reason that it towered to the sky as a superb and enduring symbol of the possibilities open to every man in the great American republic, no matter how handicapped by circumstance of birth or early fortune."[50]

To further promote the building's reputation, it was accorded the same official consideration usually reserved for a national monument. To inaugurate its opening, a sumptuous dinner was held in honor of Cass Gilbert. A message was simultaneously telegraphed to President Wilson in Washington, who pressed a button which illuminated the building, to the eager anticipation of all the notables present. As part of the ceremony, a speech was given on "The Woolworth and the Artist," in which the building was likened to the great architectural wonders of the past. According to the writer, "aspiring souls" naturally drawn to the lofty values epitomized by the skyscraper

> Will look through nature up to God
> And strive, in word and form to speak
> The beauty it was born to seek.[51]

The building's association with spiritual concerns was prompted, no doubt, by its Gothic design, which earned it the nickname "the cathedral of commerce."[52] This was reinforced by a sculpture in the lobby of Cass Gilbert in the guise of the benevolent donor, offering the people of New York a beautiful building rather than an exploitive symbol of business.

Although the artistic rendition of the building was publically encouraged, Stieglitz chose not to photograph it. However, he admitted later that the Flatiron appeared rather unattractive to him after viewing skyscrapers such as the Woolworth.[53] Despite his decision not to record its lofty tower, he was quick to defend Marin's numerous renditions to those that visited the "291" gallery in 1913. An interesting anecdote concerns one viewer who came expressly to examine Marin's Woolworth views. Stieglitz noted the marked disturbance of a well-dressed man who stood in front of the works. Sensing the man's confusion before the painter's unorthodox interpretations, Stieglitz expounded on the nature of abstract art, describing the paintings as depictions of the Woolworth in various moods. Yet the viewer remained forlorn, repeating incredulously, "So this is the Woolworth Building?" When the gentleman finally left, Stieglitz learned to his surprise that he had been addressing Cass Gilbert, the architect. The significance of the occurrence, aside from its humor, is Stieglitz's creation of an environment in which the artistic rendition of the skyscraper, and more specifically of the Woolworth Building, was highly regarded.[54]

Marin was the most enthusiastic admirer of the Woolworth among the members of the "291" circle; Stieglitz described his interest as a passion.[55] Marin's treatment of the theme ranged from representation to total abstraction, indicating his technical versatility and conceptual sophistication. In *Woolworth #28* of 1912–13 (fig. 35), he rendered the tower under construction, employing energized brushwork which belies the architecture's static character. In *Woolworth #31* of 1912–13, portions of the completed building shift and topple, merging with the surrounding space. Marin's most radical interpretation appeared in *Woolworth #32* of 1912–13 (fig. 36), composed simply of rhythmic curvilinear lines meant to convey the skyscraper's surging upward movement.

Marin seems to have been influenced by the particular physiognomy of the building as reported in the popular press (fig. 37). Although the Woolworth was supposed to be 750 feet tall, the engineers measured it at 42 feet taller. Cass Gilbert claimed that if the calculations were correct, the building must be lopsided, and the builders should be made to straighten it up.[56] Marin's tilting of the tower suggests a humorous interpretation of the inadvertent miscalculations.

Coburn completed several views of the Woolworth. Utilizing the smoke of the city, he created the illusion that the building was situated among the clouds, a reference to its unsurpassed height (fig. 38). The image of the Woolworth situated in the upper reaches of the atmosphere was a common one. On the cover of *Above the Clouds and Old New York* (fig. 39), a book published for tourists, billowing cloud formations encompass the Gothic structure.[57] The absence of other buildings signifies that the Woolworth occupies a separate realm.

The Woolworth continued to fascinate artists, including those loosely associated with the "291" gallery. Marcel Duchamp proclaimed it a ready-made. Robert Coady featured a full-length article on the building in his periodical *The Soil*, including an interview with its chief engineer.[58] The final homage to the Woolworth by the members of the Stieglitz group occurred in the film *Manhatta* (1921) by Charles Sheeler and Paul Strand.[59] In this cinematic treatment of New York, the building is surveyed from top to bottom, perhaps a statement on its unsurpassed height. Not until the completion of the Empire State Building in 1931 was the Woolworth finally eclipsed.

The American Modernists: Marin, Weber, and Walkowitz

John Marin

Marin's adoption of the skyscraper was inspired by his contact with the photo-secessionists, revealed in his static architectural portraits of 1909–1910.[60] Yet these initial interpretations of the tall building possess a nascent energy, seen in the quick, pointillist-inspired strokes. In *Downtown from River* of 1910 (Fig. 34), the artist's familiarity with cubism is apparent in the rectilinear planes which appear to glide over the surface. By exploiting the viscosity of the watercolor medium, Marin conveys the ever-changing character of the city.

Beginning in 1911 and continuing throughout 1912, his paintings demonstrate a desire to forge a new urban vocabulary. In a letter to Stieglitz, he expressed the difficulties he was experiencing. "As you have no doubt been told . . . the skyscrapers struck a snag, for the present at least, so we have had to push in a new direction, and may be a step forward."[61]

Like traditional renderers of the skyscraper such as Pennell and Hassam, the painters associated with the "291" gallery recorded the dynamism of New York. Marin spoke of piling "these great houses one upon another with paint as they do pile themselves."[62] In *Movement, Fifth Avenue* of 1912 (fig. 40), buildings shift and collide. Instead of concentrating on the individual skyscraper, the artist conveys the dynamic aspects of city life; the crowded architecture, human congestion, construction, and traffic are interrelated.

In 1913, fourteen of Marin's watercolors of the city were shown at "291" and four were exhibited at the famed international Armory Show. The former exhibition was accompanied by a detailed catalogue statement by Marin in which he explained the works' content and style. The artist clarified his disinterest in presenting a static view of the urban scene; rather, he sought to convey how the multitude of dynamic happenings in the vast metropolis impinged upon one another. He believed that not only were people and animals alive, but so was architecture. If one accepts the premise that "a work of art is a thing alive," he contended, it is necessary to imbue one's work with the same spirit of energy. In an etching of the Woolworth Building which he entitled *The Dance*, he demonstrated that skyscrapers could assume lifelike characteristics by swaying to the beat of the urban symphony. Anthropomorphizing the skyscraper was a common theme among those affiliated with "291," perhaps their way of making it more humanly comprehensible.[63]

In response to the city's dynamism, Marin admitted that sensations were evoked in him. "It is this 'moving of me' that I try to express, so that I may recall the spell that I have been under," he maintained. In order to communicate these spontaneous reactions, he recognized the importance of developing a formal language which would reconstitute them; working imitatively proved inadequate to his purposes.

Marin acknowledged that the energy was created, in part, by the fact that New York itself was in a state of transition; old buildings were being torn down and replaced by skyscrapers. Categorizing these changes as "great forces at work, great movements," he noted "the warring of the great and small, the influence of one mass on another mass." The dilemma of recording the transformations in the urban topography was settled in favor of depicting the "pushing, pulling, sideways, downwards" and "upwards" activity in abstract terms.

Rendering one's unseen, sensory responses was promoted at "291." From the gallery's inception, Stieglitz claimed that a work of art was an externalization of an inward state, the subjective emotions which prompted it. This viewpoint was expressed in a number of articles featured in *Camera Work*. Writing on the dadaist Frances Picabia, Maurice Aisen reported that the artist concerned himself solely with psychic perceptions, or the *pensée pure*.[64]

Marin's use of the term "pull forces" and his reference to "the warring of the great and small" may have inspired by Italian futurist rhetoric. His familiarity with futurism probably resulted from the publication of their aggressive pronouncements in current magazines and newspapers. Moreover, numerous examples of their paintings were illustrated in the popular press, although it was not until 1915, on the occasion of the Panama Pacific

Exposition in San Francisco, that futurist works were actually exhibited in the United States.[65] However, in view of the publication of various articles in *Camera Work* on the depiction of nature's invisible aspects and the subjective impressions of artists, Marin was already well schooled in the theoretical basis of abstract and non-objective art. The dynamic aspects of city life were commented upon before the introduction of European modernism to these shores. Contemporaries noted the pushing, congestion, and construction, although these phenomena were still rendered in a nineteenth-century vocabulary. Thus, direct knowledge of the futurists' visual vocabulary or rhetoric was not a necessary prerequisite in Marin's interpretation of New York's office building.

From 1914 to 1919, the skyscraper was all but absent from Marin's *oeuvre*.[66] But beginning in the twenties, he approached his urban milieu anew. Often employing coarse, expressionist brushwork, he conveyed the vigorous sense of movement of the postwar decade.

Max Weber

As a result of Weber's brief affiliation with Stieglitz and the "291" gallery from 1909 to 1911, the artist was influenced by the prevailing enthusiasm for skyscraper subjects.[67] Significantly, his introduction to the photo-secessionist group occurred at the high point of the prevailing feeling of urban optimism. In 1910, Coburn's *New York* was published and, in the following year, Stieglitz's "New York" issue of *Camera Work* appeared.

The exhilaration felt toward the city in these years was reported in a fictional account, "Fifth Avenue and the Boulevard Saint-Michel," by Temple Scott. The writer, a frequent participant in the group, based his story on the experiences of Michael Weaver (Max Weber), an American modernist who had recently returned from Paris. Longing for the charm and culture of Europe, Weaver feels alienated from the rampant materialism and the seething thoroughfares of New York City. Echoing Stieglitz's ambivalence, Weaver admires the "magnificent structures, showing a barbaric daring in the architect-builder" which "appeared to him as broad columns of aspiration."[68]

On the verge of despair, he meets Finch (Stieglitz), who exhibits his paintings at the Gallery of the Golden Disk ("291"). Finch often held luncheons at the Dutch House (Holland House) for painters, intellectuals, and critics associated with the gallery.[69] At one such engagement, Finch asks the artist John Seaman (Marin) how his work is progressing. Seaman replies, "I've been working on the Flatiron building and I think I've got it, once and for all. I've got it floating in the sky, mounting into clouds of gray, and gold, and ultramarine. I was never so pleased with anything I ever did before." At this Weaver interjects, "I hope, Seaman, you'll not forget to put into that Flatiron picture of yours the feeling of its fourth dimension quality . . . the consciousness of a great and overwhelming sense of space magnitude in all directions at one time."[70]

The participants continue to debate issues involving the materialistic bent of the American art establishment, the relationship of art to the public, and the superficiality of fame. Leaving the meeting, Weaver is met by Church (Benjamin De Casseres), who identifies with his alienation, but encourages him not to denigrate the United States. Church exclaims,

> Look at the Flatiron building! There it is, stuck in the common rock. But, see, it mounts into heaven itself, a thing of beauty its sordid builders never dreamed of realizing. The sky has taken it unto itself as part of its own pageantry. Let it be the symbol of your life.
>
> And look back at this magnificent perspective! It breathes hopes from every tower and turret. . . . Let that be the symbol of your native land. So long Weaver. . . . Remember, here is your Paris![71]

The story conveys the Stieglitz circle's confidence in the skyscraper as an American symbol. It also affirms Weber's attraction to the tall building despite his misgivings about other aspects of American culture, an admiration illustrated by his characterization of tunnels, bridges, and towers as realizations of dreams or visions.[72] Weaver's advice to Seaman concerning the inclusion of the fourth dimension in his rendition of the skyscraper is perhaps the most telling aspect of the tale. One of Weber's major contributions to modern art was his ability to apply his complex theories of painting to his visual interpretations of the American urban scene.

Weber's admiration for skyscraper subjects was motivated, in part, by his friendship with Coburn. After the painter's argument with Stieglitz, he drew closer to both Coburn and the photographer Clarence White. In 1911, Coburn encouraged him to render urban America: "Don't forget that vision of New York from the Harbour. The little sketch has whetted my appetite for what you will make of it."[73] As a further incentive, Coburn sent Weber a photogravure of a skyscraper a few months later.

Heeding Coburn's advice, Weber pictured the Manhattan skyline from the bay in a small oil entitled *New York* of 1912 (fig. 41). Composed entirely of sharp-edged, geometric forms, it reveals his adaptation of aspects of cubism. The transparent quality of the faceted buildings is similar to his "crystal figures" of the previous year, reinforcing his desire to reinterpret cubism based on his own experience and introduce elements of the fourth dimension.[74] In his essay on the latter subject, published in *Camera Work* of 1910, he discussed "the space that envelops" an object.[75] However, Weber lacked the sophistication of contemporary French artists, who explored the complex relationship of matter to its surrounding space. At this time, his writings were still more progressive than his rather static skyscraper images.

Just as Coburn influenced the works of Marin, so did he affect Weber's selection of specific buildings seen from similar vantage points. The photographer's book, *New York* (1910), and his show, New York From Its Pinnacles (1913), included aerial views of the city. Weber explored the city's abstract patterns from dizzying heights in a painting erroneously titled *The Woolworth Building*. He rendered Henry Ives Cobb's Liberty Tower from above, the identical structure Coburn photographed in *The House of a Thousand Windows* (fig. 42).[76]

New York of 1913 (fig. 43) heralded a shift in his perception of the skyscraper, inspired perhaps by his theoretical inquiries, which were among the most progressive in America. The static monoliths of previous years were replaced by buildings subsumed in a cataclysmic whirl of energy. No longer based on actual skyscrapers, these buildings reflect the sensations evoked in confrontation with the dynamic metropolis, an attitude markedly different from the endeavors of the photographers and painters of "291," who often based their subjective interpretations on actual sites. The novelty of *New York* seems to coincide with the development of Weber's ideas on the nature of art. In 1913, he stated, "It lies within the domain of the plastic arts to reorganize forms and visions of forms, to reconstruct and interpret nature, to create or realize forms and visions of forms, unit by unit." This synthetic reorganization process required the energy of the inspired mind because "matter" yielded "in measure with and in degree of the intensity of the creative power of the artist."[77]

In addition to the reconstruction of physical reality, Weber conceived of art as the representation of unseen forces or a whole "universe of light and colored form in matter."[78] In his *Essays on Art* of 1916, based on lectures given at the Clarence White School of Photography two years earlier, Weber put forth a more developed theory of art. He asserted that there was a multitude of invisible processes that could be depicted, divorced from their connection with specific objects. According to Weber, matter was not chaotic, but "magnetism, energy, cohesion make form. Such forms destine matter and determine its plastic and poetic character as weight, dimension or energy . . . are elements irrespective of their specific embodiment . . . so ought these be dealt with purely as only abstract elements."[79] Weber recognized the artist's ability to perceive these unseen forces in the "spiritual domain," terminology probably borrowed from Kandinsky, whose writings were published in *Camera Work*.[80] Art came into being, according to Weber, through a communion between the imagination and external invisible elements.

The artist was obviously familiar with current information in physics and science, an area outside the scope of this discussion.[81] His and Marin's employment of similar concepts suggests that they were frequently discussed at "291." Marius De Zayas, the Mexican caricaturist and theoretician on modern art, explained in *Camera Work*:

> Formerly art was the expression of a collective or individual belief, now its principal motive is its investigations. It proceeds toward the unknown, and that unknown is objectivity. It wants to know the essence of things, and analyzes them in the phenomenon of form, following the method of experimentalism set by science, which consists in the determination of the material conditions in which a phenomenon appears. It wants to know that *significance* of plastic phenomena, and accordingly, it has had to enter into the investigation of the morphological organism of things.[82]

New York (fig. 43) not only marks the realization of Weber's aesthetic theories, but also reflects his reaction to the city's construction and upward growth. Like Marin and Coburn, he viewed New York's expansion as the complex interaction of disembodied shapes and forces. "The Eye Moment," from his book *Cubist Poems* of 1913, is similar in spirit to the writings of Gertrude Stein and conveys his reactions to New York.

> Cubes, cubes, cubes, cubes
> High, low, and high, and higher, higher
> Far, far out, out, out, far
> Planes, planes, planes
> Colours, lights, signs, whistles,
>   bells, signals, colours,
> Planes, planes, planes
> Eyes, eyes, window eyes, eyes, eyes
> Nostrils, nostrils, chimney nostrils
> Breathing, burning, puffing
> Thrilling, puffing, breathing, puffing,
> Millions of things upon things,
> Billions of things upon things,
> This for the eye, the eye of being,
> At the edge of the Hudson,
> Flowing, timeless, endless
> On, on, on, on.[83]

The poem's relationship to the painting *New York* is clarified in a letter from Coburn to Weber. The photographer verified that "the poem 'The Eye Moment' " was to appear "opposite the frontispiece of *New York*," because "its opening 'Cubes, cubes, cubes, cubes' gives a deeper meaning to the book."[84]

The poem's terminology illustrates Weber's desire to reconstruct space "unit by unit" as explained in his essay of the same year. The invisible elements of sound, time, and energy were included in his conception of the city. But the most significant aspect of the piece, revealed in the title "The Eye Moment," was the "millions of things upon things, billions of things upon things" that could only be perceived by the "the eye of being" or the mind's eye.[85]

Although the "The Eye Moment" refers to the artist's internal states, it also describes the skyscraper's multiple windows. The puffing smokestacks are likened to breathing, while the chimneys themselves are associated with nostrils. The anthropomorphizing of the tall building is reminiscent of the work of Marin, who also wished to have his skyscrapers come to life.

The reference to "high, low, and high, and higher, higher," indicates Weber's response to the constant building activity in Manhattan. Describing his painting *New York at Night* (1915), he spoke of the "electrically illumined contours of buildings, rising height upon height."[86] In *Blue New York* of 1912, a gridlike structure in the foreground of the composition is meant to evoke a steel scaffold. Weber's poem "Workmass" of 1914 intermingled the various aspects of fabrication.

> Tied to the sky mass the workmen,
> But the workmass moves, moves moves
> To there where spheres of steam and
>   smoke and buildings outblot,
> To there where the buildings from
>   out the workmass grow
> The workmass like lava flows
> Over the bridge flows, flows
> From on high the buildings look on.[87]

Weber's aesthetic response to the skyscraper was not restricted to painting and poetry. In 1916, he completed the maquette of a sculpture, *Abstraction Skyscraper (Tour d'Eiffel)* (fig. 44). The ambiguity of the title suggests that the vertical, aspiring form could relate either to an office building or to the French monument of iron. In view of Weber's view that the urban environment represented a confluence of intangible elements, the sculpture was probably meant to evoke the skyscraper's soaring movement, seen in the interaction of abrupt diagonals which point upward.

Beginning in 1918, Weber's style took a dramatic turn. Eschewing his experiments in abstract art, and the influence of both cubism and futurism, he returned to the depiction of monumental figures and still-life subjects. This seemed to coincide with his teaching at the Arts Students League and the beginning of his role as a husband and father. A more conventional home life and the realization of his ethnic identity, seen in his numerous renditions of the vignettes of Jewish life, curtailed his depiction of the modern city.

Abraham Walkowitz

Although Walkowitz returned to the United States from Europe in 1908, it was not until 1911 or 1912 that he became part of the "291" circle. The enthusiasm for the skyscraper that pervaded the group at that time and his friendship with Weber resulted in his depiction of the city's dynamism. Walkowitz's cityscapes suggest a logical stylistic progression from loose watercolors to architectonic structure to tangled linear skeins, although this development is far from conclusive.[88] As in the skyscraper views of Weber and Marin, the works are linked to his artistic theories and to his exposure to rapid city building.

Times Square of 1910 (fig. 45), executed with an amorphous, *fauve*-inspired stroke, conveys the frenetic character of urban life. Humans are reduced to a flurry of activity in the midst of looming vertical forms; all is subsumed in a vast circular motion.

This approach was replaced by architectonic structure. In *New York Abstraction* of ca. 1915 (fig. 46), undifferentiated rectilinear and triangular monoliths impinge upon and topple one another, illustrating the artist's response to the realities of urban congestion. Like the earlier works of Weber, these city scenes were not dependent on any specific site but evoke the general appearance of the metropolis. If we are to accept the interpretations of painter Oscar Bluemner as accurate reflections of the artist's aims, the similarity to both Marin's and Weber's ideas concerning the synthetic reconstitution of art are apparent. Bluemner described Walkowitz's method of work in the following terms: "he ignores the totality of nature, eliminates all the irrelevancies, dissolves the natural corporation of the remaining features and qualities and arranges them in a new composition."[89]

The inclusion of a human eye within the urban chaos conveys the desire to imbue the city with life by anthropomorphizing the buildings, an approach consistent with other members of the "291" group. Walkowitz was soon to expand upon the concept of the living skyscraper.

New York Improvisation of 1915 preserves the structure of the skyscraper but introduces the superimposition of swirling arcs.[90] Walkowitz's predilection for circular motion conveys the frantic activity which consumed the city like a maelstrom. The title, borrowed from the methods of Kandinsky, indicates that the artist was working in a more spontaneous manner, commensurate with the spirit of city life.[91] Later, he described one of his urban views as "the equivalent of what one feels going through from the Battery to Times Square, showing the buildings each saying, 'I must be higher' . . . and the people crowd like mosquitos in the street below."[92]

By 1916, Walkowitz was interested in the evocative power of line rather than structure. He exhibited a view of New York's lofty buildings composed predominantly of energized, all-over lattice work, leading in 1917 to frenetic semiautomatic fantasies (fig. 47). His explanatory remarks concerning the show illustrate his intent to imbue line with dynamic energy. "When line and color are sensitized, they seem alive with the rhythm which I felt in the thing that stimulated my imagination."[93] Like Marin and Weber, he believed that art was the product of experiences which engendered sensations. The artist's role was to translate these feelings into concrete form or the language of art.

Mention must be made of the similarity between Walkowitz's drawings of the dancer, Isadora Duncan, and his views of New York. The artist met Duncan in Rodin's studio in 1907 and recorded her repeatedly from life and memory until his death. Reminiscent of Rodin's method for sculpting *The Walking Man* (1879), Walkowitz employed dynamic, free-flowing line to capture Duncan in the process of motion (fig. 48). Similar drawings were included in his book *Improvisations of New York: A Symphony in Lines* of 1948, a collection of his interpretations of the city, dating from his return to New York.[94] Just as he studied Duncan dancing, he examined the perpetual movement of New York. As a recent biographer of the artist pointed out: "New York City and Isadora Duncan, both of which are treated as studies in motion rather than form . . . are more interesting cumulatively than as isolated works."[95] Walkowitz's fusion of people and urban motifs is consistent with his contemporaries' humanization of the skyscraper. His particular contribution lies in the exploitation of the almost electric potential of line as a vehicle to transmit his reactions to the dynamic metropolis.

New York Dada

The brief and questionable manifestation of dada in New York included the participation and interaction of both Americans and Europeans.[96] The meeting of these diverse groups at the "291" gallery and at the apartment of collector Walter Conrad Arensberg had a significant impact on the native valuation of the skyscraper. Rather than providing new insight into our arts and ideas, the Europeans' unabashed enthusiasm aided in the promotion of viewpoints first articulated by the members of the "291" circle and various other American commentators.[97] For the first time in the history of American art, Old World inhabitants travelled to the United States for creative inspiration. New York was regarded as the mecca of futurity. With the arrival of the so-called dada personalities from abroad, the previous dialogue on tradition versus innovation was settled in favor of the modernity of America.

The prior affiliations and endeavors of Francis Picabia, Marcel Duchamp, and Albert Gleizes favorably disposed these artists to Manhattan's urban, industrial milieu. Before his arrival in New York, Gleizes had been a member of the *Abbaye Créteil*, a communal, utopian group which sought to relate art to contemporary life. The *Abbaye's* publications, which included Jules Romain's *La Vie Unanime* and Henri Barzun's *Le Terrestre Tragédie*, illustrated their interest in speed, simultaneity and industry. Many of Gleizes's own paintings were based on aspects of the French urban scene.[98] Duchamp's mechanomorphic representations of humanity and his experiments in the rendition of motion addressed the impact of the machine. Their meetings at Puteaux, which also included Léger, Villon, and Delaunay, involved both lengthy inquiries concerning the newest discoveries in science and technology and the social implications of an art which mirrored current society.

Picabia appeared in Manhattan in 1913, a month before the opening of the Armory Show, followed by Duchamp and Gleizes two years later.[99] Almost immediately, the popular press seized upon these infamous celebrities of the American International Exposition as experts on contemporary painting. When questioned about their reactions to the city, they uniformly responded in glowing terms. Duchamp asserted that "New York is itself a work of art, a complete work of art"; Gleizes concurred, referring to skyscrapers as "creations in iron and stone."[100] Although this view of the office building had been articulated earlier by Americans, the dadaists' opinions received widespread coverage in the media. Once again, European artists were called upon to validate American culture; as a consequence, the skyscraper was thrust into the limelight and reappraised, resulting in a renewed enthusiasm for the steel-framed structure.

Completely contradicting the opinions of Howells and James, the dadaists maintained that the modernity of New York was superior to the antiquated character of Europe. In accord with the aggressive Italian futurists, Duchamp believed that the "idea of demolishing old buildings, old souvenirs," was indeed desirable. "The dead should not be permitted to be so much stronger than the living. We must learn to forget the past, to love our own lives in our own time," he asserted. Duchamp claimed that the art of Europe was "finished — dead" and encouraged Americans to cease relying on the Old World. "Look at the skyscraper!" he maintained, "has Europe anything to show more beautiful than these."[101]

In their search for subject matter that could best express the spirit of modern life, these artists perceived New York as the physical incarnation of twentieth-century novelty. The height of the buildings, the pace of the crowds, and the pervasiveness of industry was a source of wonder and exhilaration. As Picabia reported to the popular press: "You of New York should be quick to understand me and my fellow painters. Your New York is the cubist, the futurist city. It expresses in its architecture, its life, its spirit, the modern thought. You . . . are futurists in word and deed and thought." In another interview two years later, Picabia elaborated on his perceptions on America's inherent modernity, likening the "boundlessness of our national aspirations" to the creative process itself. He considered America the place where "art and life" discovered "a wonderful consanguinity."[102]

Marius De Zayas voiced the same opinion in the periodical *291*. Drawing an analogy between the spirit of America and that of the modern artist, he asserted that America had "the same complex mentality as the true modern artist, the same eternal emotions and sensibility to surroundings, the same continual need of expressing itself in the present."[103]

In response to the modernity of New York, Picabia and Gleizes undertook the theme of the skyscraper, while Duchamp explored the complex relationship of man and the machine. Their admiration for the city must have been fueled by the exhibition of Marin's skyscraper views at the Armory Show and the Stieglitz circle's animated discussions concerning the tall building.

Picabia began to render the skyscraper, in part, as a response to a request from a *New York Tribune* editor.[104] His article "How New York Looks to Me" provides the best explanation of the artist's approach to the depiction of the tall building. To the question, "What do you think of New York?" Picabia replied that a more appropriate question was, "How are you affected by New York?" Explaining that his art was the representation of pure feeling, he continued: "You see no form? No substance? Is it that I go out to your city and see nothing? I see much, much more, perhaps, than you who are used to see it. I see your stupendous skyscrapers, your mammoth buildings. . . . But I do not paint these things which my eye sees. I paint that which my brain, my soul sees." Like the American modernists, Picabia did not view the skyscraper in isolated terms, but as part of the dynamism of the city — its crowds, commercialism, and "atmospheric charms."[105]

In an interview of a month earlier, Picabia was more specific in his explanation of the transmutation of the skyscraper into particular sensations and forces. "I saw what you call your 'skyscrapers.' Did I paint the Flatiron Building, the Woolworth Building, when I painted my impressions of these 'skyscrapers' of your great city? No! I gave you the rush of upward movement, the feeling of those who attempted to build the Tower of Babel — man's desire to reach the heavens, to achieve infinity."[106]

Despite their improvisational character, the drawings of New York included in both articles convey in non-objective terms the verticality of the skyline and the horizontal scuttling of ships (fig. 49). The identifiability of a number of motifs is based on Picabia's reference to the New York harbor at night, its mammoth buildings, its ships, and a multitude of flags.[107] The darkened character of these drawings suggests they were meant to conjure up images of nocturnal Manhattan. The astute interviewer of the initial *New York Tribune* article reinforced Picabia's selection and transformation of specific aspects of the city.

> In M. Picabia's pictures of New York . . . we are to look, not for topography . . . but for moods expressed in form . . . if the beholder can recognize in one of these drawings New York's towering heights and sharply cut skyline, a view of its electric power houses and industrial establishments from the East River, it is not because the artist deliberately sought to reproduce them, but because the vividness of their impression has made them a salient part of his mood.[108]

The mechanomorphic imagery of both Picabia and Duchamp was also nourished by their visit to America. Although these preferences were evidenced in Europe, their presence in urban, industrialized New York inspired many of their machinist experiments. The skyscraper is not blatantly present in Duchamp's works, it is implicity so.

Albert Gleizes's depictions of the skyscraper were more specific. In *Kelly Springfield* of 1915 (fig. 50), the artist superimposed the aggressive lettering of a flashing neon sign on toppling, nondescript monoliths replete with windows.[109] The use of patterning, verbiage, and overlapping planes reveals that Gleizes borrowed many synthetic cubist conventions in his interpretation of the city. Like his American colleagues, however, the use of lettering was inspired directly by the numerous billboards in New York.

Perhaps more than his European colleagues, Gleizes was stimulated by specific New York sites, indicating the influence of the Stieglitz group. The Woolworth, the Flatiron, and the Brooklyn Bridge were among the structures he portrayed.[110] In *Sur le Flat-Iron* (fig. 51), an anachronism in 1916, Gleizes fractured the building into a composite of directional forces. In a letter to the collector John Quinn, he expressed fondness for New York's characteristic features: "I make long watercolors for prepared New York's [*sic*] picture. I want to paint a big canvas, vision synthetic of my trip in America. I think very much to Wall Street with its buildings . . . and the tumultuous harbor."[111]

However, in 1916, Gleizes's attitudes toward New York began to shift; the tall buildings were referred to as "heavy blocks of cement" and the fire escapes as cages. Criticizing the materialism of America, he inveighed against life in New York. "Modern genius — American genius consisted in persuading the greatest number of individuals to buy, with money they did not possess the greatest quantity of manufactured objects for which they had absolutely no need," he argued.[112] Although his canvases throughout 1917 provide no indication of his change of heart, his opposition to New York continued to increase. He conceived of another utopian community where the dignity of human life would be respected, achieved in 1927 with the formation of *Moly-Sabata* in Soblon, France.

The enthusiastic reactions of the *émigrés* inspired a number of Americans. Closely associated with Duchamp, Man Ray expanded on the concept of the ready-made with his constructions composed of found objects. *New York 17* (fig. 52) was the first work in which Man Ray employed disparate forms in order to create a skyscraper motif. Originally composed of wooden strips of alternate lengths found in his studio, he fastened them with a carpenter's clamp. The zigzag motif created by the uneven heights suggests the variegated contour of New York's setback skyscrapers.[113] Another work, a glass jar filled with what appears to be metal ball bearings, featured the words "New York" (fig. 53). The verticality of the container, the use of metal and glass, and the piling of rounded forms evokes the crowding of skyscraper inhabitants.

Although he was only influenced in part by dada, Robert Coady, editor of the periodical *The Soil*, sought to enhance the skyscraper's reputation.[114] As the title indicates, *The Soil* celebrated aspects of indigenous American culture, including the machine, folk art, billboards, business, and industry. In the first issue, Coady's own article on "American Art" included the skyscraper, the Woolworth, and the Metropolitan Tower as examples of native aesthetic expression. On the bottom of a page from the same issue, Coady asked, "Who will paint New York? When?" and included a photograph of skyscrapers from above by the commercial firm of Brown Brothers.[115]

In addition, Coady contrasted an excerpt from Whitman's "Crossing the Brooklyn Ferry," which predicted that others would recognize New York, with Arthur Cravan's contemporary poem celebrating the technological awesomeness of it. An excerpt from Cravan's work demonstrates his admiration for the skyscraper's grandeur, electric lighting, and elevators.

> New York! New York! I should
> like to inhabit you!
> I see there science married to
> industry,
> In an audacious modernity,
> And in the palaces,
> Globes,
> Dazzling to the retina
> By their ultra-violet rays
> The American telephone
> And the softness of elevators.[116]

The next issue included a continuation of Coady's thoughts on American art, in which he defined it as the product of the native artist in his own milieu. Invoking the old versus new debate in favor of the latter, Coady proclaimed that "an Englishman invented the Bessemer Process and we built our skyscraper," thereby encouraging Americans to acknowledge their own creativity.[117] A lengthy article on the Woolworth Building followed, featuring the opinions of the man who engineered its construction. Discussing the various structural challenges and innovations characteristic of the skyscraper in general and the Woolworth in particular, he characterized the solutions as "positively an outgrowth of American conditions."[118]

The periodical included numerous reproductions of industrial and urban images. In addition to the illustration of various machines with such captions as "Monument?" or "Moving Sculpture," Coady featured the work of Marin, Weber, and Walkowitz. Walkowitz's *New York* of 1916 and *Times Square, New York — Night* of 1910 appeared in *The Soil*.[119]

In many respects, Coady's attitudes concerning the skyscraper encompass those of the "291" gallery and the dadaist position. On the one hand, he embraced the machine and skyscraper as American contributions to the creative sphere, expanding the concept to include popular culture. Yet his presentation of artists affiliated with the Stieglitz circle in *The Soil* displays his unwillingness to offer the work of Europeans as a solution.

4

Skyscraper Mania, 1917–1931

In the third decade of the twentieth century, the skyscraper was finally perceived as a dominant part of both the American sensibility and topography. Images of the tall building abounded in art, literature, music, furniture, and stage design. The debate concerning the desirability of the skyscraper escalated to new heights due to the actual proliferation of buildings everywhere. The building boom which occurred throughout the United States after the World War I, reaching its peak between 1925 and 1931, literally thrust the skyscraper into the nation's psyche. No longer relegated to the southern tip of Manhattan, skyscrapers made their way to New York's midtown district as well as to other major cities.[1]

Omnipresent derricks and beams prompted a variety of observers to chronicle and comment on the tall building. "Titanic Forces Rear a New Skyline," an article complete with visual evidence, asserted that "every uptown thoroughfare from Lexington Avenue to Eighth Avenue" in New York had "fallen under the spell of reconstruction" (fig. 54). A host of workers were striving to complete some 350 new buildings by the winter of 1925, and 900 extant structures were in the process of rehabilitation, it was reported.[2] In *Only Yesterday* (1931), Frederick Lewis Allen observed that between 1918 and 1930, office use in large modern buildings in the midtown district multiplied tenfold.[3] The construction epidemic was not confined solely to New York. "A Census of Skyscrapers" appeared in 1929 in the architectural periodical *American City* and demonstrated that now most of the nation's metropolitan centers possessed tall steel-framed buildings, although Manhattan still took the lead with more than five times the amount of its oldest and closest rival, Chicago.[4]

As a result of the increase and domination of the lofty architecture, renditions of it increased dramatically. Several exhibitions were mounted which offered the skyscraper as the veritable keynote theme. From 1923 to 1925, the John Wanamaker Gallery of Modern Decorative Art presented three major shows on urban subjects. The first was entitled Exhibition of Paintings, Watercolors, Drawings, Etchings, Lithographs, Photographs, and Old Prints of New York City. It included the works of over fifty artists, from the cityscapes of the Ashcan artists and the abstractions of the early American moderns to the contemporary works of George Ault, Stuart Davis, Charles Sheeler, Joseph Stella, Niles Spencer, Man Ray, and Preston Dickinson.[5] The following year, a more modest second annual which reiterated the subject of the initial show was mounted at Wanamaker's.[6] Although various aspects of the city were explored, titles indicate that the early and contemporary modernists perceived New York in terms of its skyscrapers.

In 1925, the John Wanamaker store hosted The Titan City: New York. This show summarized the historical orientation of the previous two exhibitions and presented the skyscraper as a reality of the present and the future. The show was organized ostensibly to commemorate Wanamaker's new building, but it was also conceived as a "tercentenary pictorial pageant of New York."[7] Although nostalgic views of the settling and development of Manhattan were included, the skyscraper dominated the exposition. Willy Pogany's sixty-foot-high panel, entitled *The Growth of New York* (fig. 55), pictured monumental buildings at the tip of the island. Fantastic, mural-sized renderings by Harvey Wiley Corbett and Hugh Ferriss offered the skyscraper as a solution for the "City of the Future" section, an immaculate, utopian urban landscape composed of multipurpose setback structures extending entire blocks. The importance of the exhibition, in addition to its optimistic, prophetic character, was the publicity it provided for the skyscraper. One reviewer noted that "the most astounding fact is that architecture should be recognized as a subject of popular interest, and that the administration of the organization had the courage to stage an exhibit of that particular character."[8]

The presentation of the lofty building as a popular subject of interest occurred in response to the *Chicago Tribune* Competition of 1922. It engendered universal interest and enthusiasm concerning the problems of tall building design and provided a forum for examining the most progressive ideas concerning architecture in general and the skyscraper in particular. Although its importance as a repository for progressive architectural solutions has long been recognized, its role as a propagandizer and advertiser for the skyscraper has not been explored.[9] Regardless of one's feeling toward the tall building, the scope of the *Tribune* Competition engendered discussion.

The request for entries took the form of a massive publicity campaign in newspapers across the nation. Drawings were received from major architectural firms in the United States and twenty-three countries around the world. The *Tribune* reproduced renowned architecture of the past in their advertisements in order to inspire prospective entrants. Like the Woolworth

Building, which was sheathed in a Gothic facade, they hoped that Chicago's future publishing tower would possess the significance of a public monument or religious architecture. The announcement for "the most beautiful office building in the world" for the "enhancement of civic beauty" professed their concern for human values.[10]

The direct appeal of the competition in both architectural and popular spheres was seen in the numerous requests from major American museums to exhibit the original drawings. The Minneapolis Institute of Arts, the former United States National Museum, the Albright Art Gallery in Buffalo, and the Art Institute of Chicago hosted this comprehensive presentation of the image of the skyscraper.[11] In May 1923 alone, the Chicago museum reported an attendance of at least 25,000 people! General enthusiasm was so strong that one art periodical reported the numerous invitations from "commercial clubs, banks, department stores and even private individuals" to show the works.[12] Despite the fact that these were architectural renderings rather than aesthetic endeavors proper, their placement in a museum or gallery context communicated the topicality of the subject to painters, photographers, and sculptors.

Literary personalities responded to the physical presence of the skyscraper. At least four novels of the decade, including *The Cubical City* (1926) by Janet Flanner, *Manhattan Transfer* (1924) by John Dos Passos, *Flamingo* (1927) by Mary Borden, and *The Skyscraper Murder* (1926) by Samuel Spewack, either presented the skyscraper as a backdrop or as a major force in their characters' activities.[13]

Notions of design were also influenced by the tall building of the twenties. Paul Frankl's skyscraper furniture, employing the cubical massing of the new setback buildings, pointed to the inclusion of the lofty steel-framed structure into the interior and exterior spheres of American life. For the first time, the skyscraper image was made perceptible on a human scale, engendering a grasp of the building's mammoth proportions.

American music felt the impact of the skyscraper. Many observers likened the cacophonous, syncopated beat of jazz music to the clatter and rhythm of skyscraper construction. In John Alden Carpenter's 1926 ballet, *Skyscrapers*, the composer employed a jazzlike idiom to convey the building of an American city. Moreover, the staging of the dance at New York's Metropolitan Opera House pointed to the tall building's incursion on conservative strongholds of culture.

Carpenter's ballet also suggested the presence of a skyscraper existence, the tall building determining the activities of the city's inhabitants. Workers pantomimed the erection of the city while machine noises heralded and defined their tasks. The notion of one's activities being prescribed by the tall building was voiced by a number of critics of the decade, who pointed to the dehumanizing effects of such a mechanized mode of existence.

The seeming domination of the skyscraper over all aspects of American life and art prompted a variability of responses. However, most scholars continue to appraise the decade as a period of artistic acceptance of the skyscraper. Terms such as "urban optimism" and "precisionism," while useful for their explanation of a portion of twenties' urban painting, have created a onesided view of tall building imagery.[14] The latter label is particularly limiting, since it often links the use of pristine, machine-inspired forms with an accompanying positive attitude.

On the other hand, historians such as Henry May categorize the contemporary response to the decade as both "rosy and black."[15] Some were favorable to the business civilization, urban expansion, and the machine. This group included artists Charles Sheeler and Margaret Bourke-White, architects Hugh Ferriss and Harvey Wiley Corbett, historian Charles Beard, and the writer Jane Heap. In contrast, Lewis Mumford, Waldo Frank, Harold Stearns, Joseph Stella, Paul Strand, and novelist Mary Borden were suspicious of the standardization of life in the nation's urban centers. The debate concerning the viability of the skyscraper reemerged with unparalleled energy. Articles in the popular press, which included both sides of the argument, indicated the widespread nature of these tensions.[16] Unlike the previous polemical discussions concerning the skyscraper, which dealt predominantly with its architectural viability or aesthetic merit, later discussions were concerned with human issues.

In order to assess skyscraper imagery after World War I, it is necessary to explore prevailing attitudes toward the tall building. In many cases, artists reflected enthusiasms or misgivings similar to those of their counterparts in other fields. Although the stylistic and formal influences on skyscraper images have been adequately identified, the physical appearance of the city and responses to urbanism and technology require further elaboration.

Aspects of Skyscraper Enthusiasm: Rationality and Transcendence

The positive response to the skyscraper in the twenties included new rationalizations and praise. Unlike previous enthusiasts who sought to define its existence in largely nationalistic terms, contemporary supporters viewed the skyscraper as an integral part of a new, sophisticated industrial and business civilization. An understanding of the favorable reaction to the steel-framed structure in the years following World War I is linked to a larger celebration of American prosperity and technological development.

Economically, the twenties was a decade of boom and expansion. As a result of the monetary plenty, a host of mechanical labor-saving gadgets became the accepted accoutrements of every American home. As Sinclair Lewis noted condescendingly in *Babbitt* of 1922 (an observation corroborated by Robert and Helen Lynd's study *Middletown* of 1929), vacuum cleaners, electric fans, percolators, toasters, and cars became incorporated irrevocably into the American experience.[17] The necessity for procuring such items was reinforced by sophisticated advertising; newspapers, magazines, and billboards created the desire for more consumer goods. "The Age of the Machine" or the "Machine Age," appellations assigned by contemporaries, aptly described the decade's mechanical preferences.[18]

Often speaking in utopian terms, supporters of the machine civilization believed that an acceptance of technology would engender a better quality of life, liberate man from baser tasks, and provide for greater leisure and spiritual growth. Henry Ford proclaimed that "for most purposes a man with a machine is better than a man without a machine." Sheldon Cheney, art and architectural critic, was perhaps the most positive admirer of the machine's so-called humanitarian potential, envisioning an environment where the elements would be "tamed, weather tempered, transportation . . . effortless," and "cleanliness universal." Machines would ultimately "solve all men's work problems."[19]

Critics of contemporary culture were branded as retrogressive and anachronistic; Beard referred to them as "artists of a classical bent and . . . spectators of a soleful temper." Edwin Avery Park, in *New Backgrounds for a New Age* (1928), claimed: "The ancient forms of artistic expression came into being when the non-material aspects of life were alone considered worthy of song and representation. . . . Today, romance and the panoply of heroes are no longer the absorbing thing. Something else compels popular interest. It is the new world of science, industry and business through which the glamour of the past has fallen away."[20]

In this climate of confidence concerning industrial development, the businessman was applauded as the new American hero, a position reinforced by the administrations of Harding, Coolidge, and Hoover (1920–33). The prevailing Republican ideology articulated by Coolidge was epitomized in the popular slogan, "The business of America is business." Under the *laissez-faire* policies of the decade, large corporations were protected from the antitrust laws instituted during the Progressive Era. Moreover, companies like Ford and General Motors promoted a favorable image of business with the supposed institution of humane conditions in their plants. As a contemporary proclaimed: "What is the finest game? Business. The soundest science? Business. The soundest art? Business. The fullest education? Business. The fairest opportunity? Business. The cleanest philanthropy? Business. The sanest religion? Business."[21]

Favorable views toward business extended to praise of the products of industry. In the twenties, observations on the machine often encompassed the tall building. Thus, any analysis of the response to the skyscraper in the twenties must include the reaction to increased mechanization. In the opinion of skyscraper optimists, the tall building and the new industrial civilization were inextricably linked. Echoing Le Corbusier's dictum, "the house is a machine for living," Sheldon Cheney referred to the skyscraper as a "perfect business-machine," describing the efficiency of its functional components, "It is simply a series of cubicles piled thirty stories high, with efficient communication lanes between offices and to the street, electric elevators up and down, scientifically calculated halls and aisles, steel frame sheathed and baked clay, concrete floors, tile and plaster walls, metal doors and window frames, plumbing, central heat, central vacuum cleaning, and electric lights." Even as vituperative a critic as Lewis Mumford characterized the skyscraper as "an imperfect machine."[22]

The perception that the skyscraper was a mechanical object was realized both ideologically and visually in the Machine Age Exposition of 1927. It was organized by the writer and editor of the *Little Review*, Jane Heap, and a distinguished panel of artists which included Charles Demuth, Marcel Duchamp, Hugh Ferriss, Louis Lozowick, Man Ray, and Charles Sheeler. The show featured "actual machine parts, apparatuses, photographs and drawings of machines, plants, construction etc., in juxtaposition with paintings, drawings, sculpture, constructions and inventions." The most progressive works from the United States, Austria, Belgium, France, Germany, Poland, and Russia attest to its international scope. Among Heap's goals was a desire to establish an interchange between the artist and the engineer. Echoing the Italian futurist Enrico Prampolini, who had published his ideas in the *Little Review*, Heap proclaimed:

> The men who hold first rank in the plastic arts today are the men who are organizing and transforming the realities of our age into a dynamic beauty. They do not copy or imitate the machine . . . they recognize it as one of the realities. In fact, it is the engineer who has been forced in his creations to use most of the forms once used by the artist . . . the artist must now discover new forms for himself. It is this "plastic-mechanical analogy" we wish to present.[23]

Side by side with ventilators, gears, and coffee grinders were models, photographs, and paintings of the skyscraper. The catalogue reveals the tall building's important position in the show. In a foreword entitled "Architecture of the Future," the utopian renderer and architect Hugh Ferriss praised the skyscraper unconditionally. Facing the essay was a reproduction of Ferriss's *Project for a Glass Skyscraper*, a model of which appeared in the exposition. He noted that the new architecture superceded the desire for individual aggrandizement present in earlier buildings. As a result of laws passed in New York City, the shape of buildings had changed from a concern with facades to three-dimensionality. He believed that these new architectural solutions, adapted to the particular American milieu, paralleled developments in other countries. In this age of the machine, Ferriss felt that outworn formulas had been rejected in favor of a universal idiom based on technology.

Despite his attempt to link current trends in America to a new international phenomenon, Ferriss believed that New York's recent skyscrapers and other setback designs were the most progressive forms of contemporary architecture. These included "Corbett's Bush building, Harmon's Shelton Hotel, Hood's Radiator building, and Saarinen's Tribune Tower." "As these giant structures march with deliberate stride into American cities, it becomes apparent that we are facing a new architectural race," Ferriss proclaimed.[24]

Because of Ferriss's supervision, the Machine Age Exposition catalogue opened with America's contribution to architecture. Supplementing his praise of the most prominent architects of the American skyscraper— Alfred Bossom; Buchman and Kahn; Helmle and Corbett; Raymond Hood; William Lescaze; McKenzie, Vorhees and Gmelin; and Eliel Saarinen— models, photographs, and renderings of their most recent efforts were included in the show. In his selection of works for the American section, Ferriss offered examples of both current and visionary architecture. In addition to Ferriss's own glass skyscraper, Leonard Cox was represented by an *Imaginary Project for a Skyscraper to Cover 4 City Blocks*, Raymond Hood showed a plan for multileveled pedestrian traffic ways connecting tall buildings, and Knud Lönberg-Holm exhibited a *Design for a Radio Broadcasting Station* of steel, concrete, and glass.[25]

Other contributions to the exhibition included Louis Lozowick's paintings of various urban and industrial centers of the United States, his representations of New York and Chicago defined solely by their skyscrapers. Works by Charles Sheeler, the painting *Business* by Charles Demuth, and photographs by Ralph Steiner attest to the view that the tall building was an integral part of the machine sensibility.[26]

Many of the attitudes articulated in the Machine Age Exposition reflect the prevailing belief that technology and the skyscraper were symbols of both rationality and transcendence. Heap's exclamation, "THE MACHINE IS THE RELIGIOUS EXPRESSION OF TODAY," reproduced in aggressive capitals, summed up this philosophy.[27] Whereas the tall building's ability to reflect these seemingly antithetical concepts was deemed impossible by past and present critics, proponents appreciated the skyscraper's utilitarian and spiritual properties. Physical height became a metaphor for the aspiring nature of both the intellect and the quest for the supernatural.

The rationalist's position was manifested in three approaches to the skyscraper which may be categorized as the technical, the philosophical, and the practical. Providing continuity with early observers of the tall building, contemporaries viewed it as the epitome of logic and utility. Just as the beauty of the machine was praised for its clean, pristine parts, a more modern skyscraper free of decoration was thought to be more efficient. This position was promoted by architectural historians such as Fiske Kimball, who referred to the skyscraper as "the citadel of functionalism." Harold Loeb, editor of the international periodical *Broom*, articulated a similar view, referring to the tall building as the physical incarnation of purely utilitarian principles: "Office buildings, lofts and apartment houses realize to a greater degree the magnificient possibilities of steel. . . . The old decorative motifs plastered on their sides, where the windows permit, are strictly subordinated to the design enforced by structural demands."[28]

The functionalist ethic was so pronounced that a veritable machine aesthetic was encouraged as a result. These ideas were outlined comprehensively in the pages of the *Little Review*, beginning in the spring of 1923 with the publication of Fernand Léger's "The Aesthetics of the Machine." The artist conceived of a plastic beauty independent of imitation and past styles, preferring instead the utilitarian beauty of kitchen utensils and "the mechanical grace of an automobile." Echoing Léger, Edwin Avery Park observed that "there is beauty in . . . the perfect adjustment of the automobile, its parts and its whole. . . . The new shape . . . of motorboats, the body of a submarine are equally beautiful."[29]

This confidence in functional designs engendered skyscraper images similarly constructed. Many of the artistic enthusiasts of the tall building composed their works with a concern for logic and efficiency.[30] The efforts of Sheeler, Lozowick, Bourke-White, and Frankl served as analogues for the clean precision of the mechanical objects they sought to render.

A concomitant argument in favor of the skyscraper's logic was the perception that it was the product of man's highest potential, an incarnation of abstract, platonic principles. The loftiness of the tall building certainly lent itself to this comparison. These notions were explored comprehensively by Orrick Johns, architectural critic of the *New York Times*. In "The Excelsior of Architecture," Johns regarded architecture in general as the expression of "the highest reach" of "intelligence." Throughout history, he maintained, "we find a surprisingly logical and continuous growth toward certain definite ideals," culminating in the invention of the steel frame, which was inspired "with a pure idea."[31]

The view of the skyscraper as a symbol of logic was also manifested in the upsurge of interest in city planning which characterized the decade. Despite their often fantastic character, the utopian projects of Corbett and Ferriss reflected the current belief that technology could be harnessed and employed to man's advantage if proper foresight was exercised. A prerequisite to this notion was an unequivocal faith in the machine and a confidence in the human capacity to master it. Even otherwise hostile observers of urbanism like Frank Lloyd Wright acknowledged that "the machine is the architect's tool — whether he likes it or not. Unless he masters it, the machine has mastered him. The machine is an engine of emancipation or enslavement, according to the human direction or control given it."[32]

Simultaneous with those who viewed the skyscraper as the keynote of logical functionalism, others surveyed it in reverential, wondrous terms. Utopian views toward the tall building encompassed both the rational and the other worldly. Orrick Johns compared the architects of contemporary skyscrapers to builders of Gothic cathedrals, noting that both shared the "sense of having his building 'hang from Heaven.'" Similarly, in "America's Titanic Strength Expressed in Architecture," the author likened contemporary skyscrapers to eminent buildings of the past: "Man enjoys overwhelming effects of extraordinary power. The simpler these titanic expressions are, the more they satisfy him. They appeal to his imagination, to his reverence, they transcend all petty things."[33]

Similar homage accompanied descriptions of business and the machine. Antedating Heap's proclamation that "THE MACHINE IS THE RELIGIOUS EXPRESSION OF TODAY," Harold Loeb spoke of the "mysticism of money" replacing religion as the quest for truth. According to the author, "business and state" were "now as closely knit as church and state in the middle ages." *Broom's* editors described "The Age of the Machine" as "an age of spiritual change and growth as well as economic ascendancy."[34]

The sense of awe and wonderment which characterized the response to the skyscraper served as an acknowledgment that America's values were in a state of transition. It may have also relected an effort to further legitimize the tall building by couching it in religious terminology. As far as literary and visual interpretations of the skyscraper were concerned, the sublime image was adopted by optimists and pessimists alike. The numerous paintings and photographs of boundless towers rendered from disorienting perspectives were manifestations of the simultaneous amazement and inability to grasp the skyscraper's monumental proportions and symbolic implications.

Charles Sheeler and the Functional Skyscraper

Of those artists who undertook the theme of the skyscraper in the twenties, Charles Sheeler may be viewed as the quintessential optimist of the urban scene. His early career as a photographer of Philadelphia's architecture in 1912, his comprehensive visual essay of the Ford Motor Company at River Rouge in 1927, and his persistent use of the tall building throughout his career demonstrate his unequivocal regard for the urban, industrial sphere as the highlight of American civilization. Despite the infrequent praise by the artist, Sheeler's utopian views of the metropolitan scene bespeak of a clean, ordered world where glistening mechanical parts operate efficiently.

The artist's initial attraction to the productions of modern technology may be explained, in part, by his affiliation with the members of both the Stieglitz and Arensberg circles. In 1914, Sheeler met and subsequently began a correspondence with the pioneer photographer on the technical aspects of camera art. Sheeler joined these groups during a period of optimal confidence concerning Manhattan's urban expansion. The "New York" issue of *Camera Work* had recently been published and Stieglitz's letters convey his unabashed enthusiasm for New York's towers. In many respects, Sheeler's and Strand's film *Manhatta* of 1921 paid homage to Stieglitz's prior celebrations of the city.

The machine images and favorable statements of Duchamp, Picabia, and Man Ray, and the positive pronouncements on art and science by Marius De Zayas and Max Weber, provided an ideological base from which to view the skyscraper. Significantly, the often esoteric symbolism of Duchamp's glass paintings was wholly overlooked by Sheeler. Instead, he praised its mechanical components and constructive logic: "He [Duchamp] built with precision . . . an instrument for making scientific measurements. . . . He planned and executed several notable works on glass. . . . They were abstract forms in space, the outlines defined by a wire-like line of lead and painted on the background of the glass."[35]

In accord with his contemporaries of the twenties, Sheeler viewed the skyscraper as utilitarian architecture *par excellence*. Steel frame, windows, curtain wall, and height were explored in his art as optimal solutions to architectural design. Employing a formal vocabulary inspired by the pristine geometry of the machine and constructing his compositions architectonically, Sheeler created visual equivalents to the logic of the skyscraper itself. Regarding a photograph of New York (1920) which served as a source for several drawings and paintings, he is quoted as praising its functional adaptation to the metropolitan environment.

The artist felt, in the subject before him, the beauty of the architectural forms that have been created in New York to meet the fundamental necessity of providing buildings with the greatest cubic area upon the smallest possible base. He feels that because our sky- scrapers and loft buildings have been created with the adequate solution of necessity in mind, they . . . are our most vital contributions to architectural progress.[36]

Sheeler's interest in the particular features of skyscraper design is explored comprehensively in the film *Manhatta* (1921), which he collabo- rated on with Paul Strand. The film is an exploration of various aspects of the island, including its ports, skyscrapers, and commercial potential, accompanied by excerpts from various poems by Walt Whitman. The art- ists' treatment of a skyscraper was explained in *Vanity Fair*: "The photogra- phers were interested in the monotonous repetition of windows and other utilitarian details."[37] Sheeler and Strand achieved this effect in *Manhatta* by scanning the building from top to bottom, enumerating the regular geome- try of the windows for the viewer (fig. 56).

A pencil drawing entitled *New York Buildings* (fig. 57) further demon- strates Sheeler's fascination with the use of glass in urban architecture. Based on an earlier photograph taken from above, the artist further reduced the sleek, precisioned forms and concentrated on the rhythmic patterns of the rectilinear windows. Whereas the previous photographic image had been a random view of the city, the cropping and simplification of the subsequent drawing conveys Sheeler's interest in specific aspects of the skyscraper.

Sheeler's attraction to skyscrapers' logical features extends to a thor- ough exploration of the entire process of construction. This segment of the six-minute kinetic poem is introduced by the following verse by Whitman:

> The building of cities, —
> the shovel, the great
> derrick, the wall scaffold,
> the work of walls and ceilings.

The scene opens with a view of workmen hammering and digging into the earth, excavating the land that would ultimately receive the skyscraper's foundation. A brief shot of workers high atop the emergent frame follows. The rise of the steel scaffold dominates the remainder of the sequence, suggested by thin vertical beams which seem to point longingly skyward (fig. 58). In contrast to the static steel frame, cranes and derricks move across the screen, evoking the mechanical activity involved in building. From a purely visual perspective, the interaction of moving diagonals and inert verticals displays Sheeler's and Strand's experimentation with the film medium's inherent possibilities.

Construction served as the subject of Sheeler's photographs of both the Berkley Apartments (1920) and the Shelton Hotel (1924). In the former image, the selection of a point of view from above portrayed naked steel members, similar in spirit to the scaffold in *Manhatta* (fig. 59). By exposing the skeleton of the Berkley Apartments, Sheeler was commenting on the structural components which made the height of the building feasible.

The skyscraper's loftiness and monumentality, seen in the narrow, aspirant steel, is explored further in *Manhatta*. In the sequence prior to that of fabrication, the Woolworth Building is spanned from top to bottom. While the artists may have been commenting on its windows, Cass Gilbert's tower remained the tallest building in Manhattan in 1921. Whitman's verse, "High growths of iron . . . uprising toward clear skies," reiterates the skyscraper's seemingly limitless potential. Sheeler's later view of the *Delmonico Building* (1927) seen from below points to his continued interest in the loftiness of the skyscraper (fig. 60). The setback was perfectly suited to this purpose, as the tapering from base to pinnacle provided the illusion of infinite climbing.

Undecorated backs of skyscrapers are also explored in *Manhatta*, perhaps a recognition of the functionalism of the curtain wall (fig. 61). This interest in unadorned surfaces seems a realization of Sadakichi Hartmann's earlier encouragement to celebrate those aspects not seen from the street. Sheeler's and Strand's comprehensive exploration of height, windows and steel frame reinforces their attraction to the skyscraper's utilitarian features.

Sheeler's interest in the skyscraper's constructive logic was echoed in his method of picture making. He approached his works with the same rigor as an architect might plan a building, conceiving of his productions as architectonic wholes. "I favor the picture that is planned and executed with the same consideration for its parts — within the complete design as is necessary in the building of a watch or an aeroplane," he asserted.[38]

A concern for structure is manifested in the reduction of his compositions to the interaction of clean, geometric forms. In an explanation of *Church Street El*, a view of New York from the dizzying heights of the Equitable Building, he expressed a desire to simplify all natural forms to the border of abstraction, retaining only those components "indispensible to the design of the picture."[39] All traces of the human hand were suppressed, the smooth surfaces seemingly produced by mechanical means.

This had the effect of producing images of anonymity and standardization. Although Sheeler began with specific buildings and urban landscapes, the resultant paintings evoke generalized metropolitan scenes. The artist's skyscraper images resemble George Babbitt's description of his hometown: "I tell you, Zenith and her sister-cities are producing a new type of civiliza-

tion. There are many resemblances between Zenith and those other burgs.
. . . The extraordinary, growing and sane standardization of stores, offices,
streets, hotels, clothes and newspapers throughout the United States shows
how strong and enduring our type is."[40] The desire for mass uniformity
which characterized the decade, seen in the attempt of Henry Ford to create
a universal car and the efforts of Ferriss to forge an ideal city, may have
fueled Sheeler's efforts.

Sheeler's skyscraper views which picture an immaculate, well-
functioning machine devoid of human inhabitants, pollution, noise, and
congestion are statements about his unswerving regard for the tall building.[41] Like utopian urban planners' renderings, Sheeler's city views convey
perfection, all ills ameliorated by the mechanical precision of the skyscraper. Indeed, one of the premises among sociologists of the twenties was
that "utopia" was "just around the corner."[42] Sheeler sought to reflect that
belief in universal logic by the formulation of a standardized vocabulary, an
architectonic compositional structure, and a flawless view of the city.

Margaret Bourke-White and *Fortune* Magazine

Margaret Bourke-White's career as a photographer commenced with the
rendition of the American industrial scene. From the midtwenties on, factories, dynamos, and the skyscraper attracted her attention, a predilection
she attributed to her father's love of technology. Like her contemporaries,
Bourke-White admired the functional architecture of industry and urbanism: "To me . . . industrial forms were all the more beautiful because they
were never designed to be beautiful. They had a simplicity of line that came
from their direct application to a purpose. Industry . . . had evolved an
unconscious beauty—often a hidden beauty that was waiting to be discovered."[43]

Beginning in 1927, the artist began a series of photographs of the Otis
Steel Mills in Ohio and Cleveland's new Terminal Tower.[44] Both series were
independent, uncommissioned endeavors and communicate a highly
romanticized view of America's technology. In a description of the former
site, which may apply equally to her perception of the skyscraper, she spoke
of the "fog-filled bowl, brooding, mysterious, their smokestacks rising high
above them in ghostly fingers."[45] Indeed, her numerous depictions of the
lofty Terminal Tower shrouded in mist (fig. 62), its monumental proportions dwarfed by the limitless envelope of nature, are similar in spirit to the
fin de siècle efforts of Stieglitz and his colleagues.

As a result of her experiments in industrial photography, eight of her
images were selected to illustrate *The Story of Steel*, a book financed by the
Otis Steel Mills. This brought her work to the attention of Henry Luce and

his associates who, in 1929, were planning the publication of the periodical *Fortune*. The magazine, which commenced in 1930, may be viewed as both a synopsis and a culmination of the decade's celebration of business and industry. In the first issue, its planners' aims were defined: "*Fortune's* purpose is to reflect industrial life in ink and paper and word and picture as the finest skyscraper reflects it in stone and steel and architecture. Business takes *Fortune* to the tip of the wing of the airplane and through the depth of the ocean. . . . It forces *Fortune* to peer into dazzling furnaces and in the faces of bankers." To augment their support of finance and technology, they employed a photographer who could provide "the most dramatic photographs of industry that had ever been taken."[46] Thus, Bourke-White's images for *Fortune* may be viewed as both independent artistic endeavors and visual accompaniments for the periodical's editorial policies.

Fortune's support of the skyscraper was extensive and unequivocal. Beginning in July 1930 and continuing until December, every aspect of the tall building from financing to construction was explored. Appropriately entitled "Skyscrapers," the series of articles served as the basis for a separate book on the subject. While claiming to be an objective appraisal, the first article began with a subjective view of the popular response to the tall building: "Most Americans are proud of their skyscrapers. Most Americans are familiar with the silhouettes of famous towers. . . . Every Sunday paper with space for an impressionistic drawing in shafts and shadows of light has described it."[47] Bourke-White's *Toward the Sun* (fig. 63), a photograph of the Chrysler Tower before its sheathing in steel, served as an accompaniment to the article. Taken from a point of view below, the building's dramatic scale is explored. The Chrysler seemed boundless as it soared to the celestial realm, a feature suggested by the title. Observing the building through the silhouetted patterns of another structure further created an image of iconic importance.

The initial article continued with an appraisal of the skyscraper as the pinnacle of man's intelligence and effort, a prevalent view in the twenties. A single individual could neither comprehend nor physically create the monumental building type, *Fortune* maintained; rather, it involved "categories of specialized human knowledge and skill."[48] Images of the infinitely surging monolith by Bourke-White and others may be viewed as symbols of the skyscraper's entrance into these unsurpassed realms of perfection.

Concomitant with *Fortune's* belief that the skyscraper had metaphorically approximated man's omniscient potential was the equally audacious idea that the skyscraper had triumphed over nature. According to Luce and his colleagues, the tall building had superceded any single individual's control and assumed a life and identity of its own. When viewing a skyscraper, one would naturally "imagine young and arrogant and reckless men who delighted in extreme height . . . and were proud of their victories over the strength of the wind."⁴⁹

In contrast to the optimists' popular belief in standardized utopian cities, seen in the paintings of Sheeler and the renderings of Ferriss, *Fortune* attempted to revive the celebration of the distinctive single building which reflected the personality of its architect, builder, and financier. The cult of the individual hero gleaned from the above passage on skyscraper builders was reinforced in the acclamation accorded to the skyscraper investor. The efforts of such financial luminaries as Irwin Chanin, A. E. Lefcourt, and Frederick F. French were described in terms reminiscent of Horatio Alger. Moreover, William Van Alen's Chrysler Building and Raymond Hood's Daily News Building, two of the decade's boldest buildings, were singled out for special praise. An entire article was devoted to the latter building, tracing its genesis from hypothetical rendering to finished product. *Fortune* claimed that the skyscraper was not simply a well-functioning machine, but also a lasting advertisement for its owners.⁵⁰

By concentrating on these individualized buildings, the periodical displayed its absorption in the current height mania, renewed as a result of the building boom, which characterized the reaction to the skyscraper since its invention. Accompanying "Skyscrapers: The Paper Spires" was a comparative chart of the prestigious, lofty structures of the world, including the Eiffel Tower, the Chrysler and Woolworth Buildings, and the then preeminent Empire State Building. Competition for ever taller buildings was noted sarcastically in the skyscraper novel *Flamingo*. Referring to a potential customer, the architect of the story exclaimed, "Sam Bottle wanted me to build him the highest building in the world, the highest, mind you, he said, to put that poor boob Woolworth in the shade. It has to be a great big beautiful advertisement for Sam Bottle's hooks and eyes."⁵¹

The instructions given to Bourke-White as to how to photograph the Chrysler Tower demonstrate *Fortune*'s competitive spirit. Rumors raged that the Chrysler would not supercede the Bank of Manhattan, despite its height of 1,046 feet, and that it would sport an ornamental steel tower applied solely to surpass the world record. In order to prove the falsity of this charge, Bourke-White was directed to photograph the building during construction in order to demonstrate that the tower was a requisite part of the design. As a result, many of her renditions of the Chrysler centered on its loftiness. Often selecting viewpoints from below, as in *Toward the Sun*, she created the sensation of limitless soaring (figs. 63 and 64). The cropping of the image reinforced the sense of scale by paying homage to its rising verticality, while the interaction of its various geometric members lent the structure an air of logical uniformity which accorded with the wishes of her publishers.

The periodical's interest in all aspects of skyscraper construction owed, in part, to a confidence in the new materials and technological processes involved in building. The operation of the steel erector's derrick, steam shovels, and riveter's gun were described in detail. *Fortune*'s confidence in industrial methods was justified in language similar to that of the Machine Age Exposition organizers. They insisted that the bemoaning of industrial progress was both retrogressive and counterproductive.

> The trouble with all the talk about the decay of artisanship is that it is true. . . . It was true when the last wattle-weaver died and they took to building houses of brick. And it will be true when the tools and machinery of the contemporary arts are replaced by atomic explosions. It is so true that no one takes time to remark that the decay of one kind of artisanship is almost always caused by the growth of another.[52]

The last article in the series summed up *Fortune*'s unequivocal regard for the skyscraper. Dismissing common complaints that the tall building was symbolic of greed, unaesthetic, and responsible for traffic congestion, *Fortune* accused detractors such as Lewis Mumford of blaming the skyscraper for the problems which characterized any modern city. Citing both Boston and London, they claimed that these urban centers were as crowded as New York. *Fortune* insisted on viewing the skyscraper as a separate entity or a "tool of industry," a belief at the heart of the optimists' response to the city.[53] To its supporters, skyscrapers were autonomous, well functioning, mechanical, modern, and should be viewed as isolated from both the people in their midst and the problems engendered by urban living.

An accompanying painting, *Chicago Impression* by Robert Hallowell, supports this attitude. Selecting a vantage point high above the metropolitan dweller, he pictured a city of calm order and spacious vistas, devoid of human activity (fig. 65). Likewise, the skyscraper photographs of Bourke-White portrayed the tall building individually, the vertical tower of the Chrysler often separated from the surrounding architecture. These purposely myopic views supported *Fortune*'s contention that the tall building should be evaluated on its own merits, as an efficient, cost-saving, mechanical addition to commerce in the United States.

Fortune concluded with a prediction for the future, a practice common among skyscraper enthusiasts who wished to identify the tall buildings as a symbol of progress and modernity. As one might expect, a good prognosis was given for its continued existence. Acknowledging the utopian renderings of Ferriss, Corbett, Oud, Gropius, and Mies van der Rohe, *Fortune* claimed that the realization of these visions would occur in America. Praising the Empire State Building as the epitome of skyscraper excellence, the editors maintained that the city of the future would include "a city of free clear columns walled in metal and glass rising forty or sixty or eighty stories into the air, a city from which the gawky totem poles and flat-chested silhouettes of the Grand Central district will be happily absent, a city beautiful from the land and from the sea."[54]

This perception of the fantastical skyscraper as the beneficial saviour of society had its roots in the earlier pronouncements and visionary cities of Ferriss and Corbett. However, *Fortune's* favorable prophesies, articulated after the fall of the stock market, appeared to be a futile effort in view of the economic debacle which rendered even the lofty Empire State Building unrentable.

The Utopians

Similar in spirit to the optimistic images of America's painters and photographers, city planners, architectural renderers, and observers of the metropolitan scene expressed an equally positive opinion about the skyscraper. The efforts of Sheeler and Bourke-White were part of a larger movement to transform the urban sphere into a logical, ordered whole by using man's intellect to harness the power of the machine. Responding to the problems of traffic congestion, lack of sunlight, and pollution, the utopians saw the expansion of monumental skyscraper cities as a panacea to the nation's urban ills. Often, their ideas were elucidated by the use of dramatic illustrations of near perfect cities, providing philosophical and pictorial inspiration for their colleagues in the fine arts.

The utopian projections of Hugh Ferriss, the leading architectural renderer of the decade, were profoundly influential.[55] Beginning in 1921, his drawings were published repeatedly in a wide variety of newspapers, art magazines, and popular periodicals.[56] The exposure given his work in major shows such as the Titan City Exhibition and the Machine Age Exposition insured his popularity in architectural and art communities.[57]

A comparison of his depictions, of both existent and imaginary buildings, with those of other skyscraper optimists reveals significant similarities. Like Sheeler and Bourke-White, Ferriss's evocative portrayals of the tall building are devoid of human protagonists (fig. 66). Composed of ordered, geometric elements, they convey both an image of rationality and romantic grandeur. Moreover, the works of planners such as Ferriss suggest a broader context in which to evaluate the painting and photography of the decade.[58]

Ferriss imbued his futuristic musings with a feeling of the supernatural, bordering on what Mumford termed "religious awe and ecstasy."[59] Theatrical ray lines illuminate his buildings, spotlighting their loftiness, while his employment of dramatic chiaroscuro creates an air of mystery and wonderment (fig. 67). Referring to the advancement of the dawn on the sprawling metropolis, Ferriss rhapsodizes:

> There is a moment of curiosity, even for those who have seen the play before, since in all probability they are about to view some newly arisen steel skeleton, some tower or even some street which was not in yesterday's performance. And to one who had not been in the audience before—to some visitor of another land or another age—there could not fail to be at least one moment of wonder. What apocalypse is about to be revealed?[60]

Ferriss's utterly romantic city views were meant to convince the spectator to accept both the new urban sphere and a new cosmological order. Inherent in his metropolis of the future is the simultaneous belief in the superiority of controlled technology and the triumph of a new spirituality.

At the same time, Ferriss developed a highly rational approach to urban planning in collaboration with architect Harvey Wiley Corbett. At the beginning of the decade, they developed a workable solution to New York's 1916 Zoning Ordinance which stipulated that buildings could not exceed a certain height without a gradual decrease in cubic area.[61] In a four-stage process which commenced with a pyramidal sculptural mass, Ferriss stepped back his building with geometric precision (fig. 68). He claimed that his novel architectural envelope would afford the maximum amount of light and air and imbue the skyscraper with a sense of monumental three-dimensionality. The creation of a ready-made solution, easily adaptable by other architects, was viewed as the first truly American interpretation of tall building design.

Ferriss's imaginative visualizations were not only conceived as a pragmatic solution to zoning restrictions, but also as a universal panacea for urban problems in general, prompting his idealistic images of vast city complexes. It is important to note that these were contemporary with Le Corbusier's futuristic city for three million inhabitants envisioned in 1922. In "Civic Architecture of the Immediate Future," Ferriss asserted confidently that, although his renderings seemed "imaginative and fantastic," they would ultimately serve as a model for most of the world's crowded business centers. In accord with those who viewed the skyscraper as a symbol of rationality, Ferriss believed that his images would encourage thoughtful city planning. Most urban problems could be corrected if architects would only adopt his orderly approach.

> Within a generation the congested areas of large cities will be razed. The iconoclasts who will recognize and remove this debris will derive their significance from the fact that with the same gesture they will establish their constructive scheme. Tenements will present a new facade. . . . The typical apartment will include a terrace overlooking the distance. Present cubages will be so massed as to leave ground space to which Nature will return.[62]

In *The Metropolis of Tomorrow* (1929), which represented a decade of work, he reinforced his belief in the beneficial effects of the new "architectural landscape" which would provide "a free access to light and air on the part of all buildings whether high or low."[63]

This position was echoed by a number of American city planners in the twenties. Reiterating the observations of decades of detractors, Corbett believed that metropolitan chaos could be avoided by exercising foresight and erecting planned skyscraper groups.

> Of all the conglomerate, helter-skelter, jumbled up, mixed in and scattered about architectural messes, — New York . . . takes the prize. To be sure, it is fascinating, it is inspiring, at points it is exciting, — in certain lights it has great charm, from certain angles it is almost appalling — but one has the feeling that if one could only be screened, sorted, analyzed, separated, some order brought out of the present chaos, all that is really worth while [*sic*] could be retained, and the joy of it all enhanced by the sense of order that is only possible through intelligently guided community effort.[64]

Despite the ostensible logic of their pronouncements and projected solutions for New York's dilemmas, Ferriss and Corbett produced visionary images of the future metropolis. In 1924, the latter published his "Different Levels for Foot, Wheel and Rail," with illustrations by Ferriss, which were exhibited at the Titan City Exhibition. Including subterranean and aerial passageways, these layered districts were designed to alleviate congestion.[65] In *The Metropolis of Tomorrow*, such novelties as apartments on bridges, mooring masts on skyscraper pinnacles, and lofty gardens high above the concrete city were offered as further relief from the effects of overpopulation and centralization (fig. 69).[66]

Ferriss's desire to synthesize the rational and the transcendent was expressed most lucidly in *The Metropolis of Tomorrow*. He was certain that enlightened artists like himself possessed the vision to fuse these seemingly antithetical aspects of the American sensibility. "Would it not be surprising if the sense of large actualities, which is lacking in the words of both contemporary scientists and churchman, should be brought to us in the wordless device of the architect?" he inquired rhetorically.[67]

The physical incarnation of these beliefs was realized in Ferriss's employment of the crystal motif. Published in 1926 and exhibited a year later in the Machine Age Exposition, his translucent skyscrapers encompassed the logical and the spiritual (fig. 70).[68] On the one hand, glass was more functionally sound than other materials, affording minimum weight on the steel skeleton and maximum luminosity. Ferriss acknowledged that the most advanced types of glass which "ingenuity" was "already manufacturing" should be sought.[69] Yet the mathematically perfect crystal is also found in the natural landscape. This, coupled with its irradiant properties, suggests divine intervention. Since the Middle Ages, the crystal has been a symbol of God. The biblical basis is found in the Song of Songs and the final chapters of the Revelation of St. John, which speaks of the new Jerusalem as a city of "pure gold, clear as glass" and "the river of the water of life, bright as crystal."[70] It was employed extensively by German expressionist artists and architects, including Bruno Taut, Peter Behrens, and Paul Scheerbart, who viewed it as a symbol of spirituality and utopian perfection. No doubt, Mies van der Rohe's project for a crystalline office building at *Friedrichstrasse* station in Berlin served as an important source of inspiration for Ferriss's subsequent fantasies.

In *The Metropolis of Tomorrow*, art and science met in a tall vertical glass tower, christened the center of philosophy. The building was identical to the glass tower exhibited at the Machine Age Exposition. The plan of this skyscraper was based on variations of three superimposed triangles, evocative of the trinity and the rationality of mathematics. Ferriss's fusion of the fantastic and the logical is illustrated in the sublime "Night in the Science Zone," a poem celebrating the glass skyscraper.

> BUILDINGS like crystals
> Walls of translucent glass
> Sheer glass blocks sheathing
>   a steel grill.
> No gothic branch: no Acanthus
>   leaf: no recollection of the
>   plant world.
> A mineral kingdom.
> Gleaming stalagmites
> Forms as cold as ice.
> Mathematics.
> Night in the Science Zone.[71]

Ferriss's spiritual orientations are illustrated in the church's role in his futuristic society. In a photograph of the artist preparing his murals for the Titan City Exhibition, Ferriss is seen putting the finishing touches on a tall beaconed monolith which he described as "a great tower to which dirigibles will be moored and down the sides of which will run escalators for passengers" (fig. 71).[72] Evocative concentric rings and diagonal rays underline the building's cosmic importance. In *The Metropolis of Tomorrow*, the identical structure is employed for religion encompassing various denominations, "the seat of their combined and coordinated activities." The building is composed of three towers and symbolizes "the cardinal functions of the Christian host," according to the artist.[73]

Ferriss's conceptions of the metropolis' subsequent appearance seems to reconcile the prior conflict between the church and tall building. In the architect's ideal city, the religious structures themselves are skyscrapers and loom high above buildings concerned with monetary matters. Referring to an image entitled *Churches Aloft*, Ferriss asked, "Might not the office and apartment remain below and the church be raised . . . aloft?"[74]

Ferriss's influence is seen in the widespread notion that the skyscraper was the architecture of the future, removing it from mundane associations and situating it in the context of fantasy. Ferriss contributed to the belief that it was not only a phenomenon of the present, but also a symbol of progress and a better society. A wide variety of the skyscraper's utopian renderers accepted Ferriss's projections on the subsequent appearance of the urban sphere, while others offered their own visual predictions. As *Fortune* so aptly asserted, the vogue of the decade was in "crystal-gazing, palm-reading, prognostication, theomancy . . . and by plain, old-fashioned hope and fear . . . to prophesy by steel and stone."[75]

Ferriss's ideas gained wide dissemination in the architectural community; many of the historians of contemporary building either included reproductions of his work or accepted his thesis that carefully planned skyscraper cities would ameliorate all social ills. In *The American Architecture of Today* of 1928, G. H. Edgell concluded his study with an observation: "It is fascinating to toy with the possibilities of the future. Speculation is futile, but one fact we can be sure: the era of steel will work a transformation in the physiognomy of our cities which will make its marvelous beginnings look pallid and weak. In conclusion, we reproduce some imaginative drawings of Hugh Ferriss." And accompanying illustrations by Ferriss in *The New World Architecture*, Sheldon Cheney hoped: "But why not the City of Architecture—that is, as something built for perfect mechanical functioning in the service of man, with an over value of sheer pleasure-giving beauty in the building. . . . Let the vision be of a city beautiful, clean-walled, glowing with color, majestically sculptural, with a lift toward the sky."[76]

Augmenting the hypothetical discussions of architectural historians were images of the future metropolis. While many illustrations appeared in architectural publications proper, their fantastic, imaginative character belies a strict categorization of them as mere skyscraper renderings. Like the images of Ferriss, these prophetic musings are works of art in their own right.

In *The History of the Skyscraper* by Francisco Mujica, the first monograph on the subject, the author included a rendering of the *City of the Future: Hundred Story City in Neo-American Style* (fig. 72).[77] Mujica conceived of multifaceted urban centers composed of gigantic structures spanning several blocks. These geometric setback buildings are uniform in design and occur at measured intervals to allow for space and air. The metropolis is divided into various levels to accommodate diverse transportation requirements.

Perhaps the most ambitious manifestation of the decade's obsession with city planning and fantasizing was by The Regional Plan of New York Committee, which published the results of nine years of research in 1931. In order to popularize and gain acceptance for their ideas, they put forth their findings in *Creative Arts*, an entire issue of which was devoted to "New York of the Future."[78] Ostensibly, the conclusions expressed by the committee seemed to conflict with those of Ferriss. In theory, Thomas Adams, the chairman of the project, was opposed to an antiseptic, technologically advanced civilization: "Some proponents of city plans seem to consider that new building of a complete new city on logical and efficient lines would produce beauty. But logic and efficiency may lead them into creating a machine type of city and accepting a monotony of regularity that appears to others to produce ugliness. Logical unity may replace interesting irregularity with a severe and uninteresting formality." Moreover, Adams blamed the tall building for congestion and lack of light and air. Echoing *fin de siècle* commentators, individual skyscrapers such as the Woolworth and the New York Telephone Buildings were praised for providing "room to breathe," while groups of buildings were appreciated for their ability to suggest "the mass effects of mountains." Adams believed that it was necessary to recognize the tall building's limitations and social ramifications, requiring thoughtful city planning rather than continued haphazard growth. But the authors guarded against viewing themselves as futurist prophets; instead, they criticized those who concocted "impossible utopias." Adams summed up the committee's attitudes toward these undesirable dream cities.

> A utopia can be achieved only on a basis of despotism. . . . Those who proclaim the scientifically organized, the perfectly adjusted, and the logical geometric city as a sound conception of civilization overlook the fundamental conditions of life and growth in a democratic society. These conditions can be subordinated only by the destruction of freedom, which is the greater evil. Art can not be superimposed upon a people from the outside.[79]

Adams's reservations about utopian solutions and machine logic for New York were not reinforced by the fantastic projections of skyscraper cities presented both in the regional planning committee's publication and in *Creative Arts*. Corbett's and Ferriss's views were supplemented by equally inventive images of the city. Renderings by Arthur J. Frappier of the proposed revampment of Chrystie and Forsyth Streets on the lower east side of Manhattan pictured streamlined geometric towers separated by measured intervals (fig. 73). Despite the isolated nature of the buildings and the wide arcades dotted with manicured greenery, the projected appearance of the neighborhood seemed as fantastic as that of any utopian planner.

Concluding the issue of *Creative Arts* are two drawings entitled *Imaginative Conceptions of the City of the Future* by Leopold De Postels, aerial views of regularized cubical urbanscapes (fig. 74). The buildings are reduced to prefabricated, volumetric masses, devoid of all superfluous detail and embellishment. The dramatic perspective and the precision of the skyscrapers communicates the decade's preference for rational, awe-inspiring cities.

Projections on the future skyscraper were so common that popular advertising was affected. In *Fortune* magazine, the Carrier Engineering Corporation pointed to the benefits of "manufactured weather," a method to control the internal environment of the office building. The ad creates the anxiety that unless one opted for this technology, "buildings still in blueprint" would become "obsolete." The text describes the perennial pulling down of old skyscrapers which give way to taller, more modern structures, suggesting that the construction epidemic was responsible, in part, for the obsessive futuristic pronouncements which characterized the decade.[80] Accompanying Carrier's words of caution is an anonymous setback structure high above the clouds. Its placement in a nocturnal setting and the employment of a disorienting viewpoint creates an air of unreality (fig. 75). An airplane adjacent to its pinnacle indicates that the forthcoming era would also include air travel.

5

The Urban Cauldron, 1917–1931

"You have taken the world as it is, and crystallized it in your imagination as a utopia; and in perfecting what was bad you have naturally created something much worse," argued Lewis Mumford in a fictional dialogue between an urban critic and a utopian city planner.[1] Mumford, at once architectural commentator, social observer, and historian of cities, was perhaps the most vituperative interpreter of the skyscraper throughout the twenties. Articles with such provocative titles as "Is the Skyscraper Tolerable?" "Botched Cities," and "The Intolerable City" attest to his aggressive attacks on the tall building.[2] Yet Mumford was not alone in voicing such harsh complaints. Despite the brief period of acceptance of the skyscraper in the years preceding World War I, the debate concerning its viability reemerged with increased vigor.

Popular journals of the time reflected these tensions. The pros and cons of the skyscraper were often expressed in a single article. Or rhetorical inquiries such as "Is the Skyscraper a Public Nuisance?" or "Is the Skyscraper a Mistake?" pointed to the festering hostility toward an ever-expanding metropolis.[3] In the novel *Flamingo* (1927) by Mary Borden, the nature of these polemical discussions is accurately recorded.

> Laws have been passed to check the freakish egotistical antics of the buildings that are jumping up all over the place. . . . The whole population is in a fever over the subject. There are those who are enamoured of them and are all for building higher and higher ones, buildings of a hundred stories, two hundred with gardens, terraces and playgrounds in the air; and there are those who hate them and would chop their heads off.[4]

In contrast to the optimists and utopian planners who viewed the skyscraper as the solution to urban ills, others blamed the tall building as the primary cause of these problems. It was attacked on social, ideological, economic, and aesthetic grounds by a wide variety of intellectuals. Although these invectives were often aimed specifically at the skyscraper, many critics were dissatisfied with what they perceived as the superficial values of materialism, success, and the increased standardization of life pervading American society.

One of the major criticisms leveled at the tall building was its adverse impact on the life of the metropolitan dweller. This social awareness was more marked than in the earlier years of the century when negative appraisals were largely aesthetic and philosophical. The multiple problems associated with the skyscraper were simply not as pronounced in the last two decades. Now the physical expansion of the tall building to previously untrodden territory shifted the focus to its control. The impact of increased skyscraper height and the effects of zoning on the metropolitan dweller were hotly debated, topical subjects.

Mumford analyzed comprehensively the myriad ways the tall building compromised the life of the city dweller. One's unalienable right to a quality existence was addressed repeatedly in his works. He complained:

> One need not dwell upon the ways in which these obdurate overwhelming masses take away from the little people who walk in their shadows any semblance of dignity as human beings; it is perhaps inevitable that one of the greatest achievements in a thoroughly dehumanized civilization should, no doubt, unconsciously achieve this very purpose. It is enough to point out that the virtues of the skyscraper are mainly exercises in technique. They have little to do with the human arts of seeing, feeling and living.

In "The Intolerable City," Mumford traced the daily routine of a fictional Mr. Brown, who worked on the eighteenth story of a skyscraper. Despite the modernity of his office, which the author found artificial, Mr. Brown was shoved by the crowds in the subway and exposed to noxious fumes and sewage waste before returning home to "four cubicles." The age of the machine had produced an architecture fit for lathes and dynamos, not for human beings, Mumford asserted.[5]

Mumford was equally harsh on those who advocated adaptation to conditions in crowded skyscraper cities. He accused the utopian planners and urban optimists of trying to arouse awe and enthusiasm for the tall building without a concern for its inhabitants. In particular, he attacked the efforts of artists such as Charles Sheeler for their selective viewpoints, which omitted human beings: "What our critics have learned to admire in our great buildings is their photographs. . . . In an article devoted to the praise of the skyscraper in a number of *The Arts*, the majority of the illustrations were taken from a point of view that the man in the street never reaches. In short, it is an architecture, not for man but for angels and aviators." The following year, he reiterated his judgment in a review of the Titan City Exhibition, which he dubbed sarcastically "The Sacred City," observing that in all the brilliant sketches of the "ideal metropolis," not a single person was to be found.[6]

Hostility toward the stultifying physical conditions in the city and the increased standardization of American life was accompanied by a fear that man would metamorphose into a subhuman mechanical being, leading ultimately to his destruction. Following World War I, this theme was introduced in Carel Kâpek's grim drama *R.U.R.* of 1921, performed in New York the following year. In Kâpek's play, robots rebel against and subsequently destroy their human creators in a Last Judgment scene.[7] Similarly, Sophie Treadwell's play, *Machinal* (1928), is peopled with one-dimensional, automaton-like characters who speak in abrasive, repetitive monotones in the midst of the cacophonous din of numerous office machines. A young woman who cannot conform to the regimentation is driven to murder her smug employer-husband, only to be herself physically and symbolically executed by a mechanical electric chair.[8]

The extreme psychological stress caused by advanced technology was explored by a host of urban sociologists. Nels Anderson and Maurice Davie sought to define specifically the effects of urban life and the machine on the American character.[9] In part, their theories were based on the earlier observations of Georg Simmel who, in his pioneer essay "The Metropolis and Mental Life" of 1903, blamed the city for squelching individuality, fostering materialist values, and creating a blasé attitude. Going a step further, Anderson argued that the rapid pace and demands of modern life often led to "standardization of the personality," irrational behavior, and even nervous breakdowns.[10]

In addition to the regimenting and stultifying existence of the office worker, skyscrapers were blamed for urban congestion. Their close proximity to one another in the business district was cited as the cause of both vehicular and pedestrian traffic. Henry Curran, former borough president of New York and indefatigable critic of the tall building, articulated this position. "All our traffic trouble is due to skyscrapers. They draw the people in the rush hours and throw them on the streets at night," he complained. According to Curran, they were the cause of the city's "structural indigestion."[11]

Skyscrapers not only monopolized physical space but squelched such intangible elements as light and air, according to detractors. One observer maintained that this unhealthy environment was taking its toll: "Recent researchers bear out the theory that the health-giving qualities of the sun play an important part in our health, our life, and, therefore, in our happiness; and we may find that, in giving to some the privilege of erecting buildings of exaggerated height, we have given a privilege which infringes on the limits of liberty because it denies health, and thereby life and happiness, to many others."[12]

Mumford and others felt that the tall building disturbed the ecology and fostered artificiality. As early as 1922, he spoke of the creation of a new metropolitan wilderness which resulted in the defloration of the American land. In an attempt to cope with the barren countryside, the wilderness was "skinned rather than cultivated by the forces of individualism." In *The Golden Day* of 1925, he traced the legacy of America from the settler to the effects of "paved streets and starched collars and skyscrapers."[13] As an antidote to the skyscraper civilization, Mumford proposed decentralized communities of single family dwellings with ample open space and greenery.

Mumford also reintroduced the notion of the skyscraper as a symbol of greed and profit, complaining that landlords, financiers, and engineers viewed the populace as mechanical units rather than autonomous individuals. He categorized Ferriss's *The Metropolis of Tomorrow* as the "metropolis of yesterday: the infantile paper city erected by the megalopolitan businessman and the skyscraper architects of the nineteen twenties."[14]

In accord with the social and architectural critics, many novelists expressed equally hostile reactions to tall buildings. In *Manhattan Transfer* (1924) by John Dos Passos, skyscrapers were employed as oppressive symbols of capitalist exploitation. The main protagonist, Jimmy Herf, has a skyscraper nightmare in which a building is both inaccessible and predatory.

> All these April nights combing the streets alone a skyscraper has obsessed him, a grooved building putting up with unaccountable bright windows falling onto him out of the scudding sky. . . . And he walks round blocks and blocks looking for the door of the humming tinsel-windowed skyscraper, round blocks and blocks still no door. Everytime he closes his eyes the dream has hold of him. . . . One of two unalienable alternatives: go away in a dirty soft shirt or stay in a clean Arrow collar. But what's the use of fleeing the city of Destruction? What about your unalienable right . . . ?[15]

Other authors associated the tall building with failed human relations and anger. In his *Sonnets-Realities* of 1925, E. E. Cummings conveys his negative reaction to the constant hammering of office building construction by likening it to an aborted love affair.

> The dirty colors of her kiss
> have just throttled
> my seething blood, her heart's
> chatter riveted a weeping
> skyscraper in me.[16]

Perhaps the strongest reaction is seen in identifying the tall building as a symbol of death. The crime committed in *The Skyscraper Murder* (1928) occurs in an imposing twenty-six-story building, which features skyscraper furniture with concealed compartments and escape routes, perfect settings for the insidious activities of the culprit.[17]

Mary Borden's *Flamingo*, the most comprehensively critical novel concerning the skyscraper, concerns the efforts of a driven, idealistic architect who seeks to build large block-long buildings with raised sidewalks. One passage deals with a steel skeleton built by the architect which is the cause of a worker's death: "He was responsible for the steel skeleton. The great, skinny, gaunt horror had shot up in the air out of his brain. . . . He cannot rid himself of the feeling that he is in some way responsible for the workman who fell like a plummet through the air, and whose spilled life made a grease spot on the sidewalk. And there will be others, since there is no end to this business of building." This excerpt foreshadows the eventual suicide of the architect himself, crushed by the corrupt material interests of the city which prevent him from realizing his dream building. He glances one more time at his "swan song," the Radio Building, before he leaps to his death.

> He opened the window and looked out and down. All around him the profiles of the skyscrapers cut shadowy perpendicular slices out of the sky. The great towering structures seemed to be swaying. Opposite was his white Radio Building facing him, a frosted glimmering needle piercing the sky. He didn't look at it.
>
> When he jumped, no one heard his tiny cry or saw him fall, a whirling speck, rolling over and over, down the immense stone precipice, past the many tiers of dark, vacant windows.[18]

The General Failure of American Values

The attacks on urban life must be viewed in the context of a broader cultural malaise. Many intellectuals who assessed the decade viewed the prevailing society, with the skyscraper as its symbol, as the propagator of false, superficial values. They perceived that the stress was on gain and profit at the expense of spiritual concerns and human needs. The creative process seemed impossible in this vacuous environment dedicated to material expansion.

The tension between spiritual and materialist values noted earlier by James, Steffens, and Marin was reintroduced by observers of the next generation. Cultural nationalists such as Van Wyck Brooks, editor of *Seven Arts* (1916–17) and *The Freeman* (1920–24), hoped for an authentic American art based on direct experience and spiritual development. Appraising the state of native literature in *America's Coming-of-Age* (1915), Brooks pointed to the supposed impotence of our arts and letters. He differentiated between a "highbrow" and a "lowbrow" sensibility, the former firmly entrenched in elevated, Old World ideals, the latter in pragmatism and acquisitiveness. The author traced the "lowbrow" viewpoint from the efforts of the Puritans to contemporary business life, providing continuity and relevance for the present society: "The coherent ideals and beliefs of

Transcendentalism gradually faded out, resulting in . . . the current of catchpenny opportunism, originating in the practical shifts in Puritan life, becoming a philosophy in Franklin, passing through the American humorists, . . . resulting in the atmosphere of contemporary business life." Brooks believed that the theoretical and the practical were equally ineffectual in forging an authentic American art.[19]

Waldo Frank expanded upon Brook's thesis in *Our America* of 1919, reiterating the separation between the material and the spiritual. Frank was affiliated with Brooks on *Seven Arts* and an ardent apologist for Stieglitz after 1915. Contending that the country sprang from a profit-making impulse, he traced the rise of materialism to the early conditions of American life, which demanded a practical harnessing of the wilderness by the pioneer. This pragmatic approach led the early settlers to develop an "intolerant, materialistic, unaesthetic" viewpoint. Even religion was subsumed in these "empirical affairs," according to Frank. He related this sensibility to the contemporary obsession with machine technology, pointing to a negation of the inner man.

> The pioneering force increased, feeding upon itself. It meant febrile efforts: the unending outplay of nerves, the atrophy of the restraining inner powers of reserve. Above all it meant the Machine . . . the new external world — the industrial world which America had created now drove the Americans out into an endless exteriorization. A sucking monster, which as it sucked swelled larger and larger. . . . Industrialism swept the American land and made it rich. Broke in on the American soul and made it poor.[20]

Frank's appraisal of urban New York was equally caustic. Along with Stieglitz, he recognized the individual beauty and the dynamic quality of skyscrapers, but he believed that the citizens who lived among them were "lowly," "driven," and "drab." Skyscrapers were the reflection of a "towering childish soul" in which "millions of human resources" were "sucked void."[21] Even entertainment and leisure were mechanized in New York, Frank complained. The material impulse had only led to war and destruction; spiritual salvation was to be realized in communion with nature rather than the machine.

In *The Rediscovery of America* of 1929, Frank was even more vociferous in his attack on materialism and the domination of the machine over the individual, focusing specifically on conditions in the twenties. The quest for success, the idolization of the machine, the superficiality of efficiency, and the corporation's consumption of the individual were commented on in disparaging terms. According to Frank, the skyscraper symbolized these false values: "The American gods of Power have a temple. It is the best we can show as formal articulation of what we are and what we love. We call it the skyscraper. Fifty stories heaped alike one atop another express a herd

. . . the house that stands for us has immensity for its aim, and for its method sameness upon sameness."[22]

Perhaps the most ambitious account of the poverty of American culture and values was *Civilization in the United States* (1922), edited by Harold Stearns. Essays by Mumford, Brooks, H. L. Mencken, and others, in their respective areas of expertise, contained evaluations of America's failings. Stearns introduced the anthology as an effort by "like-minded men and women to see the problem of American civilization as a whole." Echoing Brooks and Frank, he identified the sharp dichotomy between "preaching" and "practice" which characterized America. After identifying the problem, Stearns described an industrial society totally out of harmony with its citizens: "The most moving and pathetic fact in the social life of America to-day is emotional and aesthetic starvation. . . . One can feel the whole industrial and economic situation as so maladjusted to the primary and simple needs of men and women."[23] "The City" by Mumford, included in the collection, reinforced Stearns's pessimism. He viewed the achievements of the material civilization as symptoms of its "spiritual failure," categorizing American life as externalized, mechanized, and far removed from nature.[24]

Adverse conditions in the United States noted by Stearns, Mumford, and Frank led many to expatriate themselves in the 1920s. Writing in *The Freeman*, Stearns's solution for the American artist was simply to "GET OUT!"[25] Malcolm Cowley's *Exile's Return* (1934) elaborated on the plight of such alienated writers and intellectuals in the years after World War I.[26] In part, Cowley blamed the decimation of war for the displacement of the creative personality. He cited the life of the writer, Harry Crosby, who had experienced the destruction firsthand at Verdun. Despite all the trimmings of success, including wealth and social status, Crosby committed suicide. Cowley conjectured that his death represented an entire generation's inability to cope with war and the destruction wrought by industrial societies.

Cowley blamed the narrow conformity and commercialism of the American literary milieu for the expatriate's inability to readjust to life in the United States. After his experience with the rebellious, irreverent spirit of Paris dada, Cowley was appalled by the opportunities available to American journalists, who became "propagandists to aid in the increasing difficult task of selling more and more commodities each year to families that were given higher and higher wages to buy them with, and therefore had to be tempted with all the devices of art, literature and science into bartering their future earnings for an automobile or a bedroom suite."[27]

After landing in the port of New York, Cowley's two trunks were symbolically sent downtown "almost in the shadow of the Woolworth Building." His initial reaction to the city was shock at the absence of anything green "to break the monotony of the square streets, the glass, brick and iron." In a chapter appropriately entitled "The City of Anger," he related a pleasant nightmare in which New York was destroyed by an earthquake, "its towers snapped like pine trees in a storm."[28] Yet Cowley admitted that in spite of his hostile feelings, he was beginning to readjust to his native milieu.

The picture of Americans as dislocated from their civilization was explored methodically by Robert and Helen Lynd in *Middletown* (1929), a sociological study of a typical midwestern town undergoing an economic and technological transition. Tracing the changes wrought by industrial growth since the 1890s, the Lynds found a society devoted to materialism. The citizens of Middletown, who were engaged predominantly in dehumanizing jobs, lost the sense of satisfaction associated with work that had characterized their lives a generation ago. This was explained in part by the gap between what people did to earn a living and the actual necessities of life. Money assumed a greater degree of importance, superceding the enjoyment of the job performed. The "dominance of the dollar" manifested itself in several ways — in the rapidity of job switching for "big money," in judging status by one's financial position, and in the increased desire for material possessions fueled by advertising and the mass media.[29]

Strand and *Manhatta* (1921): Paradigm of Urban Ambivalence

The differing sensibilities of Paul Strand and Charles Sheeler resulted in conflicting images of the city in their collaborative film endeavor, *Manhatta*. Although the exploration of the functionalist properties of the skyscraper may represent a joint effort, these sequences, when viewed in the context of both artists' *oeuvres*, appear more closely linked to the work of Sheeler. His subsequent adaptations of these subjects to paintings, and his continued preference for the logic of the machine, points to his selection of them in *Manhatta*.

Strand, in contrast, held an equivocal opinion of the city, perhaps inspired by his earlier training with Lewis Hine, whose documentary photographs convey the plight of the oppressed worker and immigrant in uncompromising terms. Strand's second mentor, Stieglitz, was also concerned with the effects of rapid urban expansion on the little man. Even while depicting the abstract shapes and glistening mechanical objects found in the metropolis, Strand photographed the poor of New York. Close-ups of a blind woman forced to beg or an indigent staring vacantly outward appeal poignantly to the viewer's sympathy.

In *Wall Street* of 1915 (fig. 76), a photograph which Strand later adopted for *Manhatta*, the dehumanizing aspects of city life are explored.

Minute people scurry past the enormous Morgan Trust Building, the discrepancy in scale communicating their powerlessness compared with the seemingly omnipotent forces of capitalism.[30] Strand described the dark rectilinear window as possessing "the quality of a great maw into which the people rush."[31] *Manhatta's* exploration of the plight of the urban dweller must have been authored by Strand in view of Sheeler's total disregard of human protagonists in his work. The film's ambivalent character is illustrated in its celebration of New York's commercial and technological aspects and their adverse impact on its citizens.

Strand probably authored the second segment of the film; its content and imagery are remarkably similar to his earlier photographs of the poor. This portion of *Manhatta* begins with Whitman's verse, "When million-footed Manhattan unpent descends to its pavement."[32] A ship arrives at the dock, its gates are flung open, and an empty gang plank is suddenly filled with the surging movement of an anonymous crowd, who clamor to enter the city. A brief view of the backs of their heads reinforces their impersonality. Shifting suddenly, the camera pans a crowded street from above, in which faceless silhouettes move to and fro in traffic, reminiscent of Strand's previous still photographs (fig. 77). The next scene takes place in a cemetery — barren, static, and uninhabited in contrast to the busy business district (fig. 78). It conjures up literal and symbolic images of death — the city as a vast repository of waste and destruction.

This is borne out by the culmination of the sequence, in which people hurry past the Morgan Trust Building (fig. 79). Bosch's *Haywain* (ca. 1493) is immediately called to mind, a painting in which people grasp and strain unwittingly to embark on a journey leading inexorably to hell. The journey by sea and the flinging open of gates in the first part of the sequence in *Manhatta* also suggests Dante's and Virgil's adventure aboard Charon's boat in the *Inferno*.

It is more difficult to assign separate authorship to the penultimate segment of the film because it includes an interest in functionalism and the plight of humanity. However, the images of dehumanization may be safely attributed to Strand. It is introduced by Whitman's verse, "Where the city's ceaseless crowd moves the live long day." Through static balustrade-like columns from atop a lofty skyscraper, infinitesimal forms are seen in motion.[33] The camera shifts briefly to the stark geometry of the backs of buildings and subsequently to a train, another attempt to contrast movement and stasis. A view from above of people interwoven with automobiles and another of a cemetery conclude the sequence, the fusion of man and the machine meant to conjure up images of death.

It would be inaccurate to suggest that Strand was unequivocally hostile to his urban milieu. Like Mumford and Frank, he was appalled by the wanton disregard of human life in favor of advancements in technology and the quest for profit. Strand maintained that it was man's responsibility to harness and control the machine's potentially destructive capabilities. He praised Stieglitz for both embracing the machine and channeling it for aesthetic ends, yet warned against the destructive properties and implications of "printing presses or poison gas." "One must beware of allowing the social structure that man has created being destroyed by the perversion of scientific knowledge," he asserted. Only through a synthesis of creativity and technology, a feat achieved in *Manhatta*, did Strand believe that the true potential of each could be realized. Identifying the rift in the American sensibility noted earlier by Brooks and Frank, he contended: "Science and expression? Are they not vital manifestations of energy, whose reciprocal hostility turns one into a destructive tool of materialism, the other into an anaemic fantasy whose coming together might integrate a true religious impulse."[34]

Death and Rebirth: Stella, Ault, and Hirsch

The hostile reaction to the skyscraper centered on the effects of the metropolis on human beings. In contrast to the slick, celebratory images of Sheeler and Bourke-White, themes of dehumanization, congestion, and disorientation were actively pursued by negative imagists of the tall building. Rather than depending on the machine for social amelioration, Joseph Stella, George Ault, and Stefan Hirsch saw a reacquaintance with the land as the ultimate solution.

Stella's interest in the detrimental effects of industry and urbanism began in the early years of the century with several commissions from the magazine *The Survey*, including a series of drawings of Pittsburgh steel mills and city views. An analysis of his *New York Interpreted* series of 1921 (fig. 80) in view of his writings reveals a continuing concern with urban problems. Although the scope and epic presentation of the massive polyptych, featuring the skyscraper theme in the central panel, possesses the drama and exaltation of a religious icon, the overriding mood is of claustrophobia and oppression.[35] Four of the five panels are jammed with vertical, prisonlike bars which screen a multilayered, convoluted world devoid of metropolitan inhabitants. Any attempt to venture into this steely jungle would result in total encompassment, swallowed by its mechanical innards. The icy coldness of the colors reinforces the impersonal, artificial character of the whole, an unhealthy environment where nature has been squelched. Not only does Stella's employment of the nocturne underline the synthetic world of electricity, but also the contrast of dark and light suggests a tenebrous and glowing inferno.[36]

This view of the series is borne out by Stella's own writings. "The Brooklyn Bridge (A page of my life)" or "New York," as the article was originally titled, provides a detailed explanation of his reactions to and his eventual rejection of his urban milieu. Significantly, this literary companion piece to his city views commences with the end of the war and his relocation to the depressing atmosphere of Brooklyn, an introduction which sets the mood of despair. A huge factory with innumerable blazing windows and smoke emissions, and the metropolis seen from the bridge, conjures up images of battle for Stella. These memories are intermingled with the building of the city, "the steely orchestra of modern construction" and the "audacity" of the climbing skyscrapers which supercede the bridges. Referring simultaneously to combat, the construction of tall buildings and his own internal turmoil, he complained that "war was raging with no end — so it seemed. There was a sense of awe, of terror weighing on everything — obscuring people and objects alike."[37]

The artist's selection of hard, cold forms as "lucid as a crystal" was explained as an effort to reflect "with impassibility — the massive density, luridly accentuated by lightning of the raging storm . . . revealing the swirling horrors of the maelstrom." In conjuction with these seemingly benign, tension-fraught shapes, Stella selected a biting line that would have "the greatest vitriolic penetration to bite with lasting unmercifulness of engravings." Unfathomable space and densely packed forms create an unhealthy environment devoid of nature and air. In keeping with Mumford, he described skyscrapers "like bandages covering the sky, stifling our breath." The facades of these buildings are perceived as impenetrable, like the Great Wall of China with "its dreadful closed windows barren of flowers."[38]

Themes of congestion which, like the endeavors of Stella, picture a city of densely packed architecture, were taken up by others in the twenties. Many of the urban views of Jan Matulka show Manhattan filled to capacity with geometric behemoths emitting fumes (fig. 81). The cramming of the space, the simultaneous vantage points, and the use of monochrome reflect an environment inaccessible to human experience.

Darkness was often explored by urban pessimists who, unlike their *fin de siècle* predecessors, use the nocturne to convey doom. Stella's rendition of the electrically illumined city at night evokes a hellish ambiance radiant with fiery drama. Referring to *New York Interpreted*, he spoke of steel and electricity as an "unmerciful violation of darkness" and of subways as "infernal recesses."[39]

In contrast to Stella, George Ault did not comment on artificial illumination, but preferred the night's bleak, mysterious character beset with chilling, lifeless overtones (fig. 82). Often lit by an eerie moon, the deathlike pallor of his cityscapes is heightened by the sterility of his skyscrapers, which loom out of the darkness like silent specters. Their lack of windows, the symbolic absence of light, and the dramatic shadows they cast add to the air of discomfort. Ault referred to tall buildings as "tombstones of capitalism" and to streets as "dark dank caverns," imbuing his works with the grimness of a graveyard. Like Strand and Stella, the artist categorized New York as "the inferno without the fire," reinforcing his selection of the nocturne to convey a metropolitan hell.[40]

Stella's and Ault's intense hostility to the urban sphere came from the perception that materialistic values were endemic to America. The former often used specific imagery to express his anger toward capitalism. As Wanda Corn pointed out, a gigantic S-shaped shadow undulates around Stella's city view, perhaps a reference to the quest for acquisition.[41] In a later skyscraper collage composed of ripped, soiled paper, Stella affixed the word "paid" in large capital letters.

Yet the city caused Stella to feel "deeply moved, as if on the threshold of a new religion or in the presence of a new DIVINITY"; and despite the *New York Interpreted* series' polyptych format, Gothic arches, and "stained glass fulgency," the city was ultimately a false idol.[42] Referring to New York as a "monstrous steely bar erected by a modern cyclops to defy the gods," he believed that spiritual awakening and renewal could be achieved in nature. His descriptions of the city are apocalyptic, reminiscent of the Revelations of St. John, in which symbolic destruction, death, and rebirth occur. After depicting New York's annihilating character, Stella reported that a "PEACE" and "A NEW ERA" ensued. An image of the resurrected virgin appeared, and in the spring came birds and flowers celebrating the beginning of a new direction in his work. Thus, salvation was realized in a rejection of the artificial city in favor of the land's renewing potential, a position encouraged by Frank and others.

Stefan Hirsch also employed cubical, congested architecture to express New York's artificiality; like Stella, he believed artistic regeneration would occur in communion with nature. After his return from Europe following the war, Hirsch was appalled. "Instead of finding the fresh, open view which I had idealistically assumed to exist from reading Walt Whitman and Thoreau, I was confronted with piles of steel and concrete that keep all the sun from the Wall St. area." He admitted that his use of monolithic, windowless structures was a purposeful attempt to convey his "recoil from the monstrosity that industrial life had become in 'megapolitana.' "[43]

Hirsch's *Plants and Towers* of 1920 (fig. 83) is both an indictment and a rebellion against current conditions in New York. Windowless, mechanized buildings, with no space to relieve the tension, dominate the background. Numerous trees and shrubs encroach upon the sterile buildings, winding their wooden tracery around the inanimate concrete. A vertical shoot competes symbolically with a lofty skyscraper for predominance. As if to reverse current trends, Hirsch allows nature to reclaim its rightful place in the man-made metropolis.

Entrapment: The Ballet *Skyscrapers* (1926)

The ballet *Skyscrapers*, first performed at New York's Metropolitan Opera House in February of 1926, seemed to sum up the decade's pessimistic views toward the tall building. Written by John Alden Carpenter, with sets by Robert Edmond Jones, the piece critiques aspects of the metropolitan scene through dance, stage design, pantomime, and the cacophonous rhythm of jazzlike music meant to simulate the construction of the city.[44] The arch culprit is the steel frame of an emergent skyscraper, stark as a deathly skeleton and often glowing like a massive inferno. Built by the inhabitants of the city, it heralds their subjugation and the demise of their individuality. Herbert Croly, the editor of *Architectural Record*, referred enthusiastically to the ballet as "the first serious attempt to explore the human implications and reverberations of skyscrapers."[45]

Originally written for Serge Diaghileff's *Ballets Russes*, it was to have opened in Monte Carlo in 1925 as "Le Chant des Gratte-Ciels."[46] It is not surprising that the Russian impresario wished to stage *Skyscrapers* since his production, *Parade* (1917), included a stage manager whose skyscraper costume was designed by Picasso, machine-inspired music by Erik Satie, and exaggerated representations of American behavior.

Carpenter's ballet did not have a conventional plot; rather, it sought to convey the most characteristic elements of the native experience. It proceeded on the assumption that "American life reduces itself to violent alterations of WORK and PLAY."[47] The performance opened with a drop curtain of aggressive black and white stripes and two red traffic lights which flashed intermittently, creating a dynamic and disorienting visual effect later explored in the op art of the sixties (fig. 84).[48] These repetitive, barlike forms suggested an inescapable prison and foreshadowed the activity to follow.

The hypnotic curtain was succeeded by the threatening image of a skyscraper at the onset of its construction (fig. 85). Within the steely skeleton, a group of faceless workmen bent and swayed, wielded hammers, and tossed rivets in robotlike gestures to the beat of music simulating the clang of building. Beneath them, another group worked above a gaping hole, from which emanated smoke and fire. Fourteen additional dancers in masks and costumes of silver also moved in mechanical fashion. The steel frame was flanked by the piercing forms of congested skyscrapers, where an

anonymous human procession moved unrelentingly, pointing to the accelerated pace of life in the city.

In order to recreate the discordant but syncopated sounds of the urban
milieu, Carpenter employed thirty-one different instruments, including a
tuba, a variety of drums, cymbals, a gong, and a compressed air whistle.[49] It
is significant to note that early in the development of jazz, observers likened
its varied and repetitive beats to both the sounds of building and the rapid
pace of the city. The auditory aspects of skyscraper fabrication were
thought to be influential on these urban symphonics. In "Jazz Brings First
Dance of the City," Irving Carter, a *New York Times* critic, spoke of a
strange galvanic tempo expressive of a new modernity and kin to steel
construction, power plants, and especially the skyscraper. The direct connection between the skyscraper and current music was noted by George
Gershwin, who employed four taxi horns in his "American in Paris" of
1927.

> I do not think there is any such thing as mechanized musical compositions without
> feeling, without emotion. . . . Mechanism and feeling will have to go hand in hand, in the
> same way that a skyscraper is at the same time a triumph of the machine and a tremen-
> dous emotional experience, almost breathtaking. Not only its height but its mass and
> proportion are the result of an emotion, as well as of calculation.[50]

Like Carpenter, detractors often linked jazz with the negative aspects
of rapid city building and industrialization. Some felt that the implied
mobility of the machine age and the new music's wanton abandon were
responsible for corrupting the morals of the nation's youth.[51] The novel *The
Skyscraper Murder* opened in a jazz club, a supposed haven for undesir-
ables.

Following the mechanical gestures of the workmen building the city to
a jazzlike beat in Carpenter's *Skyscrapers*, the scene shifted from work to
play, heralded by a crowd that moved from one door to another. Play was
signified by an amusement park, complete with sideshows, freaks, a German band, a cooch dancer, a carnival, and a black spiritual.

A sudden blackout followed, and the once gay crowd moved through a
door symbolizing work, transformed to "a stiff and relentless procession of
workmen, lockstepping to their JOB."[52] Leisure and good times were curtailed by the pressures of urban labor, pointing to the machine's regimentation of life. The workers resumed their mechanized movements and pantomimed the erection of the city, metaphorically entrapped within the piercing
forms of the steel frame, which was now almost complete (fig. 86). Borden's
description of a skyscraper scaffold in *Flamingo* may apply equally to the
gruesome picture of workmen among the girders in *Skyscrapers*. The architect of the novel surveyed the city: "There's the skeleton of a building

behind him. His attention darts out and back through the rushing crowd to where the monstrous open scaffolding of steel rises up like a spider, or like a gallows, and he sees clinging to its skinny arms . . . little men with hammers, sticking like sucking leeches."[53]

The last scene of *Skyscrapers* commenced with the shrill blast of a factory whistle. By the adept manipulation of light, the future megalopolis emerged in awesome foreboding, "a stark and ominous skeleton of red and black," according to Carpenter (fig. 87).[54] The predatory darkness of the set design, the jagged shapes, and the malevolent red glow from below foretold eternal suffering for the inhabitants of the urban inferno. A reviewer, in the periodical *Survey*, observed that the ballet spelled "despair, terrible and revealing, speaking the truth of America flayed and naked." This was "no languorous ballet" but "exposed the corrosion that lurks indeed beneath our too proud skyscrapers."[55]

Images of Removal and Disequilibrium

Their inability to cope with the sprawling, expanding metropolis led many artists to express their hostility, often inadvertently, by presenting either wildly disorienting views of impinging skyscrapers or images that were cool, serene, or far removed from the frenetic activity. These diverse responses bespeak of a new relationship with the urban sphere absent from earlier visual interpretations. There is no attempt to physically integrate the individual into these scenes; rather, the metropolitan dweller is acted upon, present by implication.[56] Unlike the disparate stimuli and multiple sensations conveyed by Marin and Weber, skyscraper views of the twenties often suggest a new psychological subjugation, a deeply felt discomfort.

In a drawing by Arnold Ronnebeck, angular structures with jagged edges converge upon the available space (fig. 88).[57] In this silent, surreal nightmare, the viewer experiences a loss of balance and claustrophobia as the looming buildings close in. Ronnebeck's vertiginous perspectives convey both the artist's internal burden and the city's adverse impact on the urban dweller. The poem "Down Town" by George S. Chappell, accompanying a similar image by Ronnebeck in *Vanity Fair*, corroborates its negativity. The purposeful splitting of the word downtown associates the skyscraper city with the infernal region.

> Down . . . town . . .
> The chasms stand
> Rock-ribbed, steel-boned
> Silent and still
> The fret of the day
> Subsides . . .

> The tide that fill
> These somber sluices
> Drain away
> Night falls . . .
> Down . . . town . . .
> The words toll like a bell
> Whose echoes spell
> Both Heaven and Hell.[58]

Gotham (Whirlpool) by William Charles McNulty (fig. 89) conveys the urban dweller's inability to comprehend the complexity and scale of the rising city. Buildings swirl and topple around the stunted urban dwellings, implying imminent catastrophe. Living in such quarters and surrounded by these massive skyscrapers engenders vertigo, causing the viewer to reel vicariously.

This is not to suggest that all artists employing dramatic viewpoints and abrupt perspectives perceived the city in adverse terms. The development of this mode of seeing in the twenties indicates a method of adapting to the perenially expanding city, ranging from fear and hostility to awe and wonderment. Artists as diverse as O'Keeffe and Bourke-White employed disorienting angles to evoke the limitless surging of the skyscraper. Others utilized these views to explore the variegated contour of the new setback. Whether positive, negative, or merely descriptive, this novel way of perceiving communicates the tall building's incomprehensibility. Borden described the sensation evoked by twenties' skyscrapers:

> The walls that seemed to rush skyward inspired the breathless feeling that one has when one is being driven at a terrific speed. Looking, one was hoisted up suddenly by the neck and flung with a twang into the blue. . . . One wondered why those small figures leaning back to look up didn't all fly out of their seats and go spinning up the slim flank of the compelling building toward the distant, hypnotic inaccessible tower.[59]

More difficult to define are the images by Stieglitz and O'Keeffe, who ostensibly communicate an enthusiasm for the city. Their numerous renditions of New York from the uppermost stories of the Shelton Hotel and other lofty buildings invite this interpretation. Yet an examination of their works in the context of their views on art, their statements concerning the city, and their periodic retreats to the country indicate a profound ambivalence toward the skyscraper. In the case of Stieglitz, these equivocations represent a continuation of his earlier dialogue with the tall building. Jointly, their repeated trips to Lake George are symptomatic of the fundamental tension artists felt between the dynamic, energizing character of the metropolis and the healthful, renewing qualities of rural living. Artists' colonies in unspoiled settings, such as Ridgefield, Woodstock, and Taos, also signify such a rift.

Stieglitz's skyscraper photographs of the late twenties and early thirties represent only a segment of his *oeuvre*. The remainder concern the ephemeral aspects of nature and portraits of friends and loved ones infused with emotion. Similarly, his views of the tall building are located in the pattern of his life. *Evening New York — Shelton* of 1931 (fig. 90) is both a slice of time and a perceptual fragment imbued with melancholy.[60] Moreover, it serves as a record of his living and working quarters and traces the changes in the external appearance of the city. Rendered from the highest reaches of New York, a vast panorama of the urban landscape is encompassed. A document of the transformation in external and internal reality, it contrasts with his earlier sidewalk views, where one senses an active participation with people and buildings.

His detachment from the city was inspired, in part, by his relationship with O'Keeffe and his alienation from the official art world. More importantly, his works of this time tell of a man out of pace with the heightened activity of New York. Despite his misgivings, his enthusiasm for the individual skyscraper as a symbol of progress never waned. In a letter to Sherwood Anderson of 1925, he voiced his ambivalence: "New York is madder than ever. The pace is ever increasing. But Georgia and I somehow don't seem to be of New York — nor anywhere. We live high up in the Shelton Hotel . . . The wind howls and shakes the huge steel frame — we feel as if we were out at mid-ocean. All is so quiet except the wind, and the trembling, shaking hulk of steel in which we live. It's a wonderful place."[61]

This opinion accords with those of the turn of the century. Stieglitz often rendered industrial and commercial architecture in dramatic weather conditions so as to reflect its picturesque character. Here, a skyscraper is wrenched from its urban associations and seemingly situated far out at sea. Its isolated posture, submersion in nocturnal hues, and twinkling lights shield it from the city's more vulgar aspects.

A similar feeling of removal is present in the skyscraper renditions of Georgia O'Keeffe. Her numerous depictions of the tall building from 1925 to 1932 reflect the current dialogue between a rural versus an urban milieu. In the case of O'Keeffe, this conflict was settled ultimately in her retreat to the peaceful and unpopulated landscape of New Mexico. It is well known that she preferred reclusive, rural settings to the accelerated pace of Manhattan. Her selection of an apartment in the Shelton's upper reaches separated and elevated her from the chaos below. In addition, many of her visual interpretations of the skyscraper were rendered at night, when the commotion had settled and the theatrical spectacle of the flashing, scintillating lights could be explored. She described the Radiator Building as a "tall thin bottle with colored things going up and down inside."[62] For O'Keeffe, darkness acted as a veritable curtain, imposing a harmony over the city.

Similar in spirit to Stieglitz's interpretations of New York, O'Keeffe divorces the skyscraper from its urban associations and integrates it in nature. In *The Shelton with Sunspots* of 1926 (fig. 91), the architecture is incidental to the gossamer glow of the sun's reflections over its surface, reminiscent of Monet's renditions of Rouen Cathedral.[63]

O'Keeffe's repeated use of glowing, often celestial orbs conveys her confidence in nature as a regenerative force.[64] In *New York with Moon* of 1925 (fig. 92), a skyscraper is juxtaposed with the spire of an ineffectual church, suggesting the overshadowing of the spiritual by commercial interests. But the painting also records the flux of time when the red glow of the sun is replaced by the rising moon. Perhaps the red and black spheres, which double as traffic lights, are meant to evoke base, earthly things, while the spire points to the renewing potential of the moon, whose white glow is echoed in the street lamp. O'Keeffe was able to maintain a communion with nature's climatic, temporal, and cosmic aspects despite her presence in New York's concrete environment.

O'Keeffe's contemporary paintings of flowers underscore her rebellious attitude toward the city and her persistent effort to naturalize it. To critics who assigned sexual symbolism to her floral works, she responded that she wished merely to force the rushing Manhattan mob to focus their attention on the microcosmic world of the flower.[65] In the central panel of a three-part mural entitled *New York* (1932), she affixed a flower to a skyscraper!

Despite her repeated rendition of the skyscraper in the twenties, she viewed them as products of male interests. She took pride in the fact that she could outdo men in their own arena. The name "Stieglitz" flashed from a red neon sign in her painting, *Radiator Building—Night* of 1927.[66] Finally, she terminated her dialogue with the skyscraper in favor of a total commitment to the natural landscape.

6

The Art Deco Skyscraper: Its Impact on the Visual and Decorative Arts, 1916–1931

As a result of Ferriss's and Corbett's interpretation of the 1916 Zoning Ordinance in New York City, the shape of the skyscraper changed dramatically. The setback or stepped-back building offered by these utopian planners revolutionized tall building design beginning in the midtwenties.[1] Skyscrapers which resembled massive ziggurats proliferated both in Manhattan and in cities throughout the United States.

Observers noted that the stress was no longer on the building's bulk or facade, but on the disposition of cubical masses which created a dynamic, variegated silhouette. Because of the change in the tall building's morphology, a novel mode of perceiving and rendering the skyscraper occurred. Artists, furniture designers, sculptors, and advertisers now concentrated on its geometric components and zigzag profile. Often, dramatic views were selected to maximize and exploit the creation of these shapes or "shadowy perpendicular slices" cut "out of the sky."[2] In addition, the setback engendered an anonymous "image-type" in response to the uniformity and adaptability of the design to both architecture and the visual arts.[3]

The widespread promotion of the setback explains the spread of its popularity. In addition to the efforts of Corbett and Ferriss, the *Chicago Tribune* Competition of 1922 publicized and furthered it. A sizable portion of entries were clearly influenced by the setback envelope of Corbett and Ferriss.[4] Moreover, controversy ensued concerning the first and second prize entries. Many felt that Hood's and Howell's winning design was derivative and eclectic, a recapitulation of the Gothic mode employed in the Woolworth Building, while Eliel Saarinen's second prize rendering was modern. Influenced by Ferriss's visualizations, Saarinen gracefully stepped back his structure (fig. 93). Relying on the disposition of cubical masses, his crownless building sported a profile of right angles.

The reaction to Saarinen's entry was so overwhelming that, despite its late arrival to the competition, the judges revised their earlier decision and awarded it a position of second place.[5] Others were more adamant, suggesting that primary honors were in order. Louis Sullivan complained:

> The second and the first prize stand before us side by side. One glance of the trained eye, and instant judgement comes; that judgement which flashes from inner experience in recognition of a masterpiece. The verdict of the jury of award is at once reversed, and the second prize is placed first, where it belongs by virtue of its beautifully controlled and virile power. The first prize is demoted to the level of those works evolved of dying ideas.

Agreeing with Sullivan, H. H. Kent decried the production of "dwarf 'Woolworths' with their often grotesque features." Although he believed that the skyscraper had not yet achieved a distinctive character, Saarinen's design was praised as "the nearest to America's ideal as set forth by and in Architecture."[6]

Due to the interpretation of the new ordinance by Ferriss, Corbett, and others, the actual topography of Manhattan changed. As early as 1920, a commentator noted:

> The building regulations lately adopted prescribed that above a certain height building fronts must be set-back from the street, and higher up there must be still another recession. . . . New Yorkers who have seen the first buildings of the new type approach completion have been surprised to find that our native architecture has reproduced exactly one more ancient and foreign type—the Babylonian ziggurat or temple tower of stages.[7]

Contemporary views of the midtown of New York City reveal that the setback achieved a remarkable popularity. Raymond Hood's American Radiator Building (1924), Arthur Loomis Harmon's Shelton Hotel (1924), Ralph Walker's Telephone Company Building (1926), and Ely Jacques Kahn's Two Park Avenue Building (1927) were among the most notable examples. Because of the setback's proliferation in Manhattan, many believed that the new architecture represented a New York style, even though it appeared in cities all across the United States.[8] The new tall building design superceded its local affiliations and was adopted as a symbol of modernism and Americanism.

Contemporaries proclaimed the setback the first truly American solution to a native building type. While the skyscraper itself had been acknowledged as the expression of indigenous architecture since the turn of the century, now a style had been developed to accord with the building form. A writer in the *Architectural Forum* of 1926 pronounced: "This reborn skyscraper, though still in its infancy, represents a new style of architectural design. It is based throughout on architectural principles, and neither adapts nor reproduces old-world motifs in its design. . . . The American skyscraper has come to its own! It is American now throughout!"[9] Others saw it as the utopian solution to the nation's urban ills, its regulated forms providing an alternative to the prevailing juxtaposition of discordant architectural styles. In particular, Ferriss envisioned it as an architecture of universal application.

Commentaries on the skyscraper went beyond a simple recognition of its inherent newness and American character. Many noted the differences between past and present interpretations of the tall building, noting the cubical masses, sculptural properties, and interesting profile of the latter. This was generated by Ferriss's interpretation of the 1916 Zoning Ordinance. Beginning with the rough mass of the building, he modeled it into a pyramidal form before graduating the masses, stressing both volume and contour more than ever before. Ferriss explained this reorientation in values: "The city building, up to the present day, has been a box with a two dimensional facade attached to its side; this law demolishes the box and produces the pyramid which must be sculpted in three dimensions."[10]

The architect, designer, and artist, C. Grant La Farge, son of the famed John La Farge, provided one of the most astute aesthetic analyses of the setback. His observations are not only important for their visual acuity, but virtually enumerate the preferences of numerous artists who attempted to interpret the skyscraper's changed morphology.[11] The author began by criticizing the boxlike monolith of the past, claiming that its undifferentiated walls on narrow streets did little to command attention. Instead, he pointed to the features of the current ziggurat-like structures.

What does attract the eye is interesting, *striking silhouettes; great masses* so composed that they make us *look up at them*; very especially, light. Now the virtue of the new law is that it enables the designer to treat his building as a sort of tower. Whether or not that building starts as a solid rectangle at the ground, its required offsets as it rises lead to a grouping of diminishing masses. So it acquires perforce *a profile of interest, and attracts the eye, and goes on detaching itself more and more against the sky.*

Like Ferriss, La Farge claimed that the architect's "bulk material" had become "more plastic," allowing him to grapple with large shapes. Detail could be suppressed in favor of broader masses and a stress on simplicity. He predicted that "the whole shape of the building" would "count as never before."[12]

While La Farge described those features that engendered an aesthetic response, the editors of *Vanity Fair* pointed directly to the influence of the architecture on the visual arts. Concerning photographs reproduced in their magazine, they observed that "the new zoning law means that, instead of vast clumsy boxes, we now have combinations of volumes, relations of masses which shame the cubists." The photographs which they illustrated proved what happened when "cubism meets cubism."[13]

Attracted to the setback, artists, designers, sculptors, and advertisers created an anonymous "image-type." In contrast to the earlier renditions of individual skyscrapers such as the Singer and the Woolworth, the twenties saw the emergence of the undifferentiated skyscraper image.[14] The interaction of interchangeable geometric components in the setback skyscraper, in turn, prompted three-dimensional artistic interpretations. These features are embodied in the sculpture of John Storrs and the furniture of Paul Frankl. Both Storrs and Frankl constructed or arranged cubical masses in their architectonic works.[15] In fact, the volumetric stepped-back building so captured the visual imagination of the decade that it was selected to illustrate an advertisement for chocolates, the boxes displayed in the shape of the new skyline (fig. 94).

Although Storrs and Frankl employed color and ornamentation, reflecting the prevailing art deco aesthetic, most of the visual responses to the tall building ignored surface decoration. This may have been due to a preference for clean, machinelike forms. Thus, the adoption of the "image-type," the stress on contour, and the selection of dramatic angles represented a selective response to the city's actual appearance.

John Storrs was one of the first sculptors to incorporate setback elements in his work, although scholars have previously identified his skyscraper sculpture as clusters of buildings.[16] In addition, Storrs's polychromed surfaces have been analyzed in terms of art deco, but his debt to Ferriss and Saarinen has not been fully acknowledged. The influences on the artist were multiple; cubist sculpture, New York dada, and native American rugs were instrumental in his selection of the square, triangle, and zigzag motifs.[17] However, his interest in architecture prompted the formulation of his tower forms with graduated masses.

The son of an architect, Storrs was born in Chicago under the shadow of the city's towering new office buildings.[18] While in Paris in the 1910s, he studied sculpture and architecture, which he viewed as inextricably linked. Around 1917, he began producing cubist-inspired, architectonic works formed by the interaction of geometric planes. In an article on Storrs, Louise Bryant noted that "his theory about sculpture is that it is very closely allied to architecture and believes that sculptors should build their statues with that ever in mind."[19]

By 1922, Storrs adopted skyscraper and machine motifs, elements which he believed were analogues to America's modern architecture. In sympathy with Jane Heap and the philosophies displayed in the Machine Age Exposition, he wanted his art to reflect a mechanical aesthetic in its use of form and materials. He inquired sarcastically in the *Little Review*: "Is there no one in all this monied New York who is both connoisseur and millionaire . . . to give the architects, painters and sculptors a chance to join in the creation of something that is as complete an expression of today in its way as any of these gigantic commercial structures are an expression of their way?"[20]

The issue included a number of geometric tower forms by Storrs, the most surprising of which was a vertical structure with a stepped-back contour. The current popularity of Ferriss in both art and architectural circles, the first fledgling attempts to interpret the 1916 Zoning Ordinance, and the publicity surrounding the *Chicago Tribune* Competition probably inspired Storrs's form.

New York (fig. 95) seems a direct response to Saarinen's entry in the *Tribune* contest.[21] The sculpture's almost quadripartite divisions and the employment of stretched vertical strips are reminiscent of the second prize winner's entry. However, Storr's simplified image of metallic precision reflects his desire to forge an art which would complement, rather than imitate, the technology of the skyscraper. Stripped down and sleek, *New York* may be viewed as a transition from Saarinen's design to Hood's and Howell's Daily News Building of 1931.

Although Storrs adapted the specific character of Saarinen's entry, his skyscraper sculptures most often refer to the setback in general terms. Several constructions of combined materials created between 1922 and 1924 and entitled *Forms in Space* (fig. 96) are simplifications of the geometric masses and sculptural character of New York's stepped-back buildings. By employing a variety of metals and materials, Storrs captured the dynamism of the art deco skyscraper surface while maintaining the ordered disposition of its masses.

Paul Frankl also borrowed features of the tall building in the formulation of his "skyscraper furniture."[22] By 1927, the Frankl Galleries on Fifth Avenue and Forty-Eighth Street in Manhattan were exhibiting the very latest in household and office accoutrements inspired by the new architecture. The popularity of the furniture is seen in its inclusion in the novel *The Skyscraper Murder*.

Frankl's observations on contemporary architecture provide insight into the development of his furniture. Like Ferriss, La Farge, and others, he maintained that

the modern city architect of today can hardly hope to have his work admired in all its detail by the general public. He must depend upon large masses, upon three-dimensional forms, and not divert the attention to meaningless carved detail.

The buildings that we are beginning to notice are those which seem to be painted with a wide brush against a clear sky—a sky filled with great jagged masses. . . . The characteristics of the buildings of the future will be those that are in keeping with the life of its time. The big masses will be brought out by sharp contrasts of light and shadow. The planes will not be flat but three-dimensional and cubic.

Frankl was aware that the new architecture was a result of the limitations imposed by the 1916 Zoning Ordinance. He admitted that his furniture was influenced by "the towers and set-back architecture of modern building."[23]

Frankl's ideas on the role of the decorative arts in an industrial society were similar to those of Storrs. Responding to technology in optimistic terms, he proclaimed the age as "one of invention, machinery, industry, science and commerce." Embracing mechanical production while eschewing a craftsman's approach, he insisted that the designer must create with the industrial development of the present in mind. He saw little difference between the artist and businessman; both were required to understand contemporary humanity.[24]

Frankl's "image-type" resulted from his adoption of the skyscraper as a symbol of modern America and his belief that the decorative and building arts must be unified. The latter idea was nourished by exposure in his native Vienna to *Jugendstil* and by the prevailing quest for a *Gesamtkunstwerk*, or total work of art. He sought to imbue his furniture with similar properties, insisting that harmony could only be achieved by "bringing the same spirit into American decorative art as already has been brought into and successfully developed in our architecture."[25]

Viewing Frankl's bookcases, desks, and mirrored vanity tables in their intended settings illustrates his confidence in modern skyscraper design (fig. 97). The interaction of the volumetric compartments, which create varied profiles, echoes the new architecture. The rectilinear cells are functional components, perfectly suited as repositories for objects and books. Frankl's architectonic creations are often more inventive than the skyscrapers themselves. Asymmetrical compositional ensembles and portions of varying dimension and color enliven the character of the design.[26]

The setback skyscraper's dynamic silhouette and disposition of cubical shapes was explored by photographers and painters, who often selected dizzying angles to highlight these features. Ralph Steiner and a number of artists, whose works were illustrated in *Vanity Fair* and the *Little Review*, employed disorienting views to explore the skyscraper's novel shape. Observing conventional monolithic building from such a perspective did not yield the degree of variety afforded by terraced buildings. In Steiner's rendition of the Delmonico Building (fig. 98), the vertiginous viewpoint and the use of silhouette maximize the possibilities of the profile. Its interaction with the adjacent buildings' dynamic contours points to the setback's creation of a multiplicity of shapes out of the surrounding or negative space.

Although Steiner spoke little about his architectural photographs, his illustration of Frankl's book, *New Dimensions* (1928), an explanation of the latter's thoughts on design, reveals his awareness of the setback's possibilities. The values of simplicity, massing, and contour explored by Frankl probably influenced Steiner's accompanying images. In addition, the explanatory text by Frankl beneath each photograph suggests that Steiner's skyscraper views may reflect the author's specific instructions.

Other artists employed abrupt angles to convey the monumental bulk of the new skyscraper. Ira Martin's photograph of the unfinished Chrysler tower from above (fig. 99) explores the geometric members and the disposition of massive volumes. In an image by Caesar Zwaska (fig. 100), a building's height is conveyed by rendering it from below. The setback's successive tapering evokes the sensation that it is climbing to infinity. Numerous images by such artists as O'Keeffe, Howard Cook, and Ira Martin suggest that the shape of the setback is suited to the rendition of loftiness.[27] This is not meant to suggest that the new skyscraper envelope alone prompted the multitude of images concerning scale and monumentality; rather, it points to the multiplicity of forces, both morphological and ideological, which created the skyscraper image of the twenties.

Afterword

Two months before the stock market crash, the popular press announced that the Empire State Corporation would begin construction on the tallest building in the world at Thirty-fourth Street and Fifth Avenue, the site occupied by the legendary Waldorf-Astoria. Its financiers, Pierre Du Pont and John E. Raskob, selected Alfred E. Smith, four-term governor of New York and failed Democratic presidental candidate, as the front man for the enterprise, paying him a salary of $50,000 to promote the building. This proved to be an astute public relations gesture, because Smith's popularity with the masses helped ward off the inevitable criticism heaped upon skyscrapers during the Depression's darkest days.[1]

In the view of its promoters, Shreve, Lamb, and Harmon's Empire State Building was planned not only to vertically outdistance all other lofty structures, including the French symbol of technology, the Eiffel Tower, but also to serve as the ultimate monument to American ingenuity and aspirations. Raskob wished to insure the public's awe and wonderment before the 1,250-foot, 85-story structure and, at the same time, dwarf its rival, the Chrysler Building, by adding a mooring mast where dirigibles could land. It was not sufficient for the Empire State Building to be simply of the here and now, a mere recapitulation of all that was modern. Raskob envisioned it as the harbinger of the future, the concrete embodiment of man's desire to travel skyward. Although never usable because of violent updrafts, the Empire State's mooring mast is indelibly imprinted in everyone's imagination as the site of King Kong's attempt to ward off fighter planes for love's sake.

Theatrics became part of the building's lore. For a nominal fee, one could ascend to its pinnacles and watch the spectacle of New York below. Even opening day, 1 May 1931, was treated as an extravaganza; speeches by Smith, Governor Roosevelt, Mayor Walker, and others characterized the festivities. Copying official sanctions extended to the Woolworth Building, President Hoover bestowed national recognition upon it by pushing a button which illuminated the tower.

In spite of the Empire State Corporation's slick public relations campaign and attempt to project an image of twenties' infallibility and omnipotence, Lewis Mumford's prophecies rang truer than *Fortune's*. The skyscraper was perceived as a symbol of greed and profit; the excitement surrounding it collapsed with the stock market. When the Empire State Building opened, it was only forty-six percent rented, which led vaudevillians to refer to it as the "Empty State Building."[2] Yet it was theatrics that paid off; it was rumored that income from tourist visits to the observatory kept it financially solvent. Writing in the *New Republic*, a frequent forum for Mumford's harsh attacks, an anonymous reviewer linked skyscrapers to the inflated mentality of the twenties.

> The material embodiment of the late bull market remains in our metropolitan structures of towering heights. They soar boldly above a surrounding mesa of roofs, very much as the spire-like graph of 1929 equity prices soars above the horizontal undulating line that records the market fluctuations over a long preceding period. The same causes explain both pinnacles. They are the same methods of rationalization, the same economic theory. But the spire on the graph has visibly collapsed. We can still see the buildings, they hover over the flat plateau of stability, the ironic witnesses of collapsed hopes.[3]

In spite of the economic debacle, even the most disparaging skyscraper critics acknowledged its aesthetic appeal. Mechanical functionalism and its absorption in colored lights continued to be commented on. But it was no longer seen as the bulwark of business or as a monument to American monetary prowess. Writing in the *New Republic*, Edmund Wilson called it "superfluous, ironically advertised as a triumph in the hour when the planless competitive society is bankrupt."[4]

To counteract the onslaught of negative commentary, the Empire State's financiers helped forge a new positive skyscraper image which dominated the thirties. The investment of fifty million dollars forced them to plan costs efficiently, for any delay in the building's completion meant the loss of considerable capital. To expedite the process, its 2,500 to 4,000 construction workers were given a daily blueprint of tasks. A railway system bearing individually marked steel beams indicated their exact placement; even the derrick which was to lift them in place was designated.

A spirit of teamwork and cooperation among the workers resulted, a development that the Empire State Corporation sought to capitalize on. At the opening day's festivities, Smith paid appropriate homage to "the faithful workmen that put this monument in the air."[5] Continuing in the same vein, he recalled a picture in the *Evening Post* of Tony and his mother on their East Side tenement roof. The mother pointed to the building and exclaimed, "Tony, your old man is building that!" Smith assured the crowd that he was "for the mother . . . for Tony . . . and for Tony's old man."[6]

In May 1930, Lewis Hine, the well-known photographer of workmen and immigrants, was commissioned to chronicle the Empire State Building's rise from foundation to pinnacle.[7] Unlike his earlier oppressed factory workers, Hine's skyscraper builders gain mastery over their mechanical tools. In over 1,000 images, the building serves as a mere backdrop for the triumph of human energy and courage. Sharing their excitement and daring, Hine ascended the enormous steel scaffold, often venturing out on girders high above the sprawling city. In *Men at Work* (1932), a photographic celebration of men in various industries, he explained: "This is a book of Men at Work; men of courage, skill, daring and imagination. Cities do not build themselves, machines can not make machines, unless back of them all are the brains and toil of men." Hine identified with his subjects, having "worked in many industries and associated with thousands of workers." He hoped that the public would meet these heroes, "all of whom it was a privilege to know," through his images.[8]

In marked contrast to previous skyscraper views, workmen dominate Hine's photographs. *Finishing Up the Job* (fig. 101) pictures the completion of the Empire State Building's mooring mast by two muscular personalities, "clear-eyed, poised and self-confident creatures whom Lyssipus or Phidias would have delighted to model in imperishable marble," according to one observer.[9] Despite their position "a quarter of a mile up in the clouds," which Hine captured from a swinging crane, they are undaunted.[10] One stares boldly at the viewer with arm raised like a new Statue of Liberty, while the other smiles confidently as he actively wields a hammer, transferring his strength and virility to the steel structure. Hine underscores the cooperative nature of their effort by bonding them in close proximity. Beams and scaffold both surge upward and enframe them, asserting their primary role in the skyscraper arena.

Raskob's and Smith's working-class roots, Hine's sympathetic views of the skyscraper builder, and the realities of the Depression shifted the emphasis from the businessman to the common man. In the face of rampant unemployment, the omnipotent workman was a source of hope and a role model for the struggling masses. Although the Empire State Building itself was perceived by F. Scott Fitzgerald and others as "a ruin, lonely and inexplicable as the sphinx," or as an interesting curiosity, the construction worker's efforts served as the preeminent subject for skyscraper artists until the second World War.

Fitzgerald's dapper friend, Bunny, from "The Lost City" of 1932, reflects the artists' and writers' changed view of industry and the city. Whereas Bunny had formerly epitomized a "Metropolitan spirit" and a twenties' confidence, he had recently "gone over to communism" and fretted about "the wrongs of the southern mill workers and western farmers whose voices, fifteen years ago, would not have penetrated his study walls."[11]

Figure 1.　Joseph Pennell, *The Four-Story House*, 1904.
Etching.
(Illustrated in Fredrick Keppel, Mr. Pennell's Etchings of
N.Y. "Skyscrapers," *New York: Frederick Keppel & Co.,
1905, n.p.)*

Figure 2.   Joseph Pennell, *Singer Building — Early Evening*,
ca. 1908.
Drawing.
(*Illustrated in John C. Van Dyke*, The New New York,
New York: The Macmillan Co., 1909, pl. 28)

Figure 3.   Joseph Pennell, *The City Hall and World Building*,
ca. 1908.
Drawing.
(*Illustrated in Van Dyke*, The New New York, *New
York: The Macmillan Co., 1909, pl. 8*)

Figure 4. Alvin Langdon Coburn, *St. Paul's Church and the Park Row Building*, ca. 1905.
Photograph.
(*International Museum of Photography at George Eastman House; Illustrated in Alvin Langdon Coburn, "Some Photographic Impressions of New York,"* Metropolitan Magazine *23 [February 1906], n.p.*)

Figure 5.   John Marin, *Church and Other Buildings*, 1911.
Watercolor on paper, 9-3/8″ × 11-1/2″.
(The Alfred Stieglitz Collection, 56.381. © *The Art*
Institute of Chicago, All Rights Reserved)

Figure 6. John Marin, *Saint Paul's Manhattan*, 1914.
Watercolor on paper, 15-7/8" × 18-7/8".
(The Metropolitan Museum of Art, The Alfred Stieglitz Collection 1949, 49.70.110)

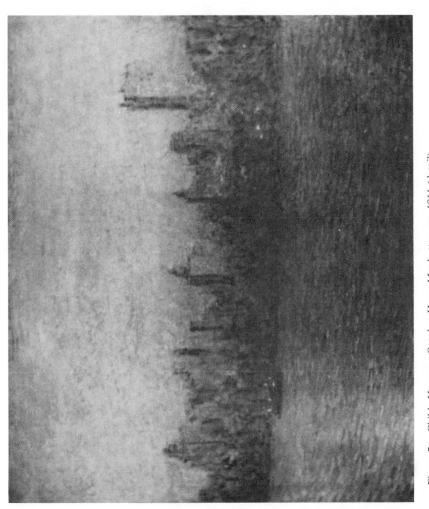

Figure 7. Childe Hassam, *October Haze: Manhattan*, ca. 1911 (detail). Oil on canvas.
(Illustrated in Annie Nathan Meyer, "A City Picture, Mr. Hassam's Latest Painting of New York," Art and Progress 11 [March 1911], p. 139)

Figure 8.   Joseph Pennell, *A Hole in the Ground*, 1904.
Etching, 11-3/4″ × 8-7/8″.
(*Illustrated in Louis A. Wuerth*, Catalogue of the Complete Etchings
of Joseph Pennell, *Boston: Little, Brown & Co., 1928, p. 118*)

Figure 9. George Bellows, *Pennsylvania Excavation*, 1907.
Oil on canvas, 34″ × 44″.
(Collection of Kidder, Peabody and Co., New York)

Figure 10. Joseph Pennell, *The Foundation — Building A
Skyscraper*, 1912.
(*Illustrated in Joseph Pennell*, The Great New York,
Boston: Le Roy Phillips, 1912, pl. 16)

Figure 11. Alfred Stieglitz, *Old and New New York*, 1910.
Photogravure.
(*Illustrated in* Camera Work, *36 [October 1911], p. 13*)

Figure 12.   Childe Hassam, *The Hovel and the Skyscraper*, 1904.
Oil on canvas, 25″ × 31″.
(*Courtesy Mr. and Mrs. Meyer Potamkin; Illustrated in
Donelson Hoopes*, Childe Hassam, *New York:
Watson-Guptill Publications, 1979*)

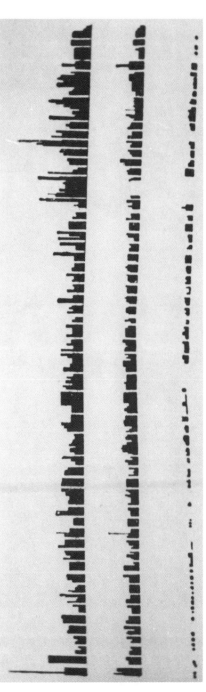

Figure 13. *New York's Changing Skyline*, ca. 1908. Chart.
(Illustrated in Joseph B. Gilder, "The City of Dreadful Heights," Putnam's Monthly 5 [November 1908], p. 143)

Figure 14.   Joseph Pennell, *Cortlandt Street Ferry*, 1908.
Sandpaper mezzotint, 11-7/8″ × 10″.
(*Illustrated in Louis Wuerth*, Catalogue of the
Complete Etchings of Joseph Pennell, *Boston: Little,
Brown and Co., 1928, p. 173*)

Figure 15. F. Hopkinson Smith, *Skyline View*, ca. 1912.
Charcoal.
(*Illustration from* Charcoals of New and Old New York, *by F. Hopkinson Smith.
Copyright 1912 by Doubleday & Company, Inc. Reprinted by permission of the
publisher.*)

Figure 16. Alvin Langdon Coburn, *The Waterfront* or *New York*,
1907.
Gum platinotype, halftone, 6.65″ × 6.49″.
(*Illustrated in* Camera Work, *21 [January 1908], p. 37*)

Figure 17.   Alfred Stieglitz, *The City of Ambition*, 1910.
Photogravure, 13–3/8″ × 10–1/4″.
(*National Gallery of Art, Washington; The Alfred
Stieglitz Collection*)

Figure 18.   Leon Kroll, *The Bridge*, 1910–11.
Oil on canvas, 36" × 45".
(*Courtesy Mr. and Mrs. Sigmund M. Hyman; Illustrated in Milton Brown, American Art from the Armory Show to the Depression, Princeton University Press, 1972*)

Figure 19.   Childe Hassam, *Lower Manhattan View down
Broad St.*, 1907.
Oil on canvas, 30-1/8″ × 16″.
(*Willard Straight Hall Collection, Cornell University,
Gift of Mrs. Leonard K. Elmhirst*)

Figure 20.   Birge Harrison, *The "Flatiron" after Rain*, ca. 1907.
Oil on canvas, 30″ ×41″.
(*Current whereabouts unknown*)

Figure 21. Albert Fleury, *Masonic Temple, Chicago*, ca. 1904.
Oil on canvas.
(*Illustrated in Maude I. G. Oliver, "A Chicago Painter:
The Work of Albert Fleury*," International Studio *22
[March 1904], p. 21*)

Figure 22.   Alfred Stieglitz, *The Flatiron*, 1902–1903.
Photograph from original negative.
(*National Gallery of Art, Washington, D.C., The Alfred Stieglitz Collection*)

Figure 23.   Edward Steichen, *The Flatiron-Evening*, 1905.
Three-color halftone, photograph.
(*Illustrated in* Camera Work, *14 [April 1906], p. 31*)

Figure 24. Alfred Stieglitz, *Icy Night, New York*, 1897.
Photograph.
*(Illustrated in Charles Caffin, Photography as a Fine Art, New York: Doubleday, Page &
Co., 1901; reprint ed., New York: American Photographic Books, Co., 1972)*

Figure 25. Alvin Langdon Coburn, *The Singer
Building — Twilight*, 1908.
Photograph.
(*Photograph from Alvin Langdon Coburn*, New York,
London: Duckworth Press, 1910)

Figure 26. Joseph Pennell, *Cliffs of West Street, New York*, 1908.
Sandpaper mezzotint, 9-7/8″ × 12-7/8″.
*(Illustrated in Joseph Pennell, The Great New York, Boston: Le Roy Phillips, 1912,
pl. 12)*

Figure 27.   Alfred Stieglitz, *Spring Showers*, 1900.
Photogravure, 310 × 127 mm.
(*National Gallery of Art, Washington, The Alfred
Stieglitz Collection. Gift of Georgia O'Keeffe and the
Alfred Stieglitz Estate*)

Figure 28.   Alvin Langdon Coburn, *Portsmouth U.S.A.* or *The
Park Row Building*, 1907.
Photograph.
(*International Museum of Photography at George
Eastman House*)

Figure 29.   Alvin Langdon Coburn, *The Octopus*, 1912.
Photograph.
(*Illustrated in Richard Cork*, Vorticism and Abstract
Art in the First Machine Age, *vol. 2, Berkeley and Los
Angeles: University of California Press, 1976, p. 497*)

Figure 30. *I Am Seeing Great Things*, ca. 1903.
Postcard.

Figure 31.   John Marin, *The Flatiron*, ca. 1909.
Watercolor on paper.
(*Private collection, Great Britain; Photograph from
Sheldon Reich*, John Marin: A Stylistic Analysis and a
Catalogue Raisonné, *Tuscson: University of Arizona
Press, 1970*)

Figure 32.   Harry M. Pettit, *King's Dream of New York*, 1908.
             Drawing.
             (*Illustrated in John Kouwenhoven*, The Columbia
             Historical Portrait of New York. *Copyright 1953 by
             Doubleday & Company, Inc.*)

Figure 33.   John Marin, *Buildings, One with Tower*, 1910.
Watercolor on paper, 21″ × 14″.

Figure 34.   John Marin, *Downtown from River*, 1910.
Watercolor on paper, 14″ × 17″.
(Private collection; Photograph courtesy of Kennedy Galleries, New York)

Figure 35. John Marin, *Woolworth Building #28*, 1912–13.
Watercolor on paper, 19-1/2″ × 16″.
(*National Gallery of Art, Washington; Gift of Eugene
and Agnes E. Meyer*)

Figure 36.   John Marin, *Woolworth Building #32*, 1912–13.
Watercolor on paper, 19-1/2″ × 16″.
(*National Gallery of Art, Washington; Gift of Eugene
and Agnes E. Meyer*)

Figure 37. John Marin, *Woolworth Building, New York, No. 3*,
1913.
Etching, 13-1/16″ × 10-5/8″.
(*Collection, The Museum of Modern Art, New York,
Purchase: Edward Warburg Fund*)

Figure 38.   Alvin Langdon Coburn, *The Woolworth Building* or
New York from Its Pinnacles, 1912.
Photograph.
(*International Museum of Photography at George
Eastman House*)

Figure 39.   *Above the Clouds and Old New York*, ca. 1913.
Cover of book by H. Bruce Addington, *Above the Clouds and Old New York*, Baltimore: Hugh McAtamney, 1913.
(**Photograph courtesy of the Museum of the City of New York**)

Figure 40. John Marin, *Movement, Fifth Avenue*, 1912.
Watercolor on paper, 16-5/8 × 13-1/2″.
(Alfred Stieglitz Collection, 49.554. © *The Art*
Institute of Chicago, All Rights Reserved)

Figure 41. Max Weber, *New York*, 1912.
Oil on canvas, 21″ × 25″.
(Courtesy William C. Janss Collection)

Figure 42.   Alvin Langdon Coburn, *The House of a Thousand Windows*, 1912.
Photograph.
(*International Museum of Photography at George Eastman House*)

Figure 43.   Max Weber, *New York*, 1913.
Oil on canvas, 101.6 × 81.3 cm.
(*Thyssen-Bornemisza Collection, Lugano, Switzerland*)

Figure 44. Max Weber, *Abstraction Skyscraper (Tour d'Eiffel)*,
1916.
Bronze, posthumous cast of 1977, 5″ high.
(*Courtesy Forum Gallery, New York*)

Figure 45. Abraham Walkowitz, *Times Square*, 1910.
Watercolor on paperboard, 24-1/2″ × 18-11/16″.
(*Hirshhorn Museum and Sculpture Garden,
Smithsonian Institution*)

Figure 46. Abraham Walkowitz, *New York Abstraction*, ca. 1915.
Charcoal on paper, 19″ × 14″.
(Courtesy Zabriskie Gallery, New York City)

Figure 47.   Abraham Walkowitz, *Cityscape*, ca. 1913.
Pencil and graphite on paper, 20″ × 13″.
(*National Collection of Fine Arts, Smithsonian Institu-
tion, gift of the artist in memory of Gertrude Vanderbilt
Whitney*)

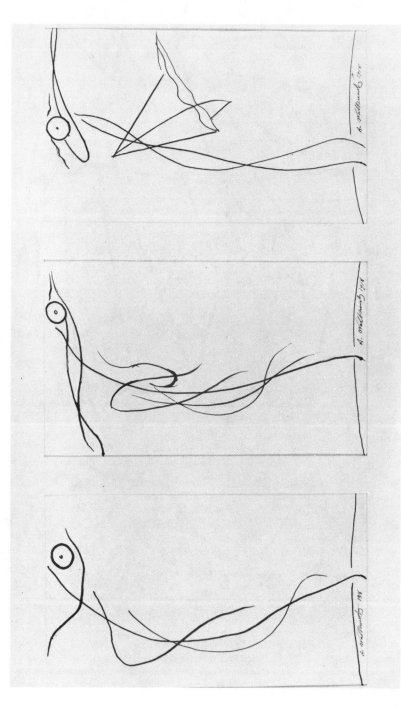

Figure 48. Abraham Walkowitz, *Improvisations of the Dance #2*, 1918. Brush and ink on paper, 10-1/2″ × 6-3/8″ each. (*Collection of the Newark Museum*)

Figure 49.   Francis Picabia, *New York (Study for a Study of New York?)*, 1913.
Pencil and ink on paper, 7″ × 6″.
(*Illustrated in* William Camfield, *Francis Picabia, Princeton: Princeton University Press, 1979;* © *ADAGP/SPADEM, Paris/VAGA, New York, 1985.*)

Figure 50.   Albert Gleizes, *Kelly Springfield*, 1915.
Gouache on board, 40-1/8″ × 30-1/8″.
(*Solomon R. Guggenheim Museum, New York; Photo:*
Robert E. Mates; © *ADAGP/SPADEM,*
Paris/VAGA, New York, 1985)

Figure 51.   Albert Gleizes, *Sur le Flat-Iron*, 1916.
Drawing, 10-5/8″ × 8-1/4″.
(*Photograph courtesy of Mr. Herbert Barrows, Ann
Arbor, Michigan;* © *ADAGP/SPADEM,
Paris/VAGA, New York, 1985*)

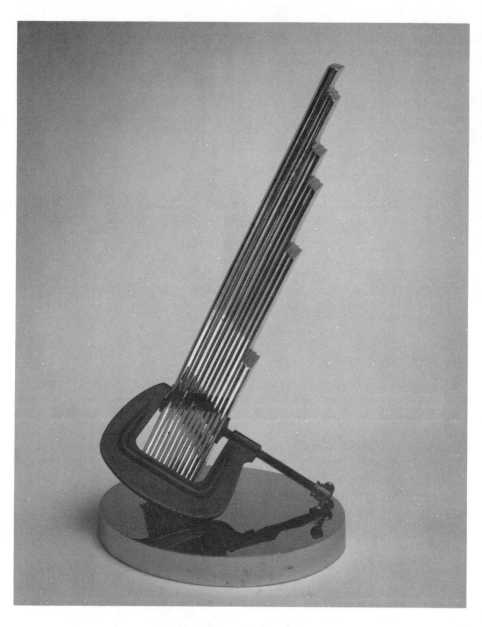

Figure 52.   Man Ray, *New York 17*, 1966.
Bronze, 17-5/8″ × 9-3/8″ × 9-3/8″.
(*Hirshhorn Museum and Sculpture Garden,
Smithsonian Institution, original lost;* ©
ADAGP/SPADEM, Paris/VAGA, New York, 1985)

Figure 53. Man Ray, *Export Commodity* or *New York*, 1920.
Metal bearings, glass jar, 11″ high.
(*Illustrated in Arturo Schwarz*, Man Ray, *New York:
Rizzoli, 1977, pl. 269;* © *ADAGP/SPADEM,
Paris/VAGA, New York, 1985*)

TITANIC FORCES REAR A NEW SKY LINE

Gigantic Structures in Many Quarters Are Transforming New York City

Sleepy West Street, Long Dozing Beside Its Piers, Has Been Invaded by a Host of Builders.

By JAMES C. YOUNG

WHEREVER the New Yorker walks through his streets, old and familiar structures come tumbling about his ears and new ones rise to uncounted floors. Turn into almost any street of the crowded mid-town section and the eye is greeted by a sight that is typical of the newer New York. Wreckers have in hand some building of yesterday, mellowed by the years. Windows are smashed, cornices torn off. Havoc prevails. Men with crowbars industriously ply their trade, heedless of the memories they rend. Acetylene torches burn through steel beams, and cranes transport squares of stone to safe resting places. This is organized destruction in the name of progress.

Trucks stand in the street, their motors chugging with the throb of power—each a Juggernaut waiting to bear away these crumbling walls. There is a thunder of bricks. The passer-by dodges by instinct. But the débris slides over his head down a long chute into a truck. Dust flies and the sidewalk throng halts to clear its eyes. Nobody is hurt, and the city moves on.

Pneumatic Drills Hammer Away

The passer-by who pauses to take account of these operations will find much that stirs imagination and prompts inquiry. It is a bit odd to note the place where a flight of stairs ran upward in some old structure when the stairs have disappeared and naught remains on the adjoining wall but the mark of their flight. Occasionally such stairs have a series of niches, one at each landing. Not many days ago such a niche still held a plaster Apollo, a hand upraised to strum his broken lyre as he gazed upon the ruin about him.

Or the scene may have advanced to the next stage, where depths yawn below the onlooker's feet. Pneumatic drills are hammering at the solid floor of Manhattan, and dynamite blasts a way through rock that was formed when glaciers passed this way. The yellow and red earth, freed from long compression beneath a building raised by man, enjoys the air and sunlight.

But that freedom will be brief. Once bedrock is made smooth and steel supports have been securely fixed, a skyscraper rises, floor by floor. Of the many wonders that go to make up the modern New York not the least is its mastery of building. Steel framework, brick trimming and marble interiors are shipped by schedule, timed to arrive precisely as needed. No sooner have the steel workers raised the skeleton of a floor than the bricklayers take possession. Behind them come the train of workers to carry on many tasks. Meanwhile the New Yorker traverses his roofed sidewalk below and usually escapes with no greater damage than an eyeful of mortar.

The remaking of New York is at full tide. Upon every hand powered-driven hammers split the air. Donkey engines whistle and shriek. Bundles of steel beams ascend to startling heights, often with a steel worker standing amid ships, his hand upon the fall of the derrick. No human agency could keep count of the unmeasured tons in steel, stone and brick that are raised day by day too upon ton, until a new skyscraper stands in the place of some lowly structure.

Now that the pleasant days of Autumn begin to run low in the glass of time, builders are hastening, with intensive effort. A host of workers is striving to complete before snow falls the 350 buildings under construction on Manhattan Island. Another army of workmen is engaged in altering no less than 900 buildings of all kinds. Daily the undertaking goes forward, driven by the hands of many artisans, working upon a vast scale.

The present period in the city's rebuilding will far surpass all periods that have gone before. Seldom in any structure of less than twelve floors erected upon a costly site. More often it will mount skyward twenty or thirty stories. Buildings erected a dozen years, embracing many of the modern facilities, give way to greater buildings embodying every improvement the engineer can devise. Relatively new structures of eight to ten floors are demolished and skyscrapers put up in their stead that will yield suitable returns. Rents rise even faster than do buildings.

Old Landmarks Go

Every quarter of the city, from Lexington Avenue to Eighth Avenue, has fallen under the spell of reconstruction. Fifth Avenue soon will be a new street for almost its entire length, and particularly in its upper reaches. Before long the visitor returning after, say, ten years' absence will have difficulty in finding a single landmark. Downtown the era of rebuilding holds sway while it flows northward into the Nineties and beyond. From Battery Place to Spuyten Duyvil New York is tearing down the old and rearing the new. Intense concentration prevails. Buildings on all sides house populations equal to those of flourishing towns. Districts of the city untouched for years are astir with enterprise. Sleepy West Street, long dozing beside its piers, has been invaded by a host of builders. One massive structure already nears completion upon a site where banana dealers and peanut venders formerly pursued their calling. The bolt of this new structure is columnal—an object that smites the eye.

Other buildings of imposing size are projected for near-by corners. West Street is awakening to the new day, but surely we may pause in the midst of so much progress to regret the doom that faces the line of two and three story buildings, their red bricks reminiscent of another time. These buildings were raised when West Street still had a nautical tang of romance. But it is doubtful if a single sailing vessel has poked her nose into West Street dock for ten years. The old-time sailors have disappeared as well.

Thus the reconstruction of New York goes on. Lower Manhattan, original home of the skyscraper, has a part in the day of greater expansion, although the downtown city no longer asserts its leadership of other years. The era of rebuilding is confined to no single section, but has shown its greatest activity in the zone bounded by Thirty-fourth and Fifty-ninth Streets, Lexington and Eighth Avenues.

Traveling uptown from City Hall, one finds little evidence of any considerable activity along the miles of streets that parallel Broadway or cross the island. This district has reached a stalemate. But the southern fringes of Greenwich Village reveal a building program that seems likely to transform that picturesque, decaying section into a land of box factories and garages.

Here the man with an hour to dream may see the old city and the new in some of its sharpest contrasts. In every street are the staid red brick houses with gable windows. Some of them are a hundred years old; a few are even older. Most of these houses were erected when Greenwich Village was a thriving residential centre. It is but a century since the Village was shining new, like any modern suburb—although it had been actually founded in Colonial times, and the homes of the early nineteenth century were raised alongside older homes put up by the Dutch.

In recent years the quiet streets and old-fashioned houses have yield-

(Continued on Page 10)

At Times Square the Eye Is Greeted by a Sight That Is Typical of the Newer New York.

Figure 54.   *Titanic Forces Rear a New Sky Line*, 1925.
(New York Times, *15 November 1925. Copyright* ©
*1925 by The New York Times Company. Reprinted by
permission*)

Figure 55.   Willy Pogany Observing His Panel *The Growth of New York*, 1925.
60″ high.
(Art, Prints and Photographs Division, The New York Public Library, Astor, Lenox and Tilden Foundations)

Figure 56. Charles Sheeler and Paul Strand, Still Photograph from the Film *Manhatta* of Buildings, 1921.
(*Use of stills from the Paul Strand film "Manhatta" courtesy of the Paul Strand Archive and Library, Silver Mountain Foundation*)

Figure 57. Charles Sheeler, *New York (Buildings)*, 1920.
Pencil on paper, 19-7/8″ × 13″.
(*Friends of American Art collection,* © *The Art Institute of Chicago, All Rights Reserved*)

Figure 58. Charles Sheeler and Paul Strand, Still Photograph from the Film *Manhatta* of Derricks and Beams, 1921.
(*Use of stills from the Paul Strand film "Manhatta" courtesy of the Paul Strand Archive and Library, Silver Mountain Foundation*)

Figure 59.   Charles Sheeler, *Berkley Apartments*, 1920.
Photograph.
(*Illustrated in* Amerika: Traum und Depression,
Akademie der Künste, Berlin, 1981)

Figure 60.   Charles Sheeler, *Delmonico Building*, 1927.
Lithograph, 9-3/4″ × 6-3/4″.
(*Courtesy of the Library of Congress*)

Figure 61.   Charles Sheeler and Paul Strand, Still Photograph from the Film *Manhatta* of the Backs
of Buildings, 1921.
(*Use of the stills from the Paul Strand film "Manhatta" courtesy of the Paul Strand
Archive and Library, Silver Mountain Foundation*)

Figure 62.   Margaret Bourke-White, *Terminal Tower, Cleveland*,
1928.
Gelatin silverprint, 13-7/16″ × 10-1/4″.
(*The Cleveland Museum of Art, Gift of Max Ratner;*
Use of photograph courtesy of Roger B. White)

Figure 63.   Margaret Bourke-White, *Toward the Sun*, ca. 1929–30.
Photograph.
(*Illustrated in* The Skyscraper from Fortune, *New
York: American Institute of Steel Construction, Inc.
1930; Use of photograph courtesy of Roger B. White*)

Figure 64. Margaret Bourke-White, *The Outside Hoist Used in the Construction of the Chrysler*, ca. 1929–30. Photograph.
(*Illustrated in* The Skyscraper from Fortune, *New York: American Institute of Steel Construction, Inc., 1930; Use of photograph courtesy of Roger B. White*)

Figure 65.   Robert Hallowell, *Chicago Impression*, 1930.
Watercolor.
(*Illustrated in* The Skyscraper from Fortune, *New York: American Institute of Steel Construction, Inc., 1930.*)

Figure 66. Hugh Ferriss, *The Clay Emerging into Practical Forms*, 1925. Drawing.
(*Illustrated in Jean Ferriss Leich, Architectural Visions: The Drawings of Hugh Ferriss, New York: Whitney Library of Design, 1980*)

Figure 67.   Hugh Ferriss, *The Chanin Building*, 1927.
Drawing.
(*Illustrated in Hugh Ferriss*, The Metropolis of
Tomorrow, *New York: Ives Washburn, 1929*)

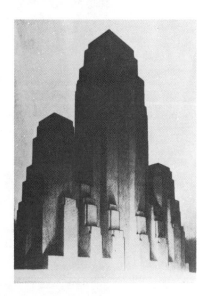

Figure 68. Hugh Ferriss, *Evolution of the Set-Back Building*,
1922.
Drawings.
(*Illustrated in Hugh Ferriss*, The Metropolis of
Tomorrow, *New York: Ives Washburn, 1929*)

Figure 69. Hugh Ferriss, *Overhead Traffic-Ways*, ca. 1929.
Drawing.
(*Illustrated in Hugh Ferriss*, The Metropolis of
Tomorrow, *New York: Ives Washburn, 1929*)

Figure 70.   Hugh Ferriss, *Glass Skyscraper*, 1926.
             Drawing.
             (*Illustrated in* The Machine Age Exposition Catalogue,
             New York: Little Review, 1927)

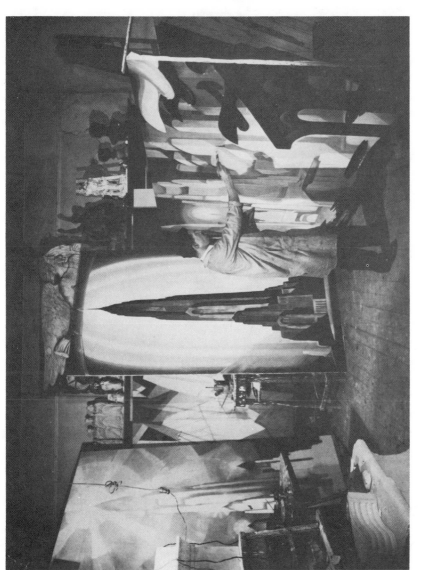

Figure 71.   Hugh Ferriss Painting *Buildings of the Future*, 1925.
Photograph.
(Art, Prints and Photographs Division, The New York Public Library, Astor, Lenox and Tilden Foundations)

Figure 72. Francisco Mujica, *City of the Future: Hundred Story City in Neo-American Style*, 1928.
Drawing.
(*Illustrated in Francisco Mujica, The History of the Skyscraper, Paris, New York:
Archeology and Architecture Press, 1929; reprint ed., New York: Da Capo Press, 1976*)

Figure 73. Arthur J. Frappier, *A Regional Plan Study of Building
Development in the Neighborhood of the
Chrystie-Forsyth Area*, 1931.
Watercolor.
(*Illustrated in* Creative Art *9 [August 1931]; Courtesy
American Federation of Arts*)

Figure 74. Leopold De Postels, *Imaginative Conceptions of the City of the Future*, ca. 1931.
Drawing.
(*Illustrated in* Creative Art *9 [August 1931]; Courtesy American Federation of Arts*)

Figure 75. *Buildings Still in Blue-Print May Be Obsolete*, 1930.
Drawing.
(*Illustrated in* Fortune *2 [April 1930]*)

Figure 76. Paul Strand, *Photograph—New York* or *Wall Street*, 1915. Photogravure. (*Illustrated in Camera Work, 48 [October 1916]*)

Figure 77. Paul Strand, *Photograph — New York*, ca. 1916.
Photogravure.
(Illustrated in Camera Work, *48 [October 1916])*

Figure 78.   Paul Strand and Charles Sheeler, Still Photograph from the film *Manhatta* of a
Cemetery, 1921.
*(Use of stills from the Paul Strand film "Manhatta" courtesy of the Paul Strand Archive
and Library, Silver Mountain Foundation)*

Figure 79. Paul Strand and Charles Sheeler, Still Photograph from the Film *Manhatta* of Wall Street, 1921.
(*Use of stills from the Paul Strand film "Manhatta" courtesy of the Paul Strand Archive and Library, Silver Mountain Foundation.*)

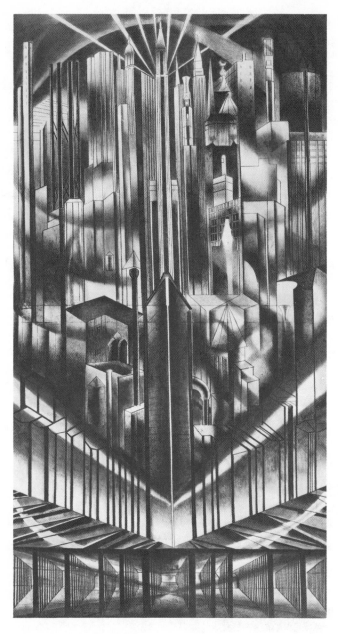

Figure 80. Joseph Stella, *New York Interpreted: The Skyscraper*, 1922 (Central Panel).
Oil on canvas, 54″ × 99-3/4″.
(*Collection of the Newark Museum*)

Figure 81. Jan Matulka, *Cityscape View of New York*, 1923.
Etching on paper, 10-1/8″ × 7-3/4″.
(*National Museum of American Art, Accession no.
1973.136, Smithsonian Institution, museum purchase*)

Figure 82.   George Ault, *Construction Night*, ca. 1923.
Oil on canvas, 29-3/8″ × 21-1/2″.
(*Courtesy Yale University Art Gallery, Gift of the*
Woodward Foundation)

Figure 83.   Stefan Hirsch, *Plants and Towers*, 1920.
Oil on canvas board, 19-3/4″ × 16-1/4″.
(*Courtesy Hirschl and Adler Galleries, New York*)

Figure 84. Robert Edmond Jones, Opening Stage Set from the Ballet *Skyscrapers*, 1926. Photograph.
(Illustrated in "Skyscrapers," Theater Arts Monthly 10 [March 1926])

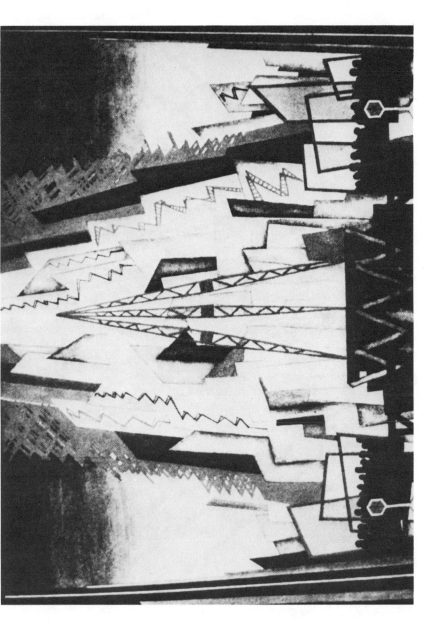

Figure 85. Robert Edmond Jones, Second Stage Set from the Ballet *Skyscrapers*, 1926. Photograph. (*Illustrated in "Skyscrapers," Theater Arts Monthly 10 [March 1926]*)

Figure 86. Robert Edmond Jones, Fifth Stage Set from the Ballet *Skyscrapers*, 1926. Photograph. *(Illustrated in "Skyscrapers," Theater Arts Monthly 10 [March 1926])*

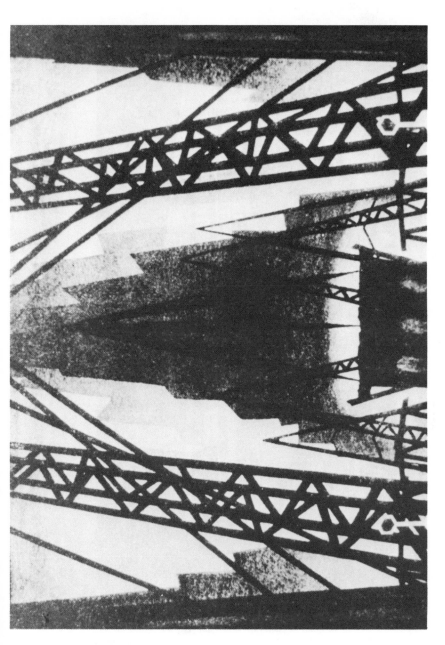

Figure 87.   Robert Edmond Jones, Final Stage Set from the Ballet *Skyscrapers*, 1926.
Photograph.
(Illustrated in "Skyscrapers," Theater Arts Monthly 10 [March 1926])

Figure 88.   Arnold Ronnebeck, *Wall Street*, ca. 1925.
Lithograph on paper, 12-1/2″ × 6-11/16″.
(*National Museum of American Art, Accession no.
1983.90.158, Smithsonian Institution, Gift of the estate
of Olin Dows*)

Figure 89.   William Charles McNulty, *Gotham (Whirlpool)*,
ca. 1928.
Etching, 12-1/2″ × 7″.
(*Current whereabouts unknown*)

Figure 90.   Alfred Stieglitz, *Evening New York — Shelton*, 1931.
Photograph.
(*National Gallery of Art, Washington; The Alfred
Stieglitz Collection*)

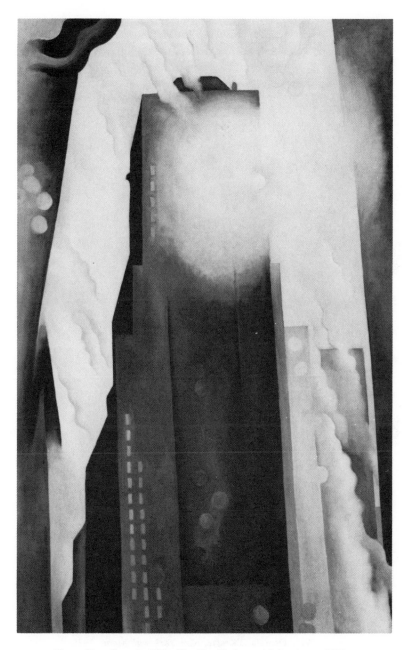

Figure 91. Georgia O'Keeffe, *The Shelton with Sunspots*, 1926.
Oil on canvas, 48-1/2″ × 30″.
(© *The Art Institute of Chicago, All Rights Reserved*)

Figure 92. Georgia O'Keeffe, *New York with Moon*, 1925.
Oil on canvas, 48″ × 30″.
(*Mr. and Mrs. Peter Meyer*)

Figure 93.   Eliel Saarinen, Second Prize Winner of the *Chicago Tribune* Competition, 1922.
Drawing.
(*Illustrated in* The International Competition for a New Administration Building for the *Chicago Tribune, Chicago: The Tribune Co., 1923, pl. 13*)

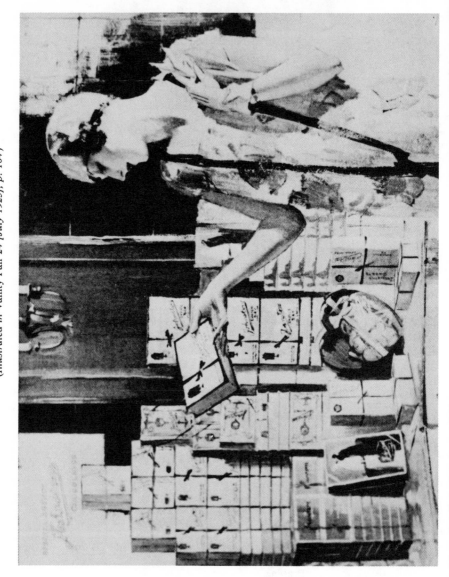

Figure 94.   Advertisement for Johnston's Chocolates, 1925.
(Illustrated in Vanity Fair 24 [July 1925], p. 104)

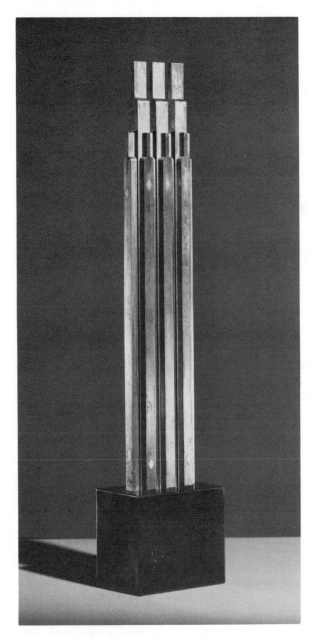

Figure 95. John Storrs, *New York*, ca. 1922–23.
Bronze and steel, 21″ high.
(*Indianapolis Museum of Art, Discretionary Fund
Purchase*)

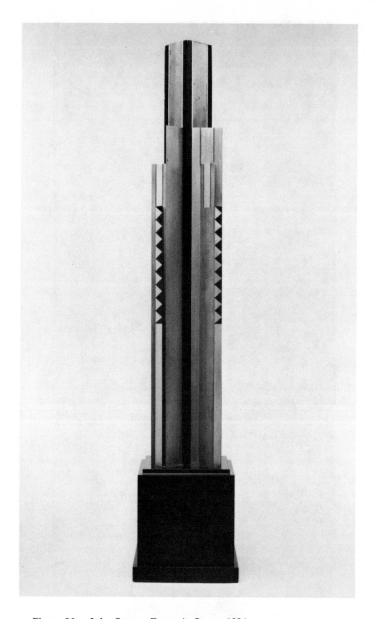

Figure 96.   John Storrs, *Forms in Space*, 1924.
Aluminum, brass, copper, wood on black marble base,
28-1/2″ × 5-1/2″ × 5-1/4″.
(*Collection of the Whitney Museum of American Art,
Acq. no. 77.58, Gift of Charles Simon*)

Figure 97.   Paul Frankl, Private Office of Payson and Clark, New York, ca. 1928.
Photograph.
(*Courtesy of* Architectural Record *64 [September 1928], p. 238*)

Figure 98. Ralph Steiner, *Delmonico Building*, ca. 1928.
Photograph.
(Illustrated in "Cubistic Phases of New York," Vanity Fair 29 [April 1928], p. 58. Courtesy Vanity Fair. Copyright © 1928, 1929 (renewed 1956, 1957) by The Condé Nast Publications, Inc.)

Figure 99. Ira Martin, *View of Skyscrapers from Above*, ca. 1929.
Photograph.
(Illustrated in "More Topless Towers for New York,"
Vanity Fair *[November 1929], p. 86. Courtesy* Vanity
Fair. *Copyright © 1928, 1929 (renewed 1956, 1957) by
The Condé Nast Publications, Inc.)*

Figure 100.   Caesar Zwaska; *New York*, ca. 1926.
Photograph.
(Illustrated in the Little Review 12 [Spring-Summer 1926])

Figure 101. Lewis Hine, *Finishing Up the Job*, 1931.
Photograph.
(*International Museum of Photography at George Eastman House*)

Notes

Introduction

1. Milton Brown, "Cubist-Realism: An American Style," *Marsyas* 3 (1945): 139–58. Martin Friedman, *The Precisionist View in American Art* (Minneapolis: The Walker Art Center, 1960).

2. Joshua Taylor, "The Image of Urban Optimism," in *America as Art* (Washington, D.C.: The National Museum of American Art, 1976), pp. 185–217. There was also a travelling show on this theme organized by Jane Farmer entitled *The Image of Urban Optimism* (Washington, D.C.: Smithsonian Institution, 1977). Friedman, *The Precisionist View in American Art*, p. 28. Barbara Zabel, in "Louis Lozowick and the Technological Optimism of the 1920s" (Ph.D. dissertation, The University of Virginia, 1978), categorized the period as "post-war technological optimism."

3. See Brown and Friedman. More recently, Susan Fillin Yeh provided a discussion of the development of the machine civilization in twenties America and analyzed Sheeler in terms of a machine aesthetic. Yeh pointed to new formal sources for Sheeler's work, including fashion photography, Raphaelle Peale, and the shapes and forms of industry itself. See "Charles Sheeler and the Machine Age" (Ph.D. dissertation, The City University of New York, 1981), "Charles Sheeler's *Upper Deck*," *Arts* 53 (January 1979): 90–94, and "Charles Sheeler: Industry, Fashion and the Vanguard," *Arts* 54 (February 1980): 154–58. In *The Precisionist Painters 1916–1949: Interpretations of Mechanical Age* (New York: Hecksher Museum, 1978), Yeh traced the sources of precisionism to Cézanne, cubism, futurism, purism, and dada.

4. Sheldon Reich, *John Marin: A Stylistic Analysis and a Catalogue Raisonné*, 2 vols. (Tucson: University of Arizona Press, 1970), and "John Marin: Paintings of New York 1912," *American Art Journal* 1 (Spring 1969): 43–52, for a discussion of the formal sources of Marin's industrial and urban images.

5. Wanda Corn's, "The New New York," *Art in America* 61 (July–August 1973): 58–65, represents a pioneer effort on this approach. My own work on the subject commenced in 1977. A lecture entitled "The Image of the Skyscraper in American Art" was delivered at The University of California, Berkeley, in the spring of 1978. See also James O'Gorman, ed., *Skyscraperism, The Tall Building Artistically Considered c.1900–1930* (Wellesley, Massachusetts: Wellesley College, February–March 1979), with a single page introduction by O'Gorman and short essays by undergraduates in his seminar.

6. Corn, "The New New York," pp. 58–65. Dominic Riciotti, in "The Urban Scene: Images of the City in American Painting, 1890–1930" (Ph.D. dissertation, University of Indiana,

1977), provided a chapter on the skyscraper. Riciotti presented similar material in "Sky-scraper: Symbol and Monument" in a paper delivered at the Midwestern American Studies Association annual meeting in 1979. Riciotti's analysis was largely chronological in format and relied mostly on secondary source material.

7. Taylor, "The Image of Urban Optimism," pp. 185–217.

8. Carl W. Condit, *The Chicago School of Architecture* (Chicago and London: The University of Chicago Press, 1964); Arnold Lehman, "The New York Skyscraper: A History of its Development, 1870–1939," 2 vols. (Ph.D. dissertation, Yale University, 1974).

9. Stanley Peter Andersen, "The Response to the Skyscraper, 1870–1939" (Ph.D. dissertation, University of Minnesota, 1960).

Chapter 1

1. See Winston Weisman, "A New View of Skyscraper History," in Henry Russell-Hitchcock et al., *The Rise of an American Architecture* (New York: Praeger, 1970), pp. 115–59, for an alternate interpretation.

2. Morton and Lucia White, *The Intellectual Versus the City* (Cambridge: Harvard University and M.I.T. Press, 1962).

3. Henry Blake Fuller, *The Cliff-Dwellers* (New York: Harper and Bros., 1893).

4. *Journalist* 12 (13 December 1890): 3; E.L. Burlingame, quoted in Frank Luther Mott, *A History of American Magazines, 1885–1905*, vol. 4 (Cambridge: Harvard University Press, 1957), pp. 9, 718.

5. The term "genteel tradition" is often used to characterize this sensibility. It was first coined by the prominent philosopher George Santayana in an essay of 1911 entitled "The Genteel Tradition in American Philosophy." Santayana asserted that this country possessed two distinct mentalities, one "a survival of the beliefs and standards of the fathers, the other an expression of the instincts, practices and discoveries of the younger generation." The former referred to the preservation of standards that were largely European in origin. See *University of California Chronicle* 13 (11 October 1911): 4ff. The above quotation was taken from George Santayana, *The Genteel Tradition, Nine Essays by George Santayana*, ed. Douglas L. Wilson (Cambridge: Harvard University Press, 1967), p. 39.

   For a further discussion of the conservative strain in American arts and letters, refer to Howard Mumford Jones, *The Age of Energy, Varieties of the American Experience 1865–1915* (New York: The Viking Press, 1970), especially the chapter on the genteel tradition. See also the chapter on the "traditionalists" in Henry Steele Commager, *The American Mind* (New Haven: Yale University Press, 1950).

6. Charles Eliot Norton quoted in Kermit Vanderbilt, *Charles Eliot Norton: Apostle of Culture in a Democracy* (Cambridge: Harvard University Press, 1959), p. 205, quoted in Brooklyn Institute of Arts and Sciences, *The American Renaissance, 1876–1917* (New York: Pantheon Books, 1976), p. 29.

7. The adoption of Mathew Arnold's philosophy was pointed out by Richard Guy Wilson in *The American Renaissance*, p. 29. See Mathew Arnold, "Numbers of the Majority and the Remnant" (1884), reprinted in *The Complete Prose of Mathew Arnold*, vol. 10, ed. R.H. Super (Ann Arbor: Michigan University Press, 1974), and Mathew Arnold, *Culture and Anarchy* (1869; reprint ed., Cambridge: Harvard University Press, 1960).

8. Richard Guy Wilson, "The Great Civilization," in *The American Renaissance*, p. 30.

9. Frank Norris, *The Pit* (New York: Curtis Publishing Co., 1902; reprint ed., New York: The Modern Library, 1934). H.B. Fuller, *The Chevalier of Pensieri-Vani* (Boston: G.P. Cupples Co., 1890), and Henry James, "The Jolly Corner," in *The Complete Tales of Henry James*, vol. 12, edited with an introduction by Leon Edel (Philadelphia and New York: J.B. Lippincott Co., 1973).

10. Norris, *The Pit*, pp. 35, 59.

11. Henry James, *The American Scene* (New York: Harper and Bros., 1907). This assessment of his native land was actually written during the winter of 1904–1905 at the suggestion of artist Joseph Pennell. On 27 June 1904, James wrote the following to Pennell: "What you say of the possibility of three or four American papers of the pictorial order, *as things by themselves*, finds me . . . very responsively disposed. . . . It is difficult for me to be positive, nonetheless, before the facts — I must be *in presence* before I can at all be sure. You must remember that you have had very recent impressions of these matters, whereas, I am practically in the dark" (Washington, D.C., Library of Congress, Prints and Photographs Division, Papers of Joseph and Elizabeth Pennell). Since Pennell was often the illustrator of literary travel guides, the letter suggests that he was to have included images. The subsequent harsh tone of James's assessment of New York probably precluded such a joint enterprise.

12. James, *The American Scene*, p. 77.

13. William Dean Howells, Letter II, 28 September 1893 in *Letters of an Altrurian Traveller* (1893–94; reprint ed., introduction by Clara M. Kirk and Rudolf Kirk, Gainesville, Florida: Scholar's Facsimile Reprints, 1961), p. 20.

14. Wilson, "The Great Civilization," p. 16.

15. The character of Frank Copperwood was based on the Chicago financier and traction magnate, Charles Yerkes (1837–1905), whose unethical business practices earned him a short term in the penitentiary. Like the fictional character, he liked to surround himself with art. His New York mansion had two large galleries filled with works obtained in Europe.

16. M.A. Lane, "High Buildings in Chicago," *Harper's Weekly* 35 (October 1891): 853; Fuller, *The Cliff-Dwellers*, pp. 2–3. The impact of the novel was probably widespread due to its serialization in *Harper's Weekly* beginning in June 1893.

17. Howells, "Plutocractic Contrasts and Contradictions," Letter V, 15 November 1893 in *Letters of an Altrurian Traveller*, p. 70. This description of New York was also included in Howells, *Impressions and Experiences* (New York, 1896; reprint ed., Freeport, New York: Books for Library Press, 1972), p. 265; James, *The American Scene*, p. 76. Many critics attributed this chaos to unchecked self-interest. The critic Charles Caffin maintained that "individualism has affected the appearance of our cities — positively by a rampant assertion of itself, and negatively by a disregard of its responsibilities to the community. Buildings are erected with reference to no other consideration than the personal interest of their promoters." To counteract this problem, Caffin encouraged a transition from individualism to civic awareness. See "Municipal Art," *Harper's Monthly* 50 (April 1900): 655–6.

    While European observers acknowledged the domination of the individual, they evaluated it in more positive terms. In Paul Bourget, *Outre-Mer*, trans. James Gordon Bennett (Massachusetts: Norwood Press, 1894), pp. 416–17, the author believed that it was the triumph of individual energy that led to democracy. Although the Englishman, William Archer, in *American Today* (New York: Charles Scribner's Sons, 1899), p. 25, stated that "the absence of unity in this architecture is a sufficient reminder that this is the country of the individual will," he did not assign negative connotations to either the initial motivation for the building or the resultant architecture.

18. "The Art Critic and the Tall Building," *Scientific American* 7 (28 January 1899): 50; James, *The American Scene*, p. 92.

19. William Merritt Chase, from a speech probably delivered in New York City, ca. 1900, quoted in Abraham Milgrome, "The Art of William Merritt Chase" (Ph.D. dissertation, University of Pittsburgh, 1969), pp. 101-2.

20. James, *The American Scene*, p. 78; Mariana Griswold Van Rensselaer noted, in "Picturesque New York," *Century* 45 (December 1892): 172, that the equanimity created by Trinity had given way to "riot and roar."

21. J. Lincoln Steffens, "The Modern Business Building," *Scribner's* 22 (July 1897): 37.

22. Howells, "Aspects and Impressions of a Plutocratic City," Letter IV, 30 October 1893 in *Letters of an Altrurian Traveller*, p. 58, also quoted in *Impressions and Experiences*, p. 249; James, *The American Scene*, p. 91; Jerome Myers, *An Artist in Manhattan*, (New York: American Artists' Group, 1940), p. 57.

23. Fuller, *The Cliff-Dwellers*, p. 4. This criticism was leveled at the industrial Chicago more than New York; Will Payne, *The Money Captain* (Chicago: Herbert S. Stone and Co., 1898), p. 1.
    Beginning in the 1890s, Chicago was the home of a number of "realist" authors who depicted the developing industrial milieu in uncompromising terms. In addition to Henry B. Fuller and Will Payne, George Ade wrote a column for the *Chicago Record* from 1893 until 1900. Accompanied by the cartoons of John McCutcheon, the humorous stories often dealt with the impact of the skyscraper on the life of the city's inhabitants. The titles included: "After the Skyscraper, What?" For further information, see George Ade, *Stories of the Streets and of the Town*, illustrations by John McCutcheon (Chicago: The Caxton Club, 1941), and William Dean Howells, "Certain of the Chicago School of Fiction," *North American Review* 176 (May 1903): 739-43.

24. "A Sunny Day in 1901," *Life* 1898, reproduced in Ray Brosseau and Ralph Andrist, *(Looking Forward): Life in the Twentieth Century as Predicted in the Pages of the American Magazines, 1895-1905* (New York: American Heritage Press, 1970), n.p. For another contemporary assessment of the pollution of Chicago, see Archer, *America Today*, pp. 106-7.

25. Edgar Saltus, "New York from the Flatiron," *Munsey's Magazine* 33 (July 1905): 382-83; James, *The American Scene*, p. 83.

26. Maxim Gorky, "The City of Mammon," *Appleton's Magazine* 8 (August 1906): 177-82; Amy Lowell, "New York at Night," (1912), *The Complete Works of Amy Lowell* (New York: Houghton Mifflin Co., 1955), quoted in John Gordon and L. Rust Hills, *New York New York: The City as Seen by Masters of Art and Literature* (New York: Shorecrest Inc., 1965), p. 247.

27. Fuller, *The Cliff-Dwellers*, p. 1; Norris, *The Pit*, p. 40. Henry James compared the pushing male crowd in the city to a war zone. "It appeared, the muddy medium, all alone with every other element and note as well, the signs of the heaped industrial battlefield." See James, *The American Scene*, p. 84, and Payne, *The Money Captain*, p. 5.

28. Saltus, "New York from the Flatiron," p. 381; Henry B. Fuller, "Chicago's Book of Days," with drawings by Albert Fleury, *Outlook* 69 (5 October 1901): 295–96; Gorky, "The City of Mammon," p. 178.

Earlier, the English illustrator John Martin had linked hell and industry in his illustrations for *The Paradise Lost* of Milton (1827) and *Illustrations of the Bible at the Brink of Chaos* from *Paradise Lost*. Martin pictured the dark abyss in similar terms to contemporary drawings of the Thames Tunnel. In *Hollow Deep of Hell*, a gaping hole in the earth bears a marked resemblance to a contemporary English iron mine.

For a comparative analysis of images of hell and industry, see Francis D. Klingender, *Art and the Industrial Revolution*, edited and revised by Arthur Elton (London: Evelyn, Adams and Mackay, 1947; reprint ed., New York: Schocken Books, 1970). Klingender also pointed out that the identification of the devil and industry had been put forth in Blake's *Milton*:

> "O Satan, my youngest born, art thou
> not Prince of Starry Hosts
> And of Wheels of Heaven, to turn the
> Mills day and night?
> ....
> Get to thy Labours at the Mills and
> leave me to my wrath
> ....
> Thy work is Eternal Death with Mills
> and Ovens and Cauldrons

William Blake, *Complete Writings*, ed. Keynes, 1966, p. 483, quoted in Klingender, p. 122.

29. George Ethelbert Walsh, "Modern Towers of Babel in New York," *Harper's Weekly* 51 (12 January 1907): 68. The author cited the leader Xelhua of Central America, who built the lofty Cholula only to have the gods destroy it by fire.

The proliferation of immigrants into New York and the variety of languages spoken led more than one critic to bemoan the bastardization of the English language. Traditionalists like William James and Henry Adams spoke of feeling displaced in their own country. See Morton and Lucia White, *The Intellectual Versus the City* (Cambridge: Harvard University Press, 1962). The erection of ever loftier skyscrapers coupled with this diversity of tongues must have rendered the image of Babel complete.

30. Mildred Stapley, "The City of Towers," *Harper's Monthly* 73 (October 1911): 698.

31. John Dewey, *School and Society* (Chicago: University of Chicago Press, 1899), quoted in White, *The Intellectual Versus the City*, p. 142.

32. Robert Henri, *The Art Spirit* (New York: J.B. Lippincott Co., 1923; reprint ed., Philadelphia: J.B. Lippincott Co., 1960), p. 7; Robert Henri, "The New York Exhibition of Independent Artists," *The Craftsman* 18 (May 1910): 162.

33. Robert Henri, *New York Sun*, 15 May 1907, quoted in William Innes Homer, "The Exhibition of 'The Eight': Its History and Significance," *American Art Journal* 1 (Spring 1969): 59.

34. Louis Sullivan, *Kindergarten Chats* (1901–1902; reprint ed., New York: George Wittenborn, Inc., 1947), p. 15; Louis Sullivan, "The Tall Building Artistically Considered," *Lippincott's* (March 1896), published in *Kindergarten Chats*, p. 208.

35. Walt Whitman, *Democratic Vistas* (London: The Walter Scott Publishing Co., 1873; reprint ed., St. Clair Shores, Michigan: Scholarly Press, 1970), p. 5; Mary Fanton Roberts [Giles Edgerton], "How New York has Redeemed Herself from Ugliness—An Artist's Revelation of the Beauty of the Skyscraper," *The Craftsman* 15 (January 1907): 458.

36. Sadakichi Hartmann, "The 'Flat-Iron' Building: An Esthetical Dissertation," *Camera Work*, no. 4 (October 1903), p. 40; Norris, *The Pit*, p. 62.

37. See Guglielmo Ferrerro, in "Artistic Aspects of the Skyscraper," *Current Opinion* 55 (April 1913): 321; Saltus, "New York from the Flatiron," pp. 389–90; Fuller, *The Cliff-Dwellers*, p. 51; Willis E. Howe, "The Work of Colin Campbell Cooper, Artist," *Brush and Pencil* 18 (August 1906): 77; John Corbin, "The Twentieth Century City," *Scribner's* 33 (March 1903): 262; Henri, quoted in Homer, "The Exhibition of 'The Eight': Its History and Significance," p. 59.

    For a feminist analysis of the exploitation of the skyscraper, suggesting "the metaphor of rape" by the "strongly phallic form," see Dolores Hayden, "Skyscraper Seduction, Skyscraper Rape," *Heresies* 1 (May 1977): 108–15. Hayden categorized the skyscraper as the manifestation of rapacious business practices legitimized by the prevalent belief in Social Darwinism. The skyscraper's antihumanitarian aspects were also evident in the numerous deaths of workers engaged in construction, according to the author.

38. Sullivan, *Kindergarten Chats*, p. 29; Santayana, "The Genteel Tradition in American Philosphy," pp. 39–40. Frank Norris voiced a similar opinion in *The Pit*, p. 59: "Ah, these men of the city, what could women ever know of them, of their lives, of what their existence through which—freed from the influence of wife or mother, or daughter or sister—they passed everyday from nine o'clock till evening. It was a life in which women had no part."

39. Alfred Stieglitz, "I Photograph the Flatiron—1902," (in Six Happenings), *Twice a Year*, nos. 14–15 (Fall-Winter 1946), p. 189; James Anderson, "The Highest Building in the World," *Metropolitan Magazine* 27 (December 1907): 389.

40. "High Buildings," in (The Field of Art) *Scribner's* 19 (January 1896): 127; and "Painter's Motifs in New York City," in (The Field of Art) *Scribner's* 20 (July 1896): 127.

41. Elia W. Peattie, "The Artistic Side of Chicago," *Atlantic Monthly* 84 (December 1899): 833–34; Sadakichi Hartmann, "A Plea for the Picturesqueness of New York," *Camera Notes* 4 (October 1900): 91–97.

42. Paul Adam, *Vues d'Amerique* (Paris: Société d'Editions Littéraires et Artistiques, 1906), quoted in "America as a Nation of Artists and Poets," *Current Literature* 41 (August 1906): 175–76.

43. Albert W. Barker, "A Painter of Modern Industrialism, The Notable Work of Colin Campbell Cooper," *Booklover's Magazine* ca. 1905, Washington, D.C., National Museum of American Art, File on Colin Campbell Cooper.

    Colin Campbell Cooper (1856–1937) was an acknowledged renderer of the skyscraper in the early years of the century, exhibiting frequently in the Philadelphia Academy Annual Expositions. After graduating from the Pennsylvania Academy of Fine Arts, he went to Europe. Like Joseph Pennell, he often etched the renowned monuments. After studying briefly at the Académie Julian and visiting Holland, Belgium, and Normandy, he returned to Philadelphia in 1901, only to embark once again to study Europe's cathedral towns. Immediately after his return in 1902, he undertook the theme of the skyscraper, according to Howe, "The Work of Colin Campbell Cooper, Artist," p. 78.

Colin Campbell Cooper (1856–1937) was an acknowledged renderer of the sky-scraper in the early years of the century, exhibiting frequently in the Philadelphia Acad-emy Annual Expositions. After graduating from the Pennsylvania Academy of Fine Arts, he went to Europe. Like Joseph Pennell, he often etched the renowned monuments. After studying briefly at the Académie Julian and visiting Holland, Belgium, and Normandy, he returned to Philadelphia in 1901, only to embark once again to study Europe's cathe-dral towns. Immediately after his return in 1902, he undertook the theme of the sky-scraper, according to Howe, "The Work of Colin Campbell Cooper, Artist," p. 78.

Cooper received the following honors: a bronze medal at the Atlantic Exposition of 1895, a gold medal at the American Art Society of Philadelphia, and the Sesman Prize at the Pennsylvania Academy of Fine Arts in 1904. He was mof many of the leading art clubs of the country. These awards attest to a member of the jury of awards at the St. Louis Exposition in 1904 and a the increasing acceptance of the skyscraper by the con-servative art establishment.

44. Maude I.G. Oliver, "A Chicago Painter: The Work of Albert Fleury," *International Studio* 22 (March 1904): 21.

Fleury was born in 1848. He was introduced to the city of Chicago in 1888, when he was commissioned to cover two lunettes on the side walls of Louis Sullivan's Auditorium hall. His works were so successful that he was soon appointed an instructor at the Art Institute of Chicago. Soon after, he chose the United States as his permanent residence. His early training in Paris was in architecture, but he abandoned it to become a painter, exhibiting at the Salon for seven years. His early technical training may explain his predilection for the new architecture of the United States. In 1888, he accompanied the artist Renouf to the United States to accept a commission to paint the Brooklyn Bridge. As Renouf's assistant, he made studies of the river, the bridge, and portions of the adjacent city.

45. Roland Rood, "The Origin of the Poetical Feeling in Landscape," *Camera Work*, no. 11 (July 1905), pp. 22–25.

46. Jesse Lynch Williams, "The Waterfront of New York," illustrations by Henry McCarter, W.R. Leigh, Jules Guerin, Shipley, Charles Hinton, and E.C. Peixotto, *Scribner's* 26 (October 1899): 392; Childe Hassam in "New York the Beauty City," *The Sun*, 23 Febru-ary 1913, p. 16, quoted in Washington, D.C., Archives of American Art, New York Public Library Papers on Childe Hassam, Reel NAA 1.

47. "High Buildings," p. 127; Hassam, "New York the Beauty City," p. 16.

Chapter 2

1. While this is not a comprehensive list, numerous "artistic" illustrations in popular period-icals attest to an acknowledgment of the possibilities of the skyscraper prior to its accep-tance in the fine arts. These articles include: Steffens, "The Modern Business Building," illustrations by W.R. Leigh: *A View of the Skyline*, p. 37, *Broadway, the Valley of the Shadow of Business*, p. 37, *Higher than the Head of the Cross*, p. 39, *Rear View of a Neighborhood Across an Air Well*, p. 40, *Hideous High Buildings*, p. 41 (a misty noctur-nal view showing the scintillating properties of electric lighting), *The Rugged Skyline of Lower Manhattan From the Jersey Shore at Night*, p. 49, *The Night Gang at Work Pushing a Job Through*, p. 49 (a view of workers constructing a skyscraper), *The Old and New, From Lower New York Across the Bridge to Brooklyn*, p. 51, *A Deep Foundation in Rock*, p. 52 (workers constructing a skyscraper, similar in spirit to Thomas Anshutz's

Workers Noontime of 1886). M.G. Van Rensselaer, "Places in New York," *Century* 53 (January 1897) included *A City Cañon* by F.H. Lungren, p. 505 (a nocturnal view from above showing a skyscraper scaffold as well as the new electric lighting). Melville E. Stone, "Chicago," *Scribner's* 17 (June 1895), included *Washington Street* by Orson Lowell, p. 671 (a view at dusk after a rainstorm showing the reflections off wet asphalt), *The Chamber of Commerce Building* by Orson Lowell, p. 665 (a nocturnal view with hurrying pedestrian traffic), *Adams Street* by Orson Lowell, p. 67 (a snow scene). Gustav Kobbe, "Sights at the Fair," *Century* 46 (May 1893), included *A Chicago Street* by A. Castaigne, p. 647 (a nocturnal view revealing the rush of traffic amidst glowing skyscrapers). Williams, "The Waterfront of New York," included: *Down Along the Battery* by Henry McCarter, p. 389 (a view of the skyline and ships), *New New York* by Henry McCarter, p. 390 (skyline and tall ship's masts), *From the Point of View of the Jersey Commuter* by W.R. Leigh, p. 391 (a nocturnal view of the skyline complete with the flickering effects of the new electric lighting), *The End of the Bay — Looking Back at Manhattan from the Brooklyn Bridge* by W.R. Leigh, p. 395 (skyline view from the patterned cables of the Brooklyn Bridge).

2. Emily Bardack Kies, in "The City and the Machine: Urban and Industrial Illustration in America, 1880-1900" (Ph.D. dissertation, Columbia University, 1971), demonstrated that a whole iconography of the city existed prior to the acceptance of urban subjects in the fine arts. Although Kies treated the appearance of the "el" train, the bridge, and the texture of the city streets in popular illustration, she did not consider the skyscraper. However, her basic theme, that the city is explored in illustration, can easily be extended to include views of the tall building.

3. Although the phrase "ways of seeing" was borrowed from John Berger, *Ways of Seeing* (New York: The Viking Press, 1972), here it is meant to suggest that consistent themes and attitudes are reflected in the first skyscraper images in the fine arts.

    In Pat Hills, *Turn-of-the-Century America* (New York: Whitney Museum of American Art, 1977), p. 145, the author divided the artists who shaped that "raw material of city life" into three groups: those that concentrated on the building of the city, those concentrating on the formal shapes, and those concentrating on the urban people. While artists certainly focused on these aspects of city development, these categories are not mutually exclusive. Moreover, "the building activity of the city" was not only an exploration of construction, but often a measure of the multitude of transitions wrought by the change. Although Hills provides a useful framework, additional categories abound in the artistic attempt to define the urban milieu.

4. Rufus Rockwell, *New York: Old and New*, 2 vols. (Philadelphia: J.B. Lippincott Co., 1909). Others include John C. Van Dyke, *The New New York*, illustrations by Joseph Pennell (New York: The Macmillan Co., 1909), and F. Hopkinson Smith, *Charcoals of New and Old New York* (New York: Doubleday, Page and Co., 1912).

5. Van Dyke, *The New New York*, pp. vii, 15, 134.

6. Ibid., p. 139.

7. Barker, "A Painter of Modern Industrialism, The Notable Work of Colin Campbell Cooper," p. 327.

8. Stapley, "The City of Towers," p. 705.

9. Frederick Keppel, *Mr. Pennell's Etchings of New York, "Skyscrapers"* (New York: Frederick Keppell, 1905), p. 56.

10. In a letter from Joseph Pennell to John C. Van Dyke, 31 May 1908, the artist reported that "the list of subjects" for *The New New York* was "excellent and suggestive," quoted in Elizabeth Robins Pennell, *The Life and Letters of Joseph Pennell*, vol. 2 (Boston: Little, Brown and Co., 1929), p. 51.

11. Van Dyke, *The New New York*, p. 140; Mariana Griswold Van Rensselaer, "Picturesque New York," with nine etchings by F.W. Mielatz, *Century* 65 (December 1892): 175. "Picturesque New York" represented a pioneer attempt to encourage artists to render their own urban milieu.

    Apparently, Pennell knew Van Rensselaer, illustrating her book, *English Cathedrals*, from 1887 to 1890. Considering Van Rensselaer's position as a well-known art critic and the author of *American Etchers* of 1886, her friendship with Pennell was probably firmly established. In 1882, she asked him for permission to reproduce one of his prints when she was preparing an article on American etchers for *Century* magazine.

12. For further information on these skyscrapers, see Lehman, "The New York Skyscraper: A History of its Development, 1870-1939." vol. 1, pp. 74-84.

13. From 1911 until 1914, John Marin painted numerous scenes of church and skyscraper. See Reich, *John Marin, A Stylistic Analysis and a Catalogue Raisonné*, vol. 2: #11.6 *Church and Other Buildings*, #11.7 *(Church and Tall Building)*, #11.23 *(Trinity Church)*, #11.24 *Trinity Church, New York*, #12.44 *(New York City Scene)*, #12.45 *(New York City Scene)*, #12.52 *Saint Paul's Lower Manhattan*, and #12.61 *Saint Paul's, Manhattan*. At present, there has been little effort to identify the skyscrapers and other buildings that Marin selected to paint in New York. Often, the buildings are incorrectly labeled. For example, #11.23 in the Reich catalogue raisonné is entitled *(Trinity Church)*. A closer examination of the watercolor reveals that the church is, in fact, St. Paul's flanked by the Park Row and the St. Paul's Buildings.

14. John Marin, *Camera Work*, nos. 42-43 (April-July 1913), p. 18. Previously, Marin's statement has been explained in the context of futurist rhetoric. See Reich, "John Marin: Paintings of New York, 1912," pp. 43-52. However, ample evidence suggests that New York and Chicago were likened to battlegrounds before the advent of futurism.

15. John H. Girder, M.D., *Newyorkitis* (New York: The Grafton Press, 1901). For a further discussion of Rauschenbusch, see Commager, *The American Mind*, pp. 173-77. Henry Adams, in his *The Education of Henry Adams* (Cambridge: The Riverside Press, 1918), developed the theme of the usurpation of religion by the forces of industry. Adams maintained that while previously the faith in the Virgin was a source of energy, it has since been replaced by that of the dynamo.

16. Editorial Statement, *Camera Work*, no. 4 (October 1903), p. 25. To complicate matters, many of the early skyscrapers themselves were based on European prototypes. In an age of rampant eclecticism, as evidenced by the art collections and interior dwellings of America's industrial magnates of the period, many tall buildings recalled those of the Old World. Of the New York edifices, the World Building (1889-1890) sported an enormous baroque cupola, the Metropolitan Tower (1909) was based on the campanile in Venice, the Singer Building (1908) was *beaux arts* in inspiration, and the Woolworth Building (1913) resembled a Gothic cathedral. For a further discussion of the eclectic character of early skyscrapers, see Weisman, "A New View of Skyscraper History," pp. 115-19.

17. Alvin Langdon Coburn, "Contrasts," *Metropolitan Magazine*, no. 4 (March 1908), n.p.

18. Joseph Pennell, in Fitzroy Carrington, "Joseph Pennell and the Wonder of Work," *Art and Progress* 4 (November 1912): 769; Stapley, "The City of Towers," p. 700.

19. Van Dyke, *The New New York*, p. 5. See also Hartmann, "A Plea for the Picturesqueness of New York," p. 94, and O'Henry, "A Night in New Arabia," *Everybody's Magazine* 18 (March 1908): 302, quoted in Corn, "The New New York," p. 60.

A love of the exotic also characterized European taste from the 1860s on, seen in the proliferation of Japanese *objets d'art* in the Western capitals and the adoption of Japanese methods of design and composition. Unlike the European rejection of the decadence of Western civilization in favor of the so-called primitive, the American preference for the East seemed to reflect the historicism and eclecticism of the period.

20. Nathaniel Hawthorne, *The Marble Faun* (1860), quoted in Jones, *The Age of Energy*, p. 259.

21. Philip Hone, *The Diary of Philip Hone*, ed. Allan Nevins, 2 vols. (New York, 1927), p. 80, quoted in Bayrd Still, *Mirror for Gotham* (New York: New York University Press, 1956), p. 82; William Dean Howells, "Editor's Easy Chair," *Harper's Monthly* 128 (December 1913): 472, quoted in Still, *Mirror for Gotham*, p. 262.

An article by David H. Ray, "The Skyscraper of the Future," *Scientific American Supplement* 75 (8 March 1913): 148, corroborates the empirical observations cited above. The author traced the succession of buildings on the site of the Bankers Trust Building on Wall Street. In 1880, the Manhattan Trust Company erected an eight-story building. By 1891, the twenty-six-story Gillender Building took its place. In two decades, it was superceded by the Bankers Trust Building.

22. Sigfried Giedion, *Space, Time and Architecture* (Cambridge: Harvard University Press, 1941), p. 259; Mary Fanton Roberts [Giles Edgerton], "How New York has Redeemed Herself from Ugliness . . .," p. 468. For a further discussion of the skyscraper's functionalism, see Sadakichi Hartmann, " 'To the FlatIron,' " *Camera Work*, no. 4 (October 1903), p. 40, Bourget, *Outre-Mer*, and Ray, "The Skyscraper of the Future," pp. 148–50.

23. Anderson, "The Highest Building in the World," p. 387.

24. Smith, *Charcoals of New and Old New York*, p. 9; Stapley, "The City of Towers," p. 701.

25. Hartmann, "A Plea for the Picturesqueness of New York," p. 97.

26. Joseph Pennell, *The Great New York* (Boston: Le Roy Phillips, 1912), n.p.

27. Speaking of the development of an inherently American sensibility, Henri asserted that older artists should accept the new. Employing a metaphor derived from skyscraper building, Henri stated that "we should rejoice that a building is rising on the foundation that we have helped and are still helping to erect." Henri, "The New York Exhibition of Independent Artists," p. 161.

28. According to Charles Morgan, *George Bellows Painter of America* (New York: Reynal and Co., 1965), p. 88, Bellows said of *Pennsylvania Excavation*: "That picture is the best attempt I have made to locate the center of interest by strong light. Those tenement houses behind the excavation always give me the creeps."

29. Ernest Poole, "Cowboys of the Skies," *Everybody's Magazine* 19 (November 1908): 653. The article concluded with a poem, "To a Skyscraper," supposedly by a "Workman Out of Employment," p. 653:

> Colossal and austere! Through the sooty veil
> of the ebbing night thy uncouth form,
> Steel-skeletoned, immune to time and storm,
> Looms like a fragment from a world beyond hail
> . . . .

Loud rise the matins of the Metropolis.
Symbols of the age! The self same hand
That shaped thee grips my throat. But at the sight
Of thee, whom it wrought of the rolling sand,
Vanish all hatreds in the hope of future light,
And in my heart is the price of the "Wider Clan" —
Man made thee Giant and I am Man.

30. Ade, *Stories of the Streets and of the Town*, pp. 6–7.

31. Joseph Pennell, "The Wonder of Work on the Panama Canal," *International Studio* 48 (December 1912): 132.

32. For a discussion of his early interest in industrial themes, see Joseph Pennell, *The Adventures of an Illustrator* (Boston: Little, Brown and Co., 1925), p. 43.

33. Pennell, *Pictures of the Wonder of Work*, (New York: J.B. Lippincott Co., 1916) pp. 7–9. Pennell also included Meunier, Legros, Brett, Segantini, Ford Madox Brown, Hokusai, Hiroshigi, Repine, De Nittis, L'Hernette, Bastien-Lepage, Tissot, Ridley, and W.L. Wylie as renderers of the "wonder of work."

34. Ibid., p. 13.

35. Elizabeth Robins Pennell, *Joseph Pennell* (New York: The Metropolitan Museum of Art, 1926), p. 31, and *The Life and Letters of Joseph Pennell*, p. 10. Pennell's interest in building extended to a comprehensive recording of the construction of the Panama Canal.

36. Joseph Pennell, "My Views on the Wonder of Work," *The Builder*, 21 April 1916, p. 293.

37. Smith, *Charcoals of New and Old New York*, p. 9.

38. According to Donelson F. Hoopes, *Childe Hassam* (New York: Watson-Guptill Publications, 1979), p. 62, the Hassams had recently moved to 27 West Sixty-seventh Street, which possessed a colorful ethnic population as well as numerous steel scaffolds. The title, Hoopes claims, is merely symbolic. "The construction going on in the foreground represents a new parish house for a church building, . . . while the 'hovel' in the middle distance is actually the old riding stables." If Hoopes is correct, it is clear that Hassam transformed the scene in order to make a statement concerning urban expansion.

39. Van Rensselaer, "Picturesque New York," p. 168; Barr Feree, "The High Building and its Art," *Scribner's* 15 (February 1894): 318; Charles Graham, "Panorama of the New York Skyline," *New York Journal*, 3 May 1894, p. 20; Steffens, "The Modern Business Building," p. 37.

40. Montgomery Schuyler, "The Skyline of New York, 1881–1897," with drawings by Fred Pansing, *Harper's Weekly* 41 (20 March 1897): 292–93, 295.

41. Joseph B. Gilder, "The City of Dreadful Heights," *Putnam's Monthly* 5 (November 1908): 143.

42. Van Rensselaer, "Picturesque New York," p. 168; Pennell, quoted in Carrington, "Joseph Pennell and the Wonder of Work," p. 769.

43. Bourget, *Outre-Mer*, p. 17; Pennell, *The Great New York*, n.p.

44. "The American Skyscraper the Giant in Architecture: Its Purpose, Beauty and Development," *The Craftsman* 24 (April 1913): 3.

45. Pennell, in Carrington, "Joseph Pennell and the Wonder of Work," p. 769.

46. Williams, "The Waterfront of New York," p. 391.

47. Anon., quoted in Martha Lamb, *Wall Street in History* (New York: Funk and Wagnalls, 1883), p. 132. In 1799, the Bank of New York was the only bank on Wall Street. By 1840, the Wall Street district contained thirty banks. Within the next forty years, this number increased to one hundred.

48. Jesse Lynch Williams, *New York Sketches* (New York: Charles Scribner's Sons, 1902), p. 124.

49. Van Rensselaer, "Picturesque New York," p. 503; Herbert George Wells, in Alvin Langdon Coburn, *New York* (London: Duckworth Press, 1910), p. 10.

50. Pennell, *The Great New York*, n.p.; Van Dyke, *The New New York*, pp. 79–80.

51. Wells, in Coburn, *New York*, p. 10; *New York* (New York: Grollier's Club, 1915), p. 16.

52. As Aaron Scharf noted in *Art and Photography* (London: The Penguin Press, 1968), pp. 169ff, impressionist paintings of urban scenes from above may have been influenced by the popular snapshots of the 1860s. According to Scharf, blurred images of moving pedestrians revealed the shortcomings of the new medium, rather than an accurate depiction of the urban dweller.

53. Birge Harrison, quoted in Charles Louis Borgemeyer, "Birge Harrison—Poet Painter," *Fine Art Journal* 29 (October 1913): 604.

54. Hassam, "New York the Beauty City," p. 16; Anon. reviewer of the Montross Gallery Show of 1907, *New York American*, 13 December 1907, n.p., Washington, D.C., Archives of American Art, New York Public Library Papers on Childe Hassam, Reel NAA 1; Howe, "The Work of Colin Campbell Cooper," p. 75.

55. Birge Harrison painted at least three different views of the Flatiron Building. These include: *The Flatiron After Rain, The Flatiron in a Blizzard*, and *The Flatiron at Twilight*. The dating of these works is problematic since one must rely on extant exhibition catalogues to determine their initial showings. The earliest record of *The Flatiron After Rain* appeared in an Exhibition of Painting by Birge Harrison, The Art Institute of Chicago, 1–20 January 1907. *The Flatiron in a Blizzard* was shown at the Century Club in a group exhibition of the works of Kenneth Frazier, Birge Harrison, William H. Hyde, and Allen Tucker, 17 February–1 March 1909. *The Flatiron at Twilight* was exhibited in A Retrospective of Paintings in Oil by Two American Artists—Mr. Alexander Harrison N.A. and Mr. Birge Harrison at The City Art Museum, St. Louis, beginning 9 November 1913. It is significant to note that all three versions of the Flatiron appeared in the latter show. Washington, D.C., Archives of American Art, Collection of Exhibition Catalogues Pertaining to Birge Harrison, Reel 51, frs. 250–54, 729–32, Reel 526, frs 96–109, Reel 50, frs. 4–6, Reel 52, frs. 133–35, 992–93, and Reel 517, frs. 263–64.

56. Van Dyke, *The New New York*, p. 53; James, *The American Scene*, p. 80.

57. Wanda Corn, *The Color of Mood: American Tonalism, 1880–1910* (San Francisco: M.H. DeYoung Museum, 1972), p. 1.

58. George Inness, quoted in Nicolai Cikovsky, *George Inness* (New York, 1971), p. 55, quoted in Corn, *The Color of Mood: American Tonalism, 1880–1910*, p. 5.

59. See Peter Bermingham, *American Art in the Barbizon Mood* (Washington, D.C.: Smithsonian Institution Press, 1975). Bermingham established a direct link between American artists such as Inness and William Morris Hunt and the masters of the Fountainbleau forest. As the author demonstrated, collectors were particularly interested in

the new French painting. Birge Harrison, in *Landscape Painting* (New York: Charles Scribner's Sons, 1909), p. 243, was to exclaim later: "Yet in France today, we will search in vain for any such body of painters as made up the wonderful school of Barbizon, which, in the fifty years beginning with 1830, and ending with 1880, gave the world the greatest art since the Italian, Dutch and Spanish Renaissance of the sixteenth century."

The photo-secessionists were particularly influenced by symbolist aesthetics. The leading art critic of *Camera Work* in the early years, Sadakichi Hartmann, had met Mallarmé in Paris and held his own "evenings" in New York with the poet Stuart Merrill. Hartmann's evocative prose, as well as the employment of soft focus techniques, and the use of disembodied heads and evocative ambiances in many of the photographs in the periodical, displayed their awareness of symbolism. An important component of the tonalist aesthetic was certainly imported from Europe.

60. Edgar Allen Poe, "Dreamland," in *Poems* (Chicago: W.B. Conkey, ca. 1890s), p. 186. Other poems by Poe dealing with the nocturne include: "The Sleeper," "A Dream Within a Dream," and "Silence."

61. Edward Steichen, interview with Wayne Miller, 1954, Washington, D.C., Archives of American Art.

62. Edward Steichen to Alfred Stieglitz, ca. 1903, p. 4, New Haven, Connecticut, Yale University, the Collection of American Literature, the Beinecke Rare Book and Manuscript Library, Alfred Stieglitz Archives.

63. An examination of the four images of the Flatiron by Steichen included in the 1978 show on the collection of Alfred Stieglitz at the Metropolitan Museum of Art reveal that the following colors and techniques were employed: #477 brown pigment gum-bichromate over gelatine silver, #478 gelatine silver touched with black, green and yellow, #479 blue-green gum-bichromate over platinum, and #480 greenish-blue pigment gum-bichromate over gelatine silver. See Weston Naef, *Fifty Pioneers of Modern Photography, The Collection of Alfred Stieglitz* (New York: The Metropolitan Museum of Art, 1978), pp. 453–56.

64. In 1880, the first electric power plant opened on Pearl Street in New York, launching the era into the age of electricity. For more information on the development of lighting at the turn of the century, see Kathy Rosalyn O'Dell, "New York Night Imagery, 1900–1942" (Seminar Paper, University of California, Berkeley and Stanford University, Winter 1981). See also Corn, "The New New York," p. 61, for a discussion of the variety of illumination.

65. Williams, "The Waterfront of New York," p. 394.

66. Smith, *Charcoals of New and Old New York*, p. 98.

67. Wells, in Coburn, *New York*, p. 10.

68. Harrison, *Landscape Painting*, p. 248; Van Dyke, *The New New York*, p. 55; Hartmann, " 'To the Flatiron,' " p. 40 (italics mine).

69. Childe Hassam exhibited in a show of 1910 entitled Luminists. Unlike the earlier measured, pristine paintings of the nineteenth-century luminists (see Barbara Novack, *American Painting of the Nineteenth Century* [New York: Praeger, 1969], and John Wilmerding et al., *American Light: The Luminist Movement, 1850–1875* [Washington, D.C.: National Gallery of Art, 1890]), the later "luminists" employed a loose brush technique similar to that of the impressionists. Yet these late "luminists" had something in common

with their nineteenth-century precursors. Both stressed the expressive power of color and light, instead of the pseudo-scientific recording of nature.

70. Fuller, *The Cliff Dwellers*, p. 1; Williams, *New York Sketches*, p. 6.

71. Van Dyke, *The New New York*, p. 6; Alfred Lord Tennyson, quoted in "Artistic Aspects of the Skyscraper," p. 323.

72. An examination of Pennell's rendition of mountains reveals a similarity to his skyscraper images. See #155 *Williams Street* and #252 *The Sentinel From the River* in Louis A. Wuerth, *Catalogue of the Lithographs of Joseph Pennell* (Boston: Little, Brown and Co., 1931).

73. James, *The American Scene*, p. 77; Hassam, quoted in "A Leader in the Open Air School," *The Evening Post*, 12 December 1907, n.p., Washington, D.C., Archives of American Art, New York Public Library Papers on Joseph Pennell, Reel NAA 1; Pennell, *The Great New York*, n.p.

74. Uvedale Price, *Essays on the Picturesque*, vol. 2 (London: Hereford, 1798), pp. 221, 302–3; William Gilpin, *Three Essays on Picturesque Beauty* (London: R. Blamire, 1972), p. 7.

75. Mariana Griswold Van Rensselaer (1851–1934) took an early interest in art, archaeology, and architecture. At age seventeen, she went to Dresden with her family, where she completed her education. Resolved to become a writer, by 1876 she had published both poetry and art criticism. More than fifty of her articles appeared in *The American Architect* before 1884; and from 1884 to 1886, *Century* published her series on American architecture. Her book on *Henry Hobson Richardson and His Works* (1888) is still regarded as an important pioneer study. She also published a book on English cathedrals in 1892. Her expertise in architecture and her fondness for the Barbizon masters explains her encouragement to render the skyscraper in picturesque terms. For more information on Van Rensselaer, see Cynthia D. Kinnard, "Mariana Griswold Van Rensselaer (1854–1934): America's First Professional Art Critic," in Claire Richter Sherman and Adele M. Holcomb, eds., *Women as Interpreters of the Visual Arts, 1820–1979* (Westport, Connecticut: Greenwood Press, 1981).

76. Van Rensselaer, "Picturesque New York," pp. 164–65, 168. Other urban sites considered picturesque by the author include the "billowy rush of white steam from an elevated train" and "the sweep of the great bridge by starry sparks."

77. "Painter's Motifs in New York City," p. 127; Corbin, "The Twentieth Century City," p. 260.

78. Harrison, *Landscape Painting*, p. 251.

79. Albert Fleury, *Picturesque Chicago*, The Art Institute of Chicago (11–30 October 1900); Alfred Stieglitz, *Picturesque Bits of New York and Other Studies* (New York: R.H. Russell, 1897), includes *Winter on Fifth Avenue, Reflections Night — New York*, and *The Glow of Night — New York*.

80. Christopher Hussy, "The Picturesque," *Encyclopaedia of World Art*, vol. 11 (New York: McGraw Hill, 1966), pp. 336–37. See also Christopher Hussey, *The Picturesque* (London: Frank Cass and Co., 1927; reprint ed. with a new preface by the author, London: Archon Books, 1967); Price, *Essays on the Picturesque*, vol. 2, p. 275.

81. Pennell, *The Wonder of Work*, p. 16.

82. According to Earl A. Powell III, in "The Picturesque," *Arts* 52 (March 1978): 110–11, which concerns the impact of the picturesque on Frederick Church, Gilpin's essay was published in the United States as early as 1793. "Gilpin's other tours were published in London in several editions and all seemed to have made their way to library shelves in America." See also William D. Templeton, *The Life and Work of William Gilpin* (Urbana, Illinois, 1939), pp. 295–98, for a discussion of the impact of Gilpin on midnineteenth-century intellectuals such as Thoreau.

   Van Rensselaer's dependence on the theories of Uvedale Price attest to the availability of the essays to cultured intellectuals in America.

Chapter 3

1. Alfred Stieglitz, "The Photo-Secession," in *Bausch and Lomb Lens Souvenir* (Rochester: Bausch and Lomb Optical Co., 1903), p. 3.

2. Dorothy Norman, ed., "From the Writings and Conversation of Alfred Stieglitz," *Twice a Year*, no. 1 (Fall–Winter 1938), p. 104. Stieglitz's predilection for experimentation extended to his early employment of various processes to manipulate the photographic print. Prior to his insistence on "straight" photography, for which he is best known, many of his prints in the years 1896–1902 display his adoption of the gum-bichromate process and the hand-manipulated glycerine developing method. For a further discussion of Stieglitz's attitude toward and employment of the various developing procedures, see Naef, *The Collection of Alfred Stieglitz*, pp. 69–71.

3. Dorothy Norman, *Alfred Stieglitz: An American Seer* (New York: Random House, 1960), p. 34; Alfred Stieglitz, "A Plea for Art Photography in America," *Photographic Mosaics* 28 (1892): 135.

4. Stieglitz, "A Plea for Art Photography in America," p. 136; Gertrude Kasebier, "Studies in Photography," *The Photographic Times* 30 (June 1898): 270.

5. Charles Caffin, *Photography as a Fine Art* (New York: Doubleday, Page and Co., 1901; reprint ed., American Photographic Books Co., 1972), p. 39.

6. Norman, "From the Writings and Conversations of Alfred Stieglitz," p. 96; Norman, *Alfred Stieglitz: An American Seer*, p. 35.

7. Norman claimed that Stieglitz "felt a deep nostalgia for the hand-made. . . . This can be sensed in his early New York photographs of isolated, old-fashioned workmen trapped, just as he was, in an ever changing society charged with unforseen conflicts and tensions. To his dismay he no longer found typical those who performed their tasks 'with all of themselves' " (*Alfred Stieglitz: An American Seer*, p. 38).

8. Alfred Stieglitz, "Pictorial Photography," *Scribner's* 26 (November 1899): 537; Editorial Comment, "The Pictures in This Number," *Camera Work*, no. 1 (January 1903), p. 63.

9. Charles Baudelaire, *The Mirror of Art*, trans. Jonathan Mayne (London: Phaidon Press, 1955), p. 230.

10. *Camera Notes*, no. 1 (July 1897), p. 3. In another context, Stieglitz stated: "The quality of *touch* in its deepest living sense is inherent in my photographs. When that sense of touch is lost the heartbeat of the photograph is extinct." *An American Place*, 11 November 1921, quoted in Fred J. Ringle, ed., *America as Americans See It* (New York: Harcourt, Brace and Co., 1933), p. 257; Theodore Dreiser and Alfred Stieglitz, in Dreiser, "A Remarkable Art," *The Great Round World* 19 (May 1902): 434.

11. Norman, "From the Writings and Conversations of Alfred Stieglitz," p. 97; see chapter 2, note 80. Other images of New York included *A Winter Sky — Central Park*. The *Incoming Boat* was missing from this rare volume; thus, it could not be determined whether this image was of New York.

12. Alfred Stieglitz, *Photographs at an American Place*, 15 February–5March 1932, hand-written checklist, Stieglitz Album in The Museum of Modern Art Library.

13. In the winter of 1902–1903, Stieglitz photographed the Flatiron several times. Three of the images are preserved in the Prints and Photography Division of the National Gallery, Washington, D.C. The image that was finally published in *Camera Work* is a cropped version of a smaller snapshot which originally included other buildings. Another 11″ × 14″ enlargement was one of a series of prints he had in mind for a series called *Fifty Prints of New York*.

    Stieglitz, "I Photograph the Flatiron — 1902," p. 189. Of course, his cognizance of technology is not the only interpretation of this statement. His use of the term "lightness" may relate to the soaring quality of the building, enhanced by its triangular shape. In addition, his employment of misty veils added an air of buoyancy and unreality to the image.

14. Japanese principles of design were an important influence on the members of the "291" group. The writings of Arthur W. Dow were particularly important, especially his *Composition* of 1899, which was in Stieglitz's library. The latter's photograph *Going to the Start* of 1899 included a bridgelike motif, placed parallel to the picture plane to suggest depth, borrowed from Japanese prints.

15. Alfred Stieglitz to Marsden Hartley, 12 May 1914, and Alfred Stieglitz to Sadakichi Hartmann, 25 May 1915, Yale University, Collection of American Literature, the Beinecke Rare Book and Manuscript Library, Alfred Stieglitz Archives.

16. Alfred Stieglitz to Paul Strand, 14 August 1917, and 10 September 1917, the Beinecke Rare Book and Manuscript Library, Alfred Stieglitz Archives.

17. T. Cusack, "Architectural Photography," *The American Amateur Photographer* 5 (September 1893): 447–55.

18. *Winter Fifth Avenue* and *Telegraph Poles* appeared in *Camera Notes* 4 (September and October 1900, respectively), p. 146 and image facing p. 1. *Midst Steam and Smoke* was featured in *Camera Notes* 5 (July 1901), n.p. Goodwillie's and Heim's photographs were mentioned in *Camera Notes* 5 (October 1901), p. 144, as was Charles Loeber's image of the Brooklyn Bridge. *Spring Showers* by Stieglitz appeared in *Camera Notes* 6 (January 1902).

19. These included: *The Bridge* by John Francis Stauss, no. 3 (July 1903), *The Street* by Stieglitz, no. 3 (July 1903), *The Flat-Iron* by Stieglitz, no. 4 (October 1903), *Midst Steam and Smoke* by Prescott Adamson, no. 5 (January 1904), *Winter, Fifth Avenue* of 1893 by Stieglitz, no. 12 (October 1905), *The Flat-Iron — Evening* by Edward Steichen, no. 14 (April 1906), *Snapshot from My Window, New York* by Stieglitz, no. 20 (October 1907), *Snapshot in the New York Central Yards* by Stieglitz, no. 20 (October 1907), *New York* by Alvin Langdon Coburn, no. 21 (January 1908), *Over the House-Tops — New York* by William Wilmerding, no. 24 (October 1908). The no. 36 (October 1911) issue included the following urban scenes by Stieglitz: *The City of Ambition* (1910), *The City Across the River* (1910), *Old and New New York* (1910), *Lower Manhattan, Excavating New York, The Hand of Man* (1893), *In the New York Central Yards* (1903), *The Terminal* (1892), *Spring Showers* (1900). Other city images included: *The Asphalt Paver,*

New York by Stieglitz, no. 41 (January 1913), *Two Towers—New York* by Stieglitz, no. 44 (October 1913, published March 1914), two views entitled *New York At Night* by Paul B. Haviland, no. 46 (April 1914). The no. 48 (October 1916) issue included the five urban views by Paul Strand entitled *Photograph—New York*, and the no. 47 (June 1917) issue included two urban views entitled *Photograph—New York* by Strand. Other photographs of people in this issue were given the same title.

20. Hartmann, "The 'Flat-Iron' Building: An Esthetical Dissertation," p. 39; Hartmann, " 'To the 'Flatiron,' " p. 40.

21. Joseph Keiley, "Landscape A Reverie," *Camera Work*, no. 4 (October 1903), pp. 45–46.

22. Hartmann, "The 'Flat-Iron' Building: An Esthetical Dissertation," p. 36.

23. Alvin Langdon Coburn, "The Relation of Time to Art," *Camera Work*, no. 36 (October 1911), p. 72.

24. Alvin Langdon Coburn (1882–1966) became part of the Stieglitz circle in 1902. Yet he had to wait until 1907 for his first one-man show at "291." Prior to that date, he and his cousin, the photographer F. Holland Day, took part in the New School of American Photography Exhibition in London in 1900. There they met Steichen, Evans, Eugene, Demachy, and Puyo, the major international pictorialists. Although he opened a studio on Fifth Avenue in 1902, he achieved fame in Europe with the support of George Bernard Shaw and H.G. Wells.

25. Alvin Langdon Coburn, "Some Photographic Impressions of New York," *Metropolitan Magazine* 23 (February 1906), n.p.

26. Alvin Langdon Coburn, "Is the Photographer the Best Judge of His Own Work?" *Photographic News* 51 (1 February 1907): 84. *Portsmouth U.S.A.* first appeared in *The Photographic News*, 1 February 1907, n.p. *New York* of 1907 was published in *Camera Work*, no. 21 (January 1908).

27. Alvin Langdon Coburn to Alfred Stieglitz, 3 November 1909, Yale University, Collection of American Literature, the Beinecke Rare Book and Manuscript Library, Alfred Stieglitz Archives.

28. Wells, in Coburn, *New York*, p. 9.

29. *Portsmouth U.S.A.* was included as *The Park Row Building*, and *New York* of 1907 was retitled *The Waterfront*.

30. Coburn's *Singer Night* appeared in the advertisement section of the no. 32 (October 1910) issue of *Camera Work*. Coborn, "The Relation of Time to Art," pp. 72–73.

31. *New York From Its Pinnacles*, Goupil Gallery, London, 1913, included a checklist of Coburn's New York photographs, seventeen images taken at the Grand Canyon, and an introductory statement by the artist. The tallest building to which Coburn referred was the Singer. In reality, Le Brun and Sons' Metropolitan Tower (1909) was loftier. Rochester, New York, The International Museum of Photography at George Eastman House, Alvin Langdon Coburn Collection.

32. Ibid.; Max Weber, "The Filling of Space," *Platinum Print* 1 (December 1913): 6. Coburn and Weber were close friends, maintaining a correspondence from 1907 until 1960. See Washington, D.C., Archives of American Art, Max Weber Papers.

33. Alvin Langdon Coburn, "The Future of Pictorial Photography," in *Photograms of the Year* (London: The Royal Photographic Society, 1916), p. 23. Coburn asserted: "In last

years exhibition of the Royal Photographic Society there was a little group of prints by American workers, mostly entitled 'Design'. . . . They were groups of various objects photographed because of their shape, colour, value, and with no thought of their sentimental associations. . . . The idea was to be as abstract as possible with the camera. Max Weber, the Cubist painter, was responsible for the idea of these designs." A catalogue for the exhibition listed three photographs entitled *Design* by Alice Choate and *Diagonals of Brooklyn Bridge* and *Diagonals of Greenwich Village* by Arthur Chapman. An inquiry to the Royal Photographic Society provided no information on these American experiments.

While Stieglitz was advocating "straight" photography, Weber and Coburn were exploring the abstract potential of the medium. Weber's role in the formulation of abstract photography deserves further exploration.

34. The selection of the Flatiron Building was not limited to the members of the Stieglitz coterie, yet their renditions demonstrate an awareness of each other's work absent from the endeavors of isolated artists. Others who rendered the Flatiron include John Sloan, Joseph Pennell, Ernest Lawson, Colin Campbell Cooper, and Birge Harrison.

35. Quoted in Grace M. Mayer, *Once Upon a City* (New York: The Macmillan Co., 1958), p. 1. See Van Rensselaer, "Picturesque New York," for a discussion of the picturesque aspects of Madison Square.

36. Stieglitz, "I Photograph the Flatiron — 1902," p. 189; Hughes, *The Real New York*, p. 26; Mary Fanton Roberts [Giles Edgerton], "How New York has Redeemed Herself from Ugliness — An Artist's Revelation on the Beauty of the Skyscraper," p. 469.

37. Rupert Hughes, *The Real New York* (New York: The Smart Set Publishing Co., 1904), p. 28.

38. "Sues 'Flatiron' Owners — Clothier Says Winds Deflected by Big Building Wrought Havoc," *New York Times*, 23 January 1903, p. 3:4; "Flatiron Building Wind," *New York Times*, 6 February 1903, p. 8:3 (another article on the clothier); "Wind Causes Boys Death — Blows Him Under an Automobile Near Flatiron Building," *New York Times*, 6 February 1903, p. 1:3; "High Winds Upset Woman and a Horse," *New York Times*, 15 April 1903, p. 2:4 (another mishap near the Flatiron); "Furious Gales Lash City and Harbor," *New York Times*, 17 September 1903, p. 1:6 (article reported that the Flatiron was the storm's center); "Flatiron's Fallen Stone," *New York Times*, 11 September 1903, p. 14:2 (a two hundred-pound stone fell from the top of the building); "Took Poison in Flatiron," *New York Times*, 12 September 1904, p. 14:3.

39. Alfred Stieglitz to Paul Strand, 28 March 1919, Yale University, Collection of American Literature, the Beinecke Rare Book and Manuscript Library, Alfred Stieglitz Archives; Herbert Seligmann, ed., *Alfred Stieglitz Talking: Notes on Some of his Conversations 1925-1931* (New Haven: Yale University Press, 1966), p. 128.

40. Edward Steichen to Alfred Stieglitz, ca. 1904, Yale University, Collection of American Literature, the Beinecke Rare Book and Manuscript Library, Alfred Stieglitz Archives.

41. Following the tendency not to identify the particular skyscrapers in Marin's works unless titled by the artist, #09.5 in Reich's catalogue raisonné is listed simply as *(City Scene)*, although it is clearly an image of the Flatiron.

42. The primary Marin scholar, Sheldon Reich, has evaluated the artist's urban scenes in the context of European modernism, especially Italian futurism and French orphism. See Reich, "John Marin: Paintings of New York, 1912," pp. 43–52. To date, the skyscraper

renditions of the artist have not been analyzed in the context of his affiliations with artists of the "291" gallery. Moreover, it should be noted that Marin was interested in urban subjects prior to his return to the United States and the advent of both orphism and futurism. *London Omnibus* of 1908, rendered in a pointillist-inspired style, captured the motion of the city's trams.

43. The building was referred to as the Singerhorn in Gilder, "The City of Dreadful Heights," p. 141, and "Towered Cities," *The Living Age* 42 (2 January 1909): 45. Walsh, in "Modern Towers of Babel in New York," p. 68, claimed that the Singer was taller than the biblical tower. "From the Singer Tower," *New York Times*, 24 June 1908, p. 1.

44. Moses King, *King's Views of New York 1896–1915 and Brooklyn 1905* (Boston, 1908; reprint ed., New York: Arno Press, 1977), p. 1; Otto F. Semsch, ed., *A History of the Singer Building* (New York: Shumway and Beattle, 1908); "Tower 1000 Feet High," *New York Times*, 19 July 1908, p. 1.

    Transportation by air was thought to be the future mode of urban travel. It was the decade of the Wright brothers, who kept the Kitty Hawk aloft for fifty-nine minutes in 1903. In 1908, the same year as the completion of the Singer, the United States army purchased its first dirigible.

45. Alvin Langdon Coburn to Max Weber, 15 September 1910, and March/April 1911, Archives of American Art, Max Weber Papers.

46. Coburn, *New York From Its Pinnacles*, n.p.

47. Reich, *John Marin: A Catalogue Raisonné and Stylistic Analysis*, vol. 2, #10.16, #10.17, #10.18, #10.19, #10.20, #10.21, and #10.39.

48. Montgomery Schuyler, quoted in "Artistic Aspects of the Skyscraper," p. 323.

49. "Woolworth Building on Broadway Will Eclipse Singer Tower in Height," *New York Times*, 3 November 1910, sec. 8, p. 1 (this article included a projected view of the Woolworth Building); "2,000,000 Broadway Building," *New York Times*, 1 July 1910, sec. 6, p. 9; "55-Story Building in Lower Broadway," *New York Times*, 30 January 1911, p. 5; "Highest Building Contract Let," *New York Times*, 20 April 1911, sec. 8, p. 25; "Woolworth Building Will Be World's Greatest Skyscraper," *New York Times*, 7 May 1911, sec. 8, p. 3 (this article also included a projected view of the building); "Foundation Work for Big Building," *New York Times*, 28 May 1911, sec. 8, p. 2; "Flag to Fly 830 Feet Up," *New York Times*, 30 June 1912, p. 10; "Artistic Terra Cotta Effects," *New York Times*, 28 July 1912, sec. 8, p. 2; "100-Story Building Entirely Possible," *New York Times*, 20 October 1912, sec. 3, p. 4; "Visits Woolworth Tower," *New York Times*, 20 October 1912, sec. 3, p. 6; "55-Story Building Opens in a Flash," *New York Times*, 25 April 1913, p. 20; "The Woolworth Building," *New York Times*, 6 June 1913, p. 10; "Thunderbolt Hits the France in Bay—Woolworth Tower Hit," *New York Times*, 13 December 1912, p. 12; "57-Story Tower Flooded on a Test," *New York Times*, 9 June 1913, p. 18.

50. *Dinner Given to Cass Gilbert, Architect, by Frank W. Woolworth* (New York: Hugh McAtamney, 1913), p. 23.

51. William Winter, "The Artist," in *Dinner Given to Cass Gilbert by Frank W. Woolworth*, p. 69.

52. Edwin A. Cochran, *The Cathedral of Commerce* (New York: Woolworth Building, 1916).

53. Stieglitz, "I Photograph the Flatiron—1902," p. 190.

54. This incident was recorded in Norman, *Alfred Stieglitz: An American Seer*, p. 99.

55. Ibid.

56. "55-Story Building Opens in a Flash," p. 20.

57. H. Bruce Addington, *Above the Clouds and Old New York* (Baltimore: Hugh McAtamney, 1913).

58. Marcel Duchamp, *Salt Seller: The Writings of Marcel Duchamp [Marchand du Sel]*, ed. Michel Sanouillet and Elmer Peterson (New York: Oxford University Press, 1973), p. 75. J. B., "The Woolworth," *The Soil* 1 (January 1917): 61–65.

59. A copy of the film is located in The Film Archives of the Museum of Modern Art, New York. Both the National Film Institute, London, and the Museum of Modern Art possess stills. Unfortunately, they do not have any of this particular sequence of the film.

60. Marin travelled in Europe from 1907 until 1910. He returned briefly in 1909 on the occasion of an exhibition of his work at "291." Weber was in Europe from 1905 until 1909. Walkowitz left for Europe in the fall of 1906 and returned to the United States late in 1907.

61. John Marin to Alfred Stieglitz, ca. 1911, Yale University, Collection of American Literature, the Beinecke Rare Book and Manuscript Library, Alfred Stieglitz Archives.

62. Ibid.

63. Martin, quoted in *Camera Work*, nos. 42–43 (April–June 1913), p. 18. Quotes in the next two paragraphs of the text are based on this passage. Carl Sandburg also put forth the notion that the tall building was alive:

> By day the skyscraper looms in the smoke and sun and has
> a soul.
> Prairie and valley, streets of the city, pour people into
> it and they mingle among its twenty floors and are
> poured out again back to the streets, prairies and
> valleys.
> It is the men and women, boys and girls so poured in
> and out all day that gave the building a soul of
> dreams and thoughts and memories.
> (Dumped in the sea or fixed in a desert, who would care
> for the building or speak its name or ask a policeman
> the way to it?)

"Chicago Poems," 1916, in *The Complete Works of Carl Sandburg* (New York: Harcourt, Brace, Jovanovich, 1969), p. 31.

64. This viewpoint was expressed in a number of articles featured in *Camera Work*. In the no. 36 (October 1911) issue, pp. 20–21, an excerpt from Henri Bergon's "Laughter" was included in which he stressed feelings and sensations. Maurice Aisen, "The Latest Evolution of Art and Picabia," special no. (June 1913), p. 18. This was reinforced by Gabrielle Buffet in "Modern Art and the Public," which appeared in the same issue. She asserted that art was not the chronicling of nature but the rendition of feelings. Marius De Zayas and Paul B. Haviland stated that primitive art is the work most closely related to feelings in *A Study of the Modern Evolution of Plastic Expression* (New York: 291,1913), p. 20.

65. Catalogue of the 1912 Futurist Exhibition which travelled through France, Germany, and England, quoted in Reich, "John Marin: Paintings of New York, 1912," p. 45. According to Reich, p. 47: "The February 25, 1912 issue of the *New York Sun* reproduced the 1910 futurist manifesto; *The Literary Digest*, March 23, 1912, carried an illustrated essay on futurism containing long quotations from the 1912 exhibition catalogue." See also John Oliver Hand, "Futurism in America: 1909–1914," *Art Journal* 41 (Winter 1981): 337–42 for a more thorough exploration.

66. The only views of New York from 1914 until 1919 include #14.11 *East River, Brooklyn, New York*, #14.39 *Lower Manhattan*, #14.54 *New York From the Ferry*, and #14.61 *St Paul's Manhattan*, in Reich, *John Marin: A Catalogue Raisonné and Stylistic Analysis*, vol. 2.

67. Weber and Stieglitz had an argument concerning the price the artist wanted to charge for his paintings, a fee Stieglitz found too expensive. A letter from Weber to a Mrs. Schubart of 21 January 1911, Yale University, Collection of American Literature, the Beinecke Rare Book and Manuscript Library, Alfred Stieglitz Archives, illustrated the strength of the ill feelings:

    My Dear Mrs. Schubart,

    I am happy to learn that you have seen my studies at the gallery. I am also very sorry not to have seen you there as well as a few more friends; but I have not been there for a week. Mr. Stieglitz ordered me out of the place — and I left — with feelings such as can not be described — never to return. . . . *Nothing* will bring me back.

68. Temple Scott, "Fifth Avenue and the Boulevard Saint-Michel," *The Forum* 45 (July–December 1910): 665–83. There is also a manuscript in the Max Weber Papers, The Archives of American Art, by Temple Scott entitled "The Faubourg Saint-Bronnex: A Study of a Post Impressionist Artist," 9 pp., concerning the artist Michael Weaver, who had just returned from Paris. Temple Scott's presence in the group is reinforced by the publication of his article "The Terrible Truthfulness of Mr. Shaw," *Camera Work*, no. 29 (January 1910), pp. 17–20.

69. Finch is described in the article as possessing a "great shock of grizzled hair, and brown eyes glinting through *pince-nez*," p. 670. Paul Haviland, in "The Home of the Golden Disk," *Camera Work*, no. 25 (January 1909), pp. 21–28, described the moving of the "291" gallery across the hall.

    In addition to Finch and Weaver, the protagonists at the luncheon included "little podgy-faced Church" (probably Benjamin De Casseres, whose statements in the article resemble those put forth in *Camera Work*; see "American Indifference," *Camera Work*, no. 28 [October 1909], p. 24, and "The Physiognomy of the New Yorker," *Camera Work*, no. 29 [January 1910], p. 35); Xerxes, the caricaturist (an obvious reference to Marius De Zayas, the Mexican caricaturist); John Seaman, the watercolor landscape painter (John Marin); Charles Cockayne, critic and lecturer on art (probably Charles Caffin, who published widely in *Camera Work*); James Foote, the reviewer and humorist (probably J.B. Kerfoot). I have been unable to identify Hewit, the photographer; Francois Aiterre, an *amateur*; Healey, a lawyer with the taste for polite letters; Nelson Hardy, the art critic with an aggressive jaw and sharp Norwegian eyes. Stuyvesant Marsh may be Frederick Dana Marsh.

    Issues of materialism, fame, and the role of the art critic were actually discussed in *Camera Work* in 1909–1910. Refer to the aforementioned articles by De Casseres and to Herbert French, "The Measure of Greatness," no. 27 (July 1909), p. 45, Nietzsche, "To the Artist Who is Eager For Fame, His Work Finally Becomes a Magnifying Glass Which He Offers to Everyone Who Happens to Look His Way," no. 28 (October 1909), p. 39, and "The Fight for Recognition," no. 30 (April 1910), pp. 21–22.

70. Scott, "Fifth Avenue and the Boulevard Saint-Michel," p. 672.

71. Ibid., pp. 684–85.

72. Max Weber, "The Fourth Dimension From a Plastic Point of View," *Camera Work*, no. 31 (July 1910), p. 25.

73. Alvin Langdon Coburn to Max Weber, March–April 1911, Archives of American Art, Max Weber Papers. The sketch to which Coburn referred has not been preserved.

74. According to Phylis Burkely North, "Max Weber: The Early Paintings, 1905–20" (Ph.D. dissertation, The University of Delaware, 1975), p. 104, Weber developed the "crystal figure" in 1911 to set himself apart from Picasso, even though his representations of the human body resembled the latter's paintings of 1908–1909. Weber referred to his painting *The Geranium* as "an experiment in crystallizing form," in *Max Weber Retrospective Exhibition* (New York: The Museum of Modern Art, 1930), p. 7. North also pointed to the influence of Aztec temple design. See p. 116.

75. Weber, "The Fourth Dimension from a Plastic Point of View," p. 25. Willard Bohn, "In Pursuit of the Fourth Dimension: Guillaume Apollinaire and Max Weber," *Arts* 54 (June 1980): 166–69. Bohn found a copy of Weber's manuscript in the Bibliothèque Littéraire Jacques Doucet in Paris, translated entirely in Apollinaire's handwriting. A comparative analysis of the texts reinforces Apollinaire's borrowings. To date, the relationship of Max Weber's writings to his paintings has not been explored thoroughly.

76. Mary F. Dermody, "Max Weber 1881–1971," in *Skyscraperism*, p. 14, identified the Liberty Tower in the two works. As Dermody pointed out, the Liberty Tower also appeared in Charles Sheeler's *New York* of 1920.

77. Weber, "The Filling of Space," p. 6; Sadakichi Hartmann's "Structural Units," *Camera Work*, no. 36 (October 1911), pp. 17–18 was written as a response to Weber's paintings. He described Weber's works as a "harmonic relation to parts," asserting that "all great expressions are extractions, typifications, symbolizations of general laws and apparitions."

78. Weber, "The Filling of Space," p. 6. These theories were developed as early as 1912. In a letter to Leonard Van Oppen (a professor at Columbia University, a poet, and a contributor to *Camera Work*), he wrote: "Grandly you have penetrated into the *light* and color of the dark the very beautiful intervals between the molecular formation of the named thing" (8 December 1912, Archives of American Art, Max Weber Papers).

79. Weber taught at the White School from 1914 to 1916. Max Weber, *Essays on Art* (New York: W.E. Rudge, 1916), pp. 68–69.

80. Ibid. An excerpt from Kandinsky's *Concerning the Spiritual in Art* was published in *Camera Work*, no. 39 (July 1912), p. 34.

81. For a discussion of the relationship between art and science, see Linda Dalrymple Henderson, "A New Facet of Cubism: 'The Fourth Dimension' and 'Non-Euclidean Geometry' Reinterpreted," *Art Quarterly* 34 (Winter 1971): 411–33. The article is particularly useful for the current discoveries that influenced the artists of Weber's milieu in Europe. More recent and more instructive is Henderson's "Mable Dodge, Gertrude Stein, and Max Weber: A Four-Dimensional Trio," *Arts* 57 (September 1982): 106–11.

82. Marius De Zayas, "Modern Art: Theories and Representation," *Camera Work*, no. 44 (October 1913), p. 14. Other writers in the periodical also commented on the relationship of art and science. In Gabrielle Buffet's "Modern Art and the Public," the author credited the new and complex state of mind with current scientific discoveries. Charles Caffin, in the *New York American*, quoted in *Camera Work*, no. 44 (October 1913), p. 42, stated: "Now the modern artist is allying himself with the scientist and all modern thinkers in conceiving of life as universal, a miracle of movement, derived no man knows whence, which weaves the universe into a whole of related and conflicting rhythms . . . a combination of lines and tones and colors becomes the abstract conception of universal relations and conflicts."

83. Max Weber, "The Eye Moment," in *Cubist Poems* (London: Elkin Mathews, 1914), p. 11. Although the book was written in 1913, it was not published until 1914. The publisher was a friend of Coburn in London, and the latter probably assisted Weber in this regard. The book was dedicated to Coburn and his mother. The poem is quite similar to a prose piece entitled "On the Brooklyn Bridge" of 1912.

    This morning early I was on the old bridge of this New York. Midst din, crash, outwearing, outliving of its iron and steel muscles and sinews. I stood and gazed at the millions of cubes upon billions of cubes pile upon pile, higher and higher, still piled and higher with countless window eyes, befogged, chimney throats clogged by steam and smoke . . . I gazed and thought of this pile throbbing, boiling, seething, as a pile after destruction, and this noise and dynamic force created in me a peace the opposite of itself. Two worlds I had before me the inner and outer. I never felt such. I lived in both.

    Archives of American Art, Max Weber Papers.

84. Coburn to Weber, 8 January 1914, Archives of American Art, Max Weber Papers. In fact, the frontispiece of *New York* never accompanied the poem. A tree was featured on the cover of the book.

85. In response to an interviewer of 1915 who called him a futurist, Weber replied, "Certainly not! I am Max Weber. My sole desire is to express myself; to paint what I see not with my eye but with my consciousness. My work now is entirely subjective" (*Baltimore Evening Sun*, March 1915, clipping, Archives of American Art, Max Weber Papers).

86. Weber, in *Max Weber Retrospective, 1907-1930*, p. 17.

87. Max Weber, "The Workmass," quoted in *New York Evening Sun*, 5 September 1914, n.p., clipping, Archives of American Art, Max Weber Papers. "The Workmass" was not part of the *Cubist Poems*.

88. It is difficult to arrive at a consistent stylistic progression in the work of Walkowitz. Not only did he date works many years later, but he repeated themes throughout his life. The evolution of his work can be tentatively determined by relating certain trends to published reproductions. For example, *New York*, a linear, latticelike interpretation of the city, was featured in the catalogue entitled *The Forum Exhibition of Modern American Painters* for a 13-25 March 1916 exhibition (New York: Anderson Galleries, 1916). We can safely assume that compositions similar in spirit probably date from 1916.

89. Oscar Bluemner, "Kandinsky and Walkowitz," *Camera Work*, no. 44 (March 1914), p. 37.

90. The date of 1915 seems plausible since this work resembles the cover Walkowitz designed for the periodical *291*, no. 3 (May 1915).

91. Oscar Bluemner's comparison of the two artists probably reveals Walkowitz's admiration. In addition to titling his works "Improvisation," he called others "Symphony," another tribute to Kandinsky.

92. Abraham Walkowitz, in Allan Reagan, "All Rules of Art Violated in Show at the Waldorf," 9 March 1929, no source given, Archives of American Art, Abraham Walkowitz Papers.

93. "Third Walkowitz Exhibition: On His Exhibition," *Camera Work*, no. 48 (October 1916), p. 11 (from A Walkowitz Exhibition at "291," 14 February–6 March 1916), also published in *The 1916 Forum Exhibition of Modern Painters*, n.p.

94. Abraham Walkowitz, *Improvisations of New York—A Symphony in Lines* (Girard, Kansas: Haldeman-Julius Publications, 1948).

95. Martica Sawin, "Abraham Walkowitz, Artist," *Arts* 38 (March 1964): 44.

96. There is some question in the scholarship whether dada actually existed in New York. According to numerous scholars, a dada sensibility could be detected in the interaction of Europeans and Americans at the gatherings of Walter Conrad Arensberg. See William Agee, "New York Dada, 1910–1930," *Art News Annual* 34 (1968): 105–13. In Dickran Tashjian, *Skyscraper Primitives: Dada and the American Avant-Garde* (Middletown, Connecticut: Wesleyan University Press, 1975), the author pointed to the continued presence of a dada sensibility, and dialogue on the subject, well into the twenties. Francis Nauman, on the other hand, claimed that it existed for only a few months and that "it died almost before its birth." See "The New York Dada Movement, Better Late Than Never," *Arts* 54 (February 1980): 143–46.

97. To date, the scholarship has stressed the influence of Duchamp and Picabia on the American valuation of the machine and aesthetics. It is important to note that the Europeans arrived at the height of the enthusiasm concerning the skyscraper among Americans themselves.

98. For a more comprehensive discussion of Gleizes's affiliations with the *Abbaye Créteil*, see Daniel Robbins, "From Symbolism to Cubism: The *Abbaye Créteil*," *Art Journal* 33 (Winter 1963–1964): 111–16.

99. Picabia left and returned in 1915.

100. Marcel Duchamp, iconoclast, "A Complete Reversal of Art Opinions," *Arts and Decoration* 5 (September 1915): 428; Albert Gleizes, in "French Artists Spur on American Art," *New York Tribune*, 24 October 1915, sec. 4, p. 2.

101. Duchamp, "A Complete Reversal of Art Opinions," p. 428; Duchamp, in "The Iconoclastic Opinions of Marcel Duchamps [sic] Concerning Art and America," *Current Opinion* 9 (November 1915): 345; Gleizes, in "French Artists Spur on American Art," p. 2, proclaimed New York's skyscrapers and bridges equal to the Old World's most admired creations.

102. Francis Picabia, "How New York Looks to Me," *New York American*, 30 March 1913, magazine sec., p. 11; Picabia, in "French Artists Spur on American Art," p. 2.

103. Marius De Zayas, Statement in *291*, nos. 5–6 (July–August 1915), p. 5.

104. William Camfield, in *Francis Picabia* (Princeton: Princeton University Press, 1979), p. 47, asserted that the *New York Tribune* requested the city pictures. Camfield obtained his information from "A Post Cubist's Impression of New York," *New York Tribune*, 9 March 1913, sec. 2, p. 1, in which the paper stated that the reproductions represented

the first "post-impressionistic pictures of New York ever made. M. Picabia made them at the request of the paper."

105. Picabia, "How New York Looks to Me," p. 11.

106. "Picabia, Art Rebel, Here to Teach a New Movement," *New York Times*, 16 February 1913, p. 9. The artist's mention of the Flatiron and the Woolworth suggests that he was taking issue with the renditions of specific buildings by the members of the "291" circle.

107. Picabia, "How New York Looks to Me," p. 11.

108. Picabia, in "A Post Cubist's Impression of New York," p. 1.

109. Other paintings by Gleizes displaying these elements include *Chal Post* of 1915 and *Broadway* of 1915.

110. A rendition of the Woolworth Building is in the collection of Mr. Bayard Ewing, Providence, Rhode Island.

111. Albert Gleizes to John Quinn, 13 July 1916, The New York Public Library, Astor, Lenox and Tilden Foundations, Rare Book and Manuscript Division, John Quinn Memorial Collection.

    According to Daniel Robbins, "The Formation and Maturity of Albert Gleizes" (Ph.D. dissertation, New York University, 1975), Gleizes's writings—*Contorsions* of 1916, *Souvenirs* of 1915, and *La Tortue Emballée* of 1915-1918—included information on his responses to New York. These writings are in the possession of his widow. An inquiry to Madame Gleizes did not provide satisfactory results.

112. Gleizes, quoted in Robbins, "The Formation and Maturity of Albert Gleizes," pp. 158, 210-11.

113. Although the date of this work has always been listed as 1917, an inaccuracy is suggested. The skyscraper is rendered in a setback design, which did not become popular until the twenties. See note 17, chapter 6.

114. Robert Coady (1876-1921) was director of the Washington Square and the Coady Galleries as well as art editor of *The Soil*. His contribution to American art was his promotion of American popular art to the status of fine art. The periodical was published from December 1916 until July 1917. Its pro-dada orientation is seen in its acceptance of an art based on American technology and its inclusion of poetry by Arthur Cravan. See Cravan poem on New York, *The Soil* 1 (December 1916), p. 36, and "Oscar Wilde is Alive," *The Soil* 1 (April 1917), p. 146. Yet, *The Soil* should not be viewed as a dada periodical, but as a mouthpiece for an intrinsically American art.

    Coady's predilection for the skyscraper was supposedly the result of his friendship with Max Weber, whom he met in Paris sometime between 1905 and 1909. According to Holger Cahill, *Max Weber* (New York: The Downtown Gallery, 1930), it was the painter who pointed out the ingenuity of the tall building to the gallery owner.

    For more information on Coady, see Judith Zilczer, "Robert J. Coady, Forgotten Spokesman of Avant-Garde Art in America," *American Art Review* 2 (September-October 1975): 77-89 (chronicles the exhibition practices of his galleries), Tashjian, *Skyscraper Primitives*, pp. 71-84 (provides an account of the contents of *The Soil* and of its impact on subsequent periodicals in America), and Gorham B. Munson, "The Skyscraper Primitive," *The Guardian* 1 (March 1925): 164-78, 372-76 (a contemporary view of Coady's contribution as well as several unpublished letters).

115. R.J. Coady, "American Art," *The Soil* 1 (December 1916): 3-4; *The Soil* 1 (December 1916): 7.

116. The excerpts from Whitman's and Cravan's poems appeared in the same issue on p. 36.

117. R.J. Coady, "American Art," *The Soil* 1 (January 1917): 54.

118. J.B., "The Woolworth," pp. 61–65.

119. See the January 1917 issue for the machine photographs. The question "Monument?" is placed beneath an image of a Chamberburg Double Frame Steam Hammer. The words "Moving Sculpture" are featured beneath a crane.
    Walkowitz's *Times Square, New York—Night* appeared in the no. 5 (July 1917) issue and *New York* appeared in the no. 1 (December 1916) issue.

Chapter 4

1. Howard Chudacoff, in *The Evolution of American Urban Society* (New Jersey: Prentice-Hall, Inc., 1975), p. 183, showed that the building boom was caused, in part, by falling construction costs after 1921. Technical advances in electrical and structural engineering made loftier structures more feasible. This, coupled with the revocation of height restrictions across the country, insured the proliferation of the skyscraper.

2. James C. Young, "Titanic Forces Rear a New Skyline," *New York Times*, 15 November 1925, sec. 4, p. 6.

3. Frederick Lewis Allen, *Only Yesterday* (New York: Harper and Row, 1931), p. 287. A contemporary article in the popular press corroborated Allen's view. In "Our Billion Dollar Building Year," *New York Times*, 14 September 1924, sec. 1, p. 7, Orrick Johns described the rapid acceleration in building:
    In 1882 the total building expenditure increased at a rate of hardly more than an average of 30 percent each decade — with the exception of the world war period. . . . By 1923 this acceleration (began in 1921) is still more perceptible, amounting to something like 40 percent.
    We come now to Manhattan's share in the total of the present year. At the end of June, the building expenditure for Manhattan, for six months only, was almost equal to that of the entire preceding year.
    If the same rate of activity prevails for the remaining months of the year Manhattan's total for 1924 will lie in the neighborhood of $340,000 — one third of the city's total, an increase over last year in the same borough of about 90 percent.
    For a retrospective assessment of building trends in New York City, see Gordon D. MacDonald, *Office Building Construction Manhattan, 1901–1953* (New York: The Real Estate Board of New York, 1953), p. 1. A comparative chart is provided which demonstrates that from 1901 to 1910, 76 office buildings were constructed, 1911 to 1924 saw the erection of 29, while from 1925 to 1933, 138 structures were erected. From 1934 to 1946, at the height of the Depression, only 7 skyscrapers were built.

4. "A Census of Skyscrapers," *American City* 41 (September 1929): 130.

5. *Exhibition of Paintings, Watercolors, Drawings, Etchings, Lithographs, Photographs and Old Prints of New York*, Wanamaker Gallery of Modern Decorative Art, 19 May–15 June 1923. The checklist offered a complete list of exhibitors which included: George Ault, George Bellows, Benn Benn, Glenn O. Coleman, James Daugherty, Stuart Davis, Adolf Dehn, Preston Dickinson, John Dos Passos, Aileen Dresser, Edmund Dufy, William Glackens, Henry Glintenkamp, Bernard Gussow, Samuel Halpert, Bertram Hartmen, Robert Henri, Everett Henry, E. Hopper, Earl Horter, Nathan Isreals, Muriel

King, Leon Kroll, William La Zinsk, Adelaid Lawson, Jonas Lie, Jules Marillac, John Marin, Frederick Dana Marsh, Reginald Marsh, Jerome Myers, David Morrison, Alice Newton, Frank Osborne, Paul Outerbridge, Walter Pach, Joseph B. Platt, Abram Poole, Man Ray, Stewart Rheinhart, Louise De Gilguilliet Rogers, Rudolf Ruzicka, Allen Saalberg, H.E. Schnakenberg, Charles Sheeler, John Sloan, Niles Spencer, Joseph Stella, Albert Sterner, Florine Stettheimer, J. Torres-Garcia, A. Walkowitz, Max Weber, Marguerite Zorach, and William Zorach.

In addition to the Daniel, Bourgeois, and Modern Galleries and the Whitney Studio Club, all of which exhibited so-called precisionist painting, the role of the Wanamaker Gallery requires further exploration. The Wanamaker photographic exhibitions in Philadelphia are well known for their foresight in the recognition of precisionist photography. See Van Deren Coke, "The Cubist Photographs of Paul Strand and Morton Schamberg," in *One Hundred Years of Photographic History: Essays in Honor of Beaumont Newhall* (Albuquerque: University of New Mexico Press, 1975), pp. 36–42.

6. *Second Annual Exhibition of Paintings, Watercolors and Drawings of New York City*, Wanamaker Gallery of Modern Decorative Art, 23 April–15 May 1924 (checklist). Of those artists usually categorized as precisionists, this exposition included the works of: Preston Dickinson, George Ault, Charles Sheeler, Niles Spencer, Stefan Hirsch, and Joseph Stella. Other exhibitors included: Glenn O. Coleman, Reginald Marsh, Stuart Davis, Abraham Walkowitz, Oscar Bluemner, Edward Hopper, Samuel Halpert, and Walt Kuhn. The categorization of this show as an annual pointed to the desire to make this theme a continuing part of the gallery's agenda.

7. A catalogue was published to accompany the show. It featured a checklist and illustrations of all the works exhibited. See *Inaugurating the New Wanamaker Building and a Tercentenary Pictorial Pageant of New York* (New York, 1925).

8. Leon V. Solon, "The Titan City Exhibition," *Architectural Record* 9 (January 1926): 92.

9. For more on the architectural significance of the competition, see Vincent Scully, *American Architecture and Urbanism* (New York: Praeger Publishers, Inc., 1969), Radde, "Esthetic and Socio-Economic Factors of Skyscraper Design, 1880–1930," and Lehman, "The New York Skyscraper: A History of its Development, 1870–1939."

10. *The International Competition for a New Administration Building for the Chicago Tribune* (Chicago: The Tribune Co., 1923), p. 1.

11. The following articles in museum journals point to the popularity of the show in the art community: "The Exhibition of Competitive Drawings for the *Chicago Tribune* Tower," *Academy Notes* 18 (January–June 1923): 66–67, "The *Chicago Tribune* Building," *American Magazine of Art* 14 (February 1923): 72–74, and *Bulletin of the Minneapolis Institute of Arts* 12 (March 1923): 22. In the latter article it was reported that "the genuine interest of the general public in this exhibition was gratifying and large groups of those in allied professions visited the museum while it was on view."

12. "The Exhibition of Competitive Drawings for the *Chicago Tribune* Tower," p. 66.

13. Janet Flanner, *The Cubical City* (New York, 1926; reprint ed., New York: Putnam University Press, 1974); John Dos Passos, *Manhattan Transfer* (New York: Houghton, Mifflin Co., 1925); Samuel Spewack, *The Skyscraper Murder* (New York: The Macauley Co., 1928); Mary Borden, *Flamingo* (New York: Doubleday and Page, 1927).

14. Friedman, in *The Precisionist View in American Art*, p. 28, stated: "In the Precisionist paintings of skyscrapers, bridges and factories . . . all traces of damage and decay

disappeared, specific architectural details were vastly simplified, and these forms were recast as the proud symbols of technological splendor. . . . The Precisionist visions of the metropolis present a hard edged, invincible utopia."

Although Friedman mentioned negative interpretations of the city, Richard Cox, in "The New York Artist as a Social Critic, 1918-1932" (Ph.D. dissertation, University of Wisconsin, 1975), p. 192, was the first to attempt an interpretation of precisionism in a social context. He stated: "Almost all the American modernists responded favorably to the shapes of urban structures, but their social response was less certain." More recently, Karen Tsujimoto, in *The American Image: Precisionist Painting and Photography* (San Francisco: The San Francisco Museum of Modern Art, 1982), included a section on the negative and ambivalent view. Despite the cursory recognition that a negative reaction did exist, scholars have not explored these responses in the context of the intellectual climate of the period.

15. Henry F. May, "Shifting Perspectives in the Twenties," *Mississippi Valley Historical Review* 43 (December 1956): 409. See also Henry May, *The Discontent of the Intellectuals* (Chicago: Rand, McNally, 1963).

16. "The Skyscraper: Babel or Boon?" with an essay for the skyscraper by Harvey Wiley Corbett and an essay against the skyscraper by Henry H. Curran, *New York Times Magazine*, 5 December 1926, pp. 1-2; "Skyscrapers and Traffic Congestion," *American Architect* 313 (27 March 1927): 386-88, also included a debate between Corbett and Curran; Frank Delano, "Skyscrapers," *American City* 34 (January 1926): 1-9; Lewis Mumford, "Towers," *American Mercury* 4 (February 1925): 193-96, included a fictional debate between an architect and a critic.

17. Sinclair Lewis, *Babbitt* (New York: Harcourt, Brace and World, 1922); Robert S. and Helen M. Lynd, *Middletown* (New York: Harcourt, Brace and Co., 1929).

18. Charles A. and Mary R. Beard, *The Rise of American Civilization*, vol. 2 (New York: The Macmillan Co., 1927), p. 728. In an advertisement to encourage subscribers, the periodical *Broom* referred to the period as "The Age of the Machine." They proclaimed that "a new art and new literature would spring sturdily from the machine civilization." See *Broom* 5 (October 1923): n.p. More recently, Reyner Banham's *Theory and Design in the First Machine Age* (New York: Praeger, 1970) employed this terminology.

19. Henry Ford, *My Life and Work* (New York: Doubleday and Co., 1923), p. 68; Sheldon Cheney, *The New World Architecture* (New York: Tudor Publishing Co., 1930), p. 24. See also Charles Beard, ed., *Whither Mankind* (New York: Longmans, Green and Co., 1928), p. 24.

20. Edwin Avery Park, *New Backgrounds for a New Age* (New York: Harcourt, Brace and Co., 1930), p. 75.

21. Paul Goodman and Frank Otto Gatell, *America in the Twenties* (New York: Holt, Rinehart and Winston, 1972), p. 187; Edward Earl Purinton, "Big Ideas From Big Business," *The Independent*, 6 April 1921, p. 395, quoted in George E. Mowry, ed., *The Twenties: Fords, Flappers, and Fanatics* (Englewood Cliffs, New Jersey: Prentice-Hall, Inc., 1963), p. 4.

22. Cheney, *The New World Architecture*, p. 10; Lewis Mumford, *Sticks and Bones* (New York: Boni & Liveright, 1924), p. 163.

23. James Heap, "Machine Age Exposition," *Little Review* 2 (Spring 1925): 22. This statement was reported in the catalogue *Machine Age Exposition* (New York: The Little

Review, 1927), p. 36. Heap's ideas on a "plastic-mechanical analogy" appeared in the announcement for the show, p. 23, and in the catalogue, p. 36. The articles in the catalogue attest to the scope of Heap's interests: Enrico Prampolini, "The Aesthetics of the Machine and Mechnical Introspection in Art," pp. 9–10 (first appeared in the Autumn–Winter 1924–1925 issue of the *Little Review*), Alexander Archipenko, "The Machine in Art," pp. 13–14, Louis Lozowick, "The Americanization of Art," pp. 18–19, and André Lurcat, "French Architecture," pp. 22–23.

24. Hugh Ferriss, "Architecture of the Future," *Machine Age Exposition*, pp. 4–6. The *Little Review's* pride in the new architecture of the United States is seen in a statement from the May 1929 issue, p. 63, which described the Machine Age Exposition as the first to show modern architecture in America. Of course, this is not the case.

25. For more information on the *De Stijl* aesthetic of Knud Lönberg-Holm, especially his controversial entry in the *Chicago Tribune* Competition, see Lehman, "The New York Skyscraper: A History of its Development, 1870–1939," pp. 236–46.

26. According to an interview between Susan Fillin Yeh and Louis Lozowick in 1972, the Machine Age Exposition catalogue was not complete. He remembered that Sheeler's *Church Street El* of 1920 was in the show despite its omission in the catalogue. See Yeh, "Charles Sheeler's 'Upper Deck,' " p. 94.

27. Heap, "Machine Age Exposition," p. 23.

28. Fiske Kimball, "What is Modern Architecture?" *Nation* 119 (30 July 1924): 128. Kimball also wrote a major history entitled *American Architecture* (Indianapolis: The Bobbs-Merrill Co., 1928). Harold Loeb, "The Mysticism of Money," *Broom* 3 (September 1922): 122.

29. Fernand Léger, "The Aesthetics of the Machine," *Little Review* 9 (Spring 1923): 45–49; Heap, "Machine Age Exposition," p. 23; Park, *New Backgrounds for a New Age*, p. 95.

30. For more information on the development of a machine aesthetic in the United States and in the work of Sheeler in particular, see Susan Fillin Yeh, "Charles Sheeler and the Machine Age."

31. Orrick Johns, "The Excelsior of Architecture," with illustrations by Hugh Ferriss, *New York Times Magazine*, 20 July 1924, p. 3. Another manifestation of this position occurred in H.H. Kent's "*Chicago Tribune* Competition," *Architectural Record* 53 (April 1923): 278. Here, the author asserted that the skyscraper represented "the most appropriate expression of the noble aspirations and high ideals of the great nation which gave birth to it."

32. Frank Lloyd Wright, "The Architect and the Machine," *Architectural Record* 61 (May 1927): 394–96. See also Matthew Josephson, "Made in America," *Broom* 2 (June 1922): 269.

33. Johns, "The Excelsior of Architecture," p. 3; C. Howard Walker, "America's Titanic Strength Expressed in Architecture," *Current History Monthly* 21 (January 1925): 552.

34. Heap, "Machine Age Exposition," p. 23; Loeb, "The Mysticism of Money," pp. 115, 118; *Broom* 5 (Oct. 1923, advertisement), n.p. Other examples of the deification of the machine occurred in Lewis, *Babbitt*, p. 217 and throughout the novel, Park, *New Backgrounds for a New Age*, p. 81, and Purinton, "Big Ideas from Big Business," quoted in Mowry, *The Twenties*, pp. 3–10.

35. Washington, D.C., Archives of American Art, Charles Sheeler Papers, Reel NSH-1, n.d.

36. Charles Sheeler, quoted in "Cubist Architecture in New York," *Vanity Fair* 15 (January 1921): 72.

37. Charles Sheeler and Paul Strand, quoted in "Manhattan—'The Proud and Passionate City,'" *Vanity Fair* 18 (April 1922): 51.

38. Archives of American Art, Charles Sheeler Papers, 4 pp., n.d., Reel NSH-1. Sheeler's preference for the art of Mantegna reinforced his view of painting as an architectonic process:

    Architectural form was a consuming interest to Mantegna from first to last. Architectural form not only applied to the buildings which frequent his pictures but to all forms which play a part in his designs. Trees, rocks, draperies and even human forms took on the grandeur and finality of architecture. . . .

    This is not to say that his portrayal of people, and other living things in nature were inanimate but rather that their characteristics were clothed in eternal forms.

    "Notes on Mantegna," 5 pp., n.d.

    Lillian Docterman, in "The Stylistic Development of Charles Sheeler" (Ph.D. dissertation, State University of Iowa, 1963), pp. 78–79, maintained that the writings of Roger Fry and Clive Bell also influenced Sheeler in his formulation of an organized method of painting.

39. Archives of American Art, Charles Sheeler Papers, Reel NSH-1. This statement concerned both *Church Street El* and *Pertaining to Yachts and Yachting*.

40. Lewis, *Babbitt*, p. 184. This view was corroborated by the Beards in *The Rise of American Civilization*, p. 728.

41. According to Leo Marx, *The Machine in the Garden* (London: Oxford University Press, 1964), p. 356, Sheeler's creation of a well-ordered, silent ambiance, devoid of pollution, represented the American industrial landscape pastoralized.

42. May, "Shifting Perspectives in the Twenties," p. 407.

43. Margaret Bourke-White, *Portrait of Myself* (New York: Simon and Schuster, 1963), p. 33.

44. Bourke-White was not the first to experiment with industrial photography. In addition to the early efforts of the members of the Stieglitz circle, Edward Weston photographed the Armco Steel Works in 1922. In a passage from his journal of 1923, quoted in *Edward Weston: Fifty Years* (Millerton, New York: Aperture, Inc., 1973), p. 43, he wrote: "The Middletown visit was something to remember with auto drives. . . . But most of all in importance was my photographing of 'Armco,' the great plant and gigantic stacks of the American Rolling Mill Co." Yet Bourke-White was the first to capture industry in comprehensive detail, photographing the Otis Steel Mill from indoors without the benefit of flashbulbs, strob, or high speed developers. With the aid of a "fast"—f/3.5—lens, she accomplished this feat. Eight of her photographs were selected for Otis's *The Story of Steel*, a privately printed book sent to stockholders.

45. Bourke-White, *Portrait of Myself*, p. 46.

46. *Fortune* 1 (February 1930): 38; Bourke-White, *Portrait of Myself*, p. 63.

47. *The Skyscraper from Fortune* (New York: American Institute of Steel Construction, Inc., 1930), p. 3. The book was a reproduction of a series of articles which appeared in *Fortune* from April to December 1930.

48. Ibid.

49. Ibid., p. 6.

50. The praise of the skyscraper financiers occurred in "Skyscrapers: Pyramids in Steel and Stock," pp. 11–13, and "Skyscrapers: The Paper Spires," pp. 14–21, both chapters in *The Skyscraper from Fortune*.

51. Borden, *Flamingo*, p. 218.

52. "Skyscrapers: Builders and Their Tools," in *The Skyscraper from Fortune*, p. 27.

53. "Skyscrapers: Prophecy in Steel," in *The Skyscraper from Fortune*, p. 38.

54. Ibid., p. 40.

55. For biographical information on the artist, consult Jean Ferriss Leich, *Architectural Visions: The Drawings of Hugh Ferriss*, with essays by Paul Goldberger and a foreword by Adolf Placzek (New York: Whitney Library of Design, 1980). Ferriss's predilection for industry was evident as early as 1918 with his *Ten Drawings—(Showing Notable Architecture and Engineering Construction Wherein Pennsylvania Cement Was Used)* (New York: Pennsylvania Cement Co., 1918), a source which Leich does not mention. See also "American Capitals of Industry," *Harper's Monthly* 139 (July 1919): 217–24. The former works show a new simplified rendition of industry akin to the later works of the machine optimists.

56. Hugh Ferriss, "The New Architecture," *New York Times Magazine*, 19 March 1922, pp. 8–9, 27; Hugh Ferriss, "Civic Architecture of the Immediate Future," *Arts and Decoration* 18 (November 1922): 12–13. Ferriss's illustrations in *Vanity Fair* were extensive. They include: "Architectural Tendencies of Today" in 21 (February 1924): 44; "The Fine New Playhouse of the Theater Guild" in 22 (August 1924): 32; "The New New York" in 25 (December 1925): 66–67; "The New Architecture of Florida" in 26 (April 1926): 54–55; "The Sesqui-Centennial at Philadelphia" in 26 (July 1926): 46–47; and "New York of the Future" in 27 (September 1926): 84. Ferriss's renderings in architectural periodicals and histories are too numerous to mention.

57. Prior to the Wanamaker show, Ferriss exhibited his works at the Anderson Galleries, 13 April–25 April 1925. Archives of American Art, Metropolitan Museum of Art Papers, Miscellaneous Exhibition Catalogues, Reel N510. As a result of the Wanamaker Show or Titan City Exhibition, numerous reviews further exposed his work to the public. Consult "Pageant of New York, the Titan City, in Tercentenary Pictorial Exhibition," *Art News* 31 (October 1925), p. 10; Lewis Mumford, "The Sacred City," *New Republic* 45 (27 January 1926): 270–71; Solon, "The Titan City Exhibition," pp. 92–94; Park, *New Backgrounds for a New Age*, pp. 169–70; *New York Times*, 14 October 1925, p. 31; *New York Times* 21 October 1925, p. 24.

58. Friedman recognized "the utopian aura" of painting in the twenties but did not elaborate on this point. See *The Precisionist View in American Art*, p. 28.

59. Mumford, "Towers," p. 193.

60. Hugh Ferriss, *The Metropolis of Tomorrow* (New York: Ives Washburn, 1929), p. 15. See pp. 54 and 62 for further examples of apocalyptic language.

61. Harvey Wiley Corbett had already provided a working solution to the regulation in "High Buildings on Narrow Streets," *American Architect* (June 1921): 603–8. Here, he explicated the setback principle by means of a diagram. It was up to Ferriss to translate Corbett's theoretical diagram into workable skyscraper renderings.

The 1916 Zoning Ordinance in New York was passed to curb the wanton growth of skyscrapers vertically and to check their spread to various sections of the city. Manhattan was divided into "use districts" — residence, business, and unrestricted — with maximum height allowed on the southern tip of Manhattan. Mammoth rectilinear buildings could not rise above a certain height, but were required to set back their structures at various intervals. The amount of ascension was determined, in part, by the width of the adjacent street. For example, in the lower end of Manhattan, a building could rise 2-1/2 times the width of the street. See Louis Graves, "The New Zoning Ordinance in New York City," *Architectural Forum* 26 (January 1917): 1–6, for a summary of the new law.

62. These ideas were put forth by Ferriss in "Civic Architecture of the Immediate Future," pp. 12–13, and in the Machine Age Exposition catalogue.

63. Ferriss, *The Metropolis of Tomorrow*, p. 114.

64. Harvey Wiley Corbett, "The Birth and Development of the Tall Building," *American Architect* 129 (January 1926): 39.

65. Harvey Wiley Corbett, "Different Levels for Foot Wheel and Rail," *American City* 31 (July 1924): 2–6.

66. The Italian futurist architect, Sant' Elia, often included such features in the 1910s. It is unclear whether Ferriss was aware of Sant' Elia's work.

67. Ferriss, *The Metropolis of Tomorrow*, p. 38.

68. Ferriss's glass skyscraper was first published in the *New York Times*, 21 March 1926, p. 3. See Leich, *Architectural Visions*, p. 135.

69. Ferriss, *The Metropolis of Tomorrow*, p. 100.

70. Quoted in Wolfgang Pehnt, *Expressionist Architecture* (New York: Praeger, 1973), p. 36. See Pehnt for a discussion of the use of the crystal motif in German expressionist art, especially in the work of Bruno Taut, Peter Behrens, and Ludwig Mies van der Rohe.

71. Ferriss, *The Metropolis of Tomorrow*, p. 124.

72. Quoted in *Inaugurating the New Wanamaker Building and a Tercentenary Pictorial Pageant of New York*, n.p. In addition to the Wanamaker catalogue, original photographs are also available in the Avery Library, Columbia University.

73. Ferriss, *The Metropolis of Tomorrow*, p. 134.

74. Ibid., p. 68.

75. "Skyscrapers: Prophecy in Steel," in *The Skyscraper from Fortune*, p. 37.

76. G.H. Edgell, *The American Architecture of Today* (New York: Charles Scribner's Sons, 1928), p. 372; Cheney, *The New World Architecture*, pp. 398–99.

77. Francisco Mujica, *The History of the Skyscraper* (New York and Paris: Archeology and Architecture Press, 1929; reprint ed., New York: Da Capo Press, 1977). In his book, Mujica advocated the use of pre-Columbian architecture. He believed that the advent of the setback or "Neo-American architecture" was parallel to the "elements of primitive American architecture" and should be explored for possible motifs. This view was articulated earlier by Alfred Bossom in "New Styles in American Architecture," *The World's Work* 55 (June 1928): 189–95. Bossom pointed to the possibilities of Mayan design in particular and Mexican architecture in general. See also Bossom's "New Beauty in the Skyscraper," *Literary Digest* 93 (May 1927): 26–27, for a further discussion of his views on the influence of Mayan architecture.

78. *Creative Arts* 9 (August 1931), entire issue. For a history of the regional plan which commenced in 1922, consult George McAneny, "The Beauty of Regional Planning," pp. 133–37.

79. Thomas Adams, *Regional Plan of New York and Its Environs: The Building of the City* (New York: Regional Plan, 1931), pp. 99, 105, 110, 114, 557–78.

80. "Buildings Still in Blue-Print May Be Obsolete," *Fortune* 2 (April 1930): 155. In Rem Koolhaas's *Delirious New York* (New York: Oxford University Press, 1978), p. 6, the author coined the term "Manhattanism," which he defined as "a world totally fabricated by man, i.e., to live *inside* fantasy." That is, he defined Manhattan as a testing ground for the creation of futurist experiments and dreaming from 1890 to 1940, including colossal skyscrapers and Coney Island.

Chapter 5

1. Mumford, "Towers," p. 193.

2. Lewis Mumford, "Botched Cities," *American Mercury* 18 (October 1929): 143–50, "Is the Skyscraper Tolerable?" *Architecture* 55 (February 1927): 67–69, and "The Intolerable City," *Harper's Monthly* 152 (February 1926): 283–93.

3. These included: "Is the Skyscraper a Mistake?" *Review of Reviews* 76 (September 1927): 313–14; "High Buildings an Absurdity," *Literary Digest* 92 (22 January 1927): 25; Henry James, "Is the Skyscraper a Public Nuisance?" *The World's Work* 54 (May 1927): 66–76; "Must the Sky-Scraper Go?" *Literary Digest* 90 (14 August 1926): 23.

4. Bordon, *Flamingo*, p. 114.

5. Mumford, *Sticks and Bones*, pp. 175, 188, "The Intolerable City," pp. 283–93.

6. Mumford, "Towers," p. 193, *Sticks and Bones*, p. 174. Sheeler's photographs appeared the previous year as illustrations for Charles Downing Lay's "New Architecture in New York," *Arts* 4 (August 1923): 67–86.

7. Karel Câpek, *R.U.R. (Rossum's Universal Robots)*, trans. Raul Selver, 1921 (New York: Doubleday, Page & Co., 1923; reprint ed., in Harlan Hatcher, *Modern Continental Dramas*, New York: Harcourt, Brace & Co., 1941). The fear of robots or robotlike humans was quite widespread in the 1920s. Stuart Chase's chapter, "Robots," in *Men and Machines*, illustrated by W.T. Murch (New York: The Macmillan Co., 1929), pp. 142–68, and Murray Godwin's "A Day in the Life of a Robot," *transition*, no. 13 (Summer 1928), pp. 148–71, deal with the adverse impact of the machine on man. The term "robot" is Czech for forced labor.

8. Sophie Treadwell, *Machinal*, 1928, in Judith E. Barlow, ed., *Plays by American Women: The Early Years* (New York: Avon Books, 1981), pp. 243–328. *Machinal* originally opened at New York's Plymouth Theater in November of 1928. Its original stars were Zita Johann and the young Clark Gable. The sets were designed by Robert Edmond Jones. See Eugene R. Black, "Robert Edmond Jones: Poetic Artist of the New Stagecraft" (Ph.D. dissertation, University of Wisconsin, 1955) and *Robert Edmond Jones: Designs for the Theater*, 26 February–20 April 1958 (New York: Whitney Museum of American Art).

   Elmer Rice's play, *The Adding Machine*, was perhaps the first American play to depict the stultifying conditions of a typical office job. The oppressed main protagonist, Mr. Zero, performs the monotonous task of recording and computing sales for a department store until he is replaced, after 25 years of service, by an adding machine. The squelching of his dreams and the failure of his personal life lead to an act of passion, the murder of his boss. Rice is particularly adept at recreating an office environment, where people cross-talk, repetitively call out numbers, and dream of a happier life. Elmer L. Rice, *The Adding Machine*, with a foreword by Philip Moeller (New York: Doubleday, Page & Co., 1923).

9. Nels Anderson and Edward Lindeman, *Urban Sociology* (New York: Alfred A. Knopf, 1928); Maurice R. Davie, *Problems of City Life* (New York: John Wiley and Sons Inc., 1932); "Psychic Results," in Scott E.W. Bedford, ed., *Readings in Urban Sociology* (New York: D. Appleton and Co., 1927).

10. Georg Simmel, "Die Grosstadt un das Geistleben" [The Metropolis and Mental Life], 1903, trans. Edward A. Shils, Social Sciences III: Selections and Selected Readings, vol. 2, 14th ed.; reprint ed., *On Individuality and Social Forms*, edited with an introduction by Donald Levine (Chicago: University of Chicago Press, 1971), pp. 324–29.

    Anderson, *Urban Sociology*, pp. 212, 218, 230, 234. Refer to Dr. Herman Frank's assessment that city life leads to poorly developed mental judgment and lack of initiative in Chase's *Men and Machines*, pp. 156–57. In *This Ugly Civilization* (New York: Simon and Schuster, 1929), the economist Ralph Borsodi claimed that the machine created a "herd-minded type."

    For other negative appraisals of the effect of business and the machine on the American personality, consult Harold Stearns, ed., *Civilization in the United States* (New York: Harcourt, Brace & Co., 1922), and Robert and Helen Lynd, *Middletown* (New York: Harcourt, Brace & Co., 1929).

11. Curran, in "Skyscrapers and Traffic Congestion," p. 387; "Babel or Boon," p. 2.

12. Delano, "Skyscrapers," p. 7. This position was also put forth in Lucia Ames Mead, "What the American Woman Thinks," *The Woman Citizen* 10 (November 1925): 22–23.

13. Lewis Mumford, "The City," in Stearns, *Civilization in the United States*, pp. 16, 19–20; Mumford, *The Golden Day* lectures delivered in Geneva in 1925 (New York: Horace, Liveright, 1926), pp. 74, 80. These ideas were similar to those of Van Wyck Brooks and Waldo Frank. Mumford, "The Sacred City," p. 270.

14. Mumford, "The Sacred City," pp. 270–71, "Towers," p. 195, *The Culture of Cities* (New York: Harcourt, Brace & Co., 1938), p. 521. For more on Mumford's economic views of the skyscraper, see *Sticks and Bones*, pp. 159–60.

15. Dos Passos, *Manhattan Transfer*, p. 284.

16. E.E. Cummings, "Sonnets-Realities" (1925), in *Complete Poems, 1913–1962* (New York: Harcourt, Brace & Co., 1972), p. 132.

17. Spewack, *The Skyscraper Murder*.

18. Borden, *Flamingo*, pp. 125, 416. Mary Borden (b. 1886) grew up in Chicago, later graduating from Vassar College. She travelled extensively in Europe, finally becoming a British citizen. She received medals from the French and English during World War I for her direction of a mobile hospital. She wrote frequently in both American and British magazines.

19. Van Wyck Brooks, *America's Coming-of-Age* (New York: B.W. Huebsch, 1915), p. 9. Despite his criticism of base, material values, he acknowledged the vitality of business as "perhaps the most engaging activity of American life," p. 134. Brooks's ideas were put forth earlier in *The Wine of the Puritans* (New York: Mitchel Kennerly, 1909). Here he

differentiated between the spiritual or transcendental and the commercial aspects of the American character.

20. Frank, *Our America*, pp. 19, 24, 44.

21. Ibid., p. 171.

22. Waldo Frank, *The Re-discovery of America* (New York: Charles Scribner's Sons, 1929), pp. 90, 93.

23. Stearns, *Civilization in the United States*, pp. iii, vii.

24. Mumford, "The City," in *Civilization in the United States*, p. 9.

25. *Freeman*, vol. 1 (4 August 1920), p. 491, quoted in Frank Luther Mott, *A History of American Magazines, 1905-1930*, vol. 5 (Cambridge: Harvard University Press, 1968), p. 94.

26. Malcolm Crowley, *Exile's Return* (New York: W.W. Norton and Co., 1934), p 184.

27. Ibid., p. 216.

28. Ibid., pp. 182, 212. It is ironic to note that Cowley was an editor of the periodical *Broom*, which celebrated machine technology. Yet he claimed that he was attempting to come to grips with the city, "the picturesque American qualities of the Machine Age and the New Economic Era while living under their shadow."

29. Lynds, *Middletown*, pp. 73, 81. For a more comprehensive discussion on the findings of the Lynds, see Richard Pells, *Radical Visions and American Dreams* (New York: Harper and Row, 1973).

30. In "Paul Strand: The Early Years, 1910-1932" (Ph.D. dissertation, The City University of New York, 1978), Naomi Rosenblum contended that *Photograph — New York* or *Wall Street* was an indictment against the relationship of man to institutions of modern capitalist society. However, Rosenblum admitted that Strand was unaware of making a political statement at the time. Strand claimed that the photograph was the result of his experiments in movement.

31. Paul Strand, in Calvin Tomkins, *Paul Strand: Sixty Years of Photographs* (Millertown, New York: Aperture, Inc., 1976), p. 144.

32. Whitman's verse is from "A Broadway Pageant," first printed in the *New York Times* as "The Errand Bearers" on 27 June 1860. See Walt Whitman, *Leaves of Grass*, eds. Scully Bradley and Harold Blodgett (New York: New York University Press, 1965; reprint ed., New York: W.W. Norton & Co., Inc., 1973).

33. This individual segment was described in "Manhattan — 'The Proud and Passionate City' " as "a view of Broadway through the balustrade on the roof of the Empire Building, contrasting the flickering liveliness of movement in the street with the static architecture." This description was probably offered by the artists themselves. References to other stills in the article were presented as "the photographers were interested," which suggests that they were consulted as to the content of the piece.

34. Paul Strand, "Alfred Stieglitz and a Machine," *Manuscripts*, no. 2 (March 1922), p. 7, "Photography and the New God," *Broom* 3 (November 1922): 253.

35. Irma Jaffe, in her comprehensive work *Joseph Stella* (Cambridge: Harvard University Press, 1970), recognized Stella's hostility to the city and his love of the Italian land. Wanda Corn, in her recent "In Detail: Joseph Stella and *New York Interpreted*," *Portfolio* 1 (January-February 1982): 40-45, revived the interpretation of Stella's rapture and

empathy with New York. Corn's contribution to the scholarship is her identification of specific religious and musical influences on the painting.

36. Stella's description of Broadway at night, replete with electricity, reveals his hostility toward its artificiality: "Clamorous with lights, strident with sounds—that's Broadway, the White Way—at night, blazing and mad with pleasure-seeking" (Stella's unpublished notebooks, quoted in Jaffe, *Stella*, p. 78).

    Frank, too, complained about the "Great White Way" as an example of mechanized entertainment to which New Yorkers were accustomed. Citing Maxim Gorky, who likened our amusement parks to mournful places, Frank maintained that Americans had lost touch with the solitude of nature as a source of enjoyment. See *Our America*, pp. 174–75.

37. Joseph Stella, "The Brooklyn Bridge (A page of my life)," *transition*, nos. 16–17 (June 1929), pp. 86–88.

38. Ibid., p. 87; Quoted in Irma Jaffe, *Joseph Stella* (Cambridge: Harvard University Press, 1970), p. 78.

39. Negative comments concerning electricity are common in Stella's writings. In "Brooklyn Bridge (A page of my life)," p. 88, he spoke of it as the "alarm rung by electric light." His later "Discovery of America: Autobiographical Notes," *Art News* 59 (October 1960): 67, included a reference to electric lighting as the "bells of alarm."

40. Archives of American Art, George Ault Papers, Documentation written by Louise Ault for a collector, Reel D-247. Like Stella, Ault sought renewal in the country. Mrs. Ault recalled that after visiting New York, he would often return to Woodstock and criticize the skyscrapers.

41. Corn, "In Detail: Joseph Stella and *New York Interpreted*," p. 45.

42. Credit is due Corn for pointing out the Gothic motifs.

43. Letter from Stefan Hirsch to Martin Friedman, 16 March 1960, quoted in Friedman, *The Precisionist View in American Art*, p. 34.

44. The choreography was done by Sammy Lee, borrowed from the popular Broadway stage, in an effort to imbue the performance with a bit of American vernacular. The stage sets by Robert Edmond Jones were exhibited in the *Little Review's* International Theater Exposition of 1926. Other progressive theater pieces in this show which employed mechanical themes included: B. Aronson, *The Bronx Express*; 'Gas' with sets by Louis Lozowick; Mordecai Gorelick's sets for Câpek's *R.U.R.*; and various works by Russian constructivists. See *Little Review* 11 (Winter 1926), for a complete list of entries.

45. Herbert Croly, "Architectural Counterpoint," (in Notes and Comments), *Architectural Record* 59 (May 1926): 489. Herbert Croly's *The Promise of American Life* (New York: 1909), influential among Progressives, acknowledged that America needed a new social order in the age of corporations. He favored strong government regulation in the public interest.

46. According to Fred Austin, "Skyscrapers," *Dance Magazine* 5 (April 1926): 24–25, 58, in the spring of 1924, Diaghileff cabled Carpenter to come to Paris for a conference. At this time, Carpenter had the "embryo" of *Skyscrapers* in mind. In August of that year, he played the score of *Skyscrapers* for Diaghileff at his villa in Venice. The latter was so impressed that he agreed to produce it at Monte-Carlo in 1925 as "Le Chant des Gratte-Ciels." It is unclear why *Skyscrapers* was never produced by Diaghileff.

    The American artist Gerald Murphy also designed ballet scenery for Diaghileff in

1921. Two years later, the head of *Les Ballet Suedois*, Rolf de Maré, asked Murphy to design sets for his new work, *Quota* (1923). The ballet concerned the impressions and adventures of a Swedish immigrant to the United States, who encountered a series of American stereotypes, including a millionairess, a colored vaudeville dancer, a "dry agent," a cowboy, and "America's sweetheart." The music by Cole Porter had a "jazz base" and in one portion alluded to taxi horns. Murphy's set pictured the front page of a New York-Chicago tabloid, expanded to grandiose proportions, with a series of headlines and a view of the Woolworth Building. See William Rubin, *The Paintings of Gerald Murphy* (New York: Museum of Modern Art, 1974).

47. John Alden Carpenter, *Skyscrapers*, description and orchestral score (New York: Schirmer, Inc., 1926), n.p.

48. Although photographs of the sets have been located, the preparatory drawings by Jones have proved elusive. A few were exhibited in *Robert Edmond Jones: Designs for the Theater*. The Whitney Museum claimed that they were part of the Estate of Robert Edmond Jones and under the conservatorship of Ralph Pendleton of Wesleyan University. The latter is now deceased and all attempts to contact Wesleyan concerning the new conservator proved unsuccessful.

49. The actual incorporation of urban clatter in music was first popularized by the Italian futurist Russolo. In "The Art of Noises" of 1913, he proclaimed that futurist music was based on the screeching of factories, machines, and autos. After the Russian Revolution, a new proletariat music was created which included the mechanical din familiar to the worker. In 1922, on the fifth anniversary of the Soviet Revolution, "Symphony for Factory Whistles" was performed, including sirens, airplane engines, and machine guns. George Antheil's 1926 score for Léger's *Ballet Machanique* also evoked the restlessness of a mechanized world. This use of modern city noises is referred to as "urbanism" by musicologist Nicolas Slonimsky in *Music Since 1900*, 4th ed. (New York: C. Scribner's, 1971), p. 1500. Consult Slonimsky for further manifestations of the music of the modern city.

50. Irving Carter, "Jazz Brings First Dance of the City," *New York Times*, 14 June 1925, sec. 4, p. 9; George Gershwin, "The Composer in the Machine Age," in Oliver M. Sayler, ed., *Revolt in the Arts* (New York: Brentano's, 1930), p. 265. For another reference to music and the urban sphere, consult Flanner, *The Cubical City*, p. 73.

     The so-called "primitiveness" of jazz was also linked to the notion of an urban jungle, probably because blacks were associated with the new music. See Carter, "Jazz Brings First Dance of the City," p. 9; Flanner, *The Cubical City*, p. 24; "The Appeal of Primitive Jazz," *Literary Digest* 55 (25 August 1917): 28–29. Any discussion of primitivism and modern American art should include a discussion of the contemporary reaction to jazz.

51. "Says Autos and Jazz Ruin American Youth," *New York Times*, 11 October 1924, p. 16. See Waldo Frank, "Jazz and Folk Art," *New Republic* 49 (1 December 1926): 42–43. Here the author referred to jazz as "the art of a commerce and industry ridden people."

52. Carpenter, *Skyscrapers*, n.p.

53. Borden, *Flamingo*, p. 125.

54. Carpenter, *Skyscrapers*, n.p.

55. Alice Holdship Ware, "Skyscrapers," *Survey* 56 (1 April 1926): 35.

56. Donald B. Kuspit, in "Individual and Mass Identity in Urban Art: The New York Case," *Art in America* 65 (September–October 1977): 67–77, addressed the issue of how urban iconography "reflected the artist's own sense of identity in the city." Using Georg Simmel's 1903 essay "The Metropolis and Mental Life," he analyzed urban art from the Ashcan artists to the present. Citing the works of the early group, he contended that they represented the artist's individuality, since the protagonists in these works were engaged with the city. Beginning with Marin, this identification began to shift in favor of disengagement. Kuspit contended that the modernity of the city negated the individual. Kuspit also uses style as an indicator of a particular reaction to New York. Thus, the painterliness of the work of the Eight or the Stieglitz group evokes individuality, while more orderly works suggest estrangement — "imprecision vs. precision."

    Kuspit's essay is useful because it introduced the notion of psychological reaction among artists to the urban sphere. He realized that this personal response is often engendered by forces outside oneself, such as the increased complexity of society. Yet his linking of modes of rendering with concomitant attitudes is limited. A variety of factors produced the multiplicity of interpretations of New York, as Kuspit was reluctant to admit.

57. Several of Ronnebeck's works were published in *Vanity Fair*. In April 1925, *Trinity Church and Wall Street, Pershing Square Night*, and *The Equitable Building* were illustrated. The captions tend to support the artist's negative reactions. *Vanity Fair* claimed that Ronnebeck wished to recreate the "emotions which we experience" while travelling in the city. *Down Town* appeared in *Vanity Fair* 24 (July 1925), p. 58.

58. Ibid.

59. Borden, *Flamingo*, p. 131.

60. Titles reflect his obsessions with familiar sights from various angles. In his 1932 show, Stieglitz — Photographs, at An American Place, the following works are listed: 1–9, *From My Window at an American Place — North*; 10–16, *From My Window at the Shelton, North*; 17–18, *From My Window at the Shelton, Southeast*; and 19–28, *From My Window at the Intimate Gallery, West*.

61. Alfred Stieglitz to Sherwood Anderson, 9 December 1925, Chicago, Newberry Library, Sherwood Anderson Collection, quoted in Paynter, "The Modern Sphinx: American Intellectuals and the Machine, 1910–1940," p. 130.

62. Georgia O'Keeffe, *Georgia O'Keeffe* (New York: Viking Press, 1976), n.p. In Elizabeth Dean, "Georgia O'Keeffe's Radiator Building: Icon of Glamorous Gotham," *Revue Française d'Etudes Américaines*, no. 11 (April 1981), pp. 81–92, the author linked the theatricality of the pulsating lights to the current art deco aesthetic. For more on the theatricality of art deco, see Cervin Robinson and Rosemarie Haag Bletter, *Skyscraper Style: Art Deco New York* (New York: Oxford University Press, 1975).

63. The skyscraper in rain and snow were also favorites of O'Keeffe. Kuspit, in "Individual and Mass Identity in Urban Art: The New York Case," p. 72, claimed that she was humanizing her buildings by naturalizing them.

64. Robert Rosenblum, *Modern Painting and the Northern Romantic Tradition* (New York: Harper & Row, 1975), situated O'Keeffe in the tradition of the German Romantics, especially in her use of simplified heavenly orbs. Rosenblum claimed that the Americans, like their nineteenth-century predecessors, were seeking religious experiences outside the confines of Christian art. While it is possible to locate Americans like Dove and O'Keeffe

in the context of an international tradition, this approach ignores conflicts in the American milieu between nature and the city.

65. O'Keeffe, *Georgia O'Keeffe*, n.p.

66. Laurie Lisle, *Portrait of an Artist: A Biography of Georgia O'Keeffe* (New York: Washington Square Press, 1980), pp. 188–89.

Chapter 6

1. The setback motif was termed the "ZigZag Moderne" by David Gebhard. He traced these forms to multiple sources including: the Pueblo Southwestern Indian heritage; the pre-Columbian world of Mexico and Peru; Mayan Aztec, and Zapotec architecture; the Viennese Secession; and the 1925 Decorative Art Exposition in Paris. He saw the tall commercial building as "the most impressive architectural expression of the early ZigZag Moderne in the United States." See Gebhard's *Kem Weber: The Moderne in Southern California, 1920–1941* (Santa Barbara: University of California Art Galleries, 1969), especially the chapter on "The Moderne."

   Bletter and Robinson, in *Skyscraper Style: Art Deco New York*, also included the setback in the art deco aesthetic, defining it as primarily a commercial style. According to the authors, the setback was only one aspect of the style. Color, decorative cladding, and theatricality were also indispensible to the art deco skyscraper. Expanding on Gebhard's work, Bletter provided a comprehensive analysis of the various influences on American art deco.

2. Borden, *Flamingo*, p. 416.

3. These ideas were outlined publically in February 1979 in my lecture "The Image of the Skyscraper in American Art, 1900–1930," while I was a predoctoral fellow at the National Museum of American Art in Washington, D.C.

4. A multitude of entries of the *Chicago Tribune* Competition employed the setback motif. These included those by: Holabird and Roche (third prize); Arthur Frederick Adams (honorable mention); Edward H. Silverman and Arthur W. Hall; Robert Loebeck; Richard Yoshijiro Mine (honorable mention); Bertram Goodhue (honorable mention); Hewitt and Brown (honorable mention); Hugh Jones (honorable mention); J. Batteaux; Pierre Le Bourgeois (honorable mention); Walter Gropius and Adolf Meyer; Alex Baerwold; Karl Sieben; W. Dyck; and Max Taut.

5. For a further discussion of the controversy, see Radde, "Aesthetic and Socio-Economic Factors of Skyscraper Design, 1880–1930," p. 238.

6. Louis Sullivan, "*Chicago Tribune* Competition," *Architectural Record* 53 (February 1923): 153; H.H. Kent, "*Chicago Tribune* Competition," pp. 378–79. Another early building employing graduated masses was Bertram Goodhue's Nebraska State Capitol Building of 1922. Although the work was popular among architects, it is dubious whether artists were exposed to it.

7. "Towers of Babel," *New York Times*, 7 March 1920, sec. 2, p. 2. Radde also cited Carrère and Hastings's Fisk Rubber Building of 1919 (authored in part by Richard H. Shreve) and Benjamin Wistar Morriss's Cunard Building of 1919 (also in collaboration with Carrère and Hastings) as early examples of the setback in New York. See p. 204 of Radde's dissertation.

8. Bletter's and Robinson's *Skyscraper Style: Art Deco New York* reflects this view. Manifestations of the setback in other cities in the twenties include: Holabird and Root's Rand Tower (1929) in Minneapolis; Shreve and Lamb's R.J. Reynold's Tobacco Co. (1929) in Winston Salem, North Carolina; Smith, Hinchman, and Grylls's Union Trust Building (1929) and Penobscot Building (1928) in Detroit; Albert Kahn's Fisher Building (1928) in Detroit; Helmle, Corbett, and Harrison's Pennsylvania Poser and Light Co. Building (1925) in Allentown, Pennsylvania; C. Howard Crane's American Insurance Union Citadel (1927) in Columbus, Ohio; George Kelham's Russ Building (1928) in San Francisco; and I.R. Timlin's St. Louis Telephone Building (1926) in St. Louis.

9. Edward Rush Duer, "The Skyscraper in New York," *Architectural Forum* 44 (February 1926): 107. See also Henry S. Churchill, "The New Architecture," *Nation* 117 (14 November 1923): 552–53.

10. Ferriss, "Civic Architecture of the Immediate Future," p. 12.

11. C. Grant La Farge (1862–1938) began to draw as a small boy, often assisting his father with interior decorating projects. From 1880 to 1881, he studied architecture at the Massachusetts Institute of Technology. The following year in Boston, he was a student of H.H. Richardson. In 1891, his firm, Hein and La Farge, was hired to build the Cathedral of St. John the Divine, later taken over by Ralph A. Cram. He was president of the New York chapter of the American Institute of Architects from 1911 to 1912.

12. C. Grant La Farge, "The New Sky-line," *American Mercury* 1 (January 1924): 89–91 (italics mine). Others who commented on these features include Churchill, "The New Architecture," pp. 552–53, Cheney, *The New World Architecture*, and Paul Frankl, *New Dimensions* (New York: Payson and Clark, 1928).

13. "Cubistic Phases of New York," *Vanity Fair* 30 (April 1928): 58. See Banham, *Theory and Design in the First Machine Age*, for a discussion of the influence of cubism on architecture.

14. This may have been due to the stress on standardization by such corporations as Ford.

15. The synthetic construction of the skyscraper was attempted earlier by Max Weber, who spoke of formulating his images "unit by unit."

16. The view that Storrs was rendering groups of buildings or skyscraper clusters was put forth by Abraham Davidson in "John Storrs, Early Sculptor of the Machine Age," *Artforum* 13 (November 1974): 41. Noel Frackman, in "John Storrs and the Origins of Art Deco" (Master's thesis, The Institute of Fine Arts, New York University, 1975), p. 44, perhaps the most comprehensive work on the artist to date, described these works as "tower-skyscrapers." More recently, Jeffrey Wechsler, in "Machine Aesthetics and Art Deco," in *Vanguard American Sculpture, 1910–1930* (New Brunswick, New Jersey: Rutgers University, 1979), p. 96, referred to these works as "miniature edifices." He cited a critic who admired them for their adherence to "the new building requirements of New York City, demanding the tops of buildings recede like pyramids." Yet Wechsler did not mention the setback in this context or expand upon just what the critic meant. Rather, the observer was cited to support the notion that the sculptures were small buildings.

17. Frackman demonstrated quite convincingly that Storrs's use of indigenous American sources explained his own development of an art deco aesthetic, rather than a mere copying of a prevailing style. In addition, an interesting drawing of a ziggurat-like design appeared in his diaries of 1915, demonstrating his interest in architecture and decoration

before the advent of art deco. See Archives of American Art, John Storrs Papers, Reel 1558.

    The influence of New York dada on Storrs has not been explored. In 1923, his diary lists meetings with Man Ray and Duchamp, Reel 1548. This fact is crucial in redating Man Ray's sculpture *New York*, supposedly done in 1917. For one thing, Man Ray's use of the setback points to a later date for this piece. Storrs may have influenced him in this regard.

18. An interesting photograph of the young John Storrs pictures him appropriately among Chicago's towering edifices. Archives of American Art, John Storrs Papers, Reel 1556.

19. Louise Bryant, "John Storrs," *The Masses* (October 1917): 21.

20. John Storrs, "Museum of Artists," *Little Review* 9 (Winter 1922): 63.

21. *New York* is dated 1925 by Wechsler and ca. 1925–1926 by Frackman. It seems that this work could have been executed as early as 1922 in response to Saarinen's design. However, it did not appear in the *Little Review* of 1922 along with other illustrations of his towerlike sculpture.

22. In *New Dimensions*, the most comprehensive presentation of his ideas on design, furniture, the machine, and architecture, Frankl asserted: "Cabinets and bookcases have recently been influenced by American skyscrapers. This new departure, representing towers and set-back architecture of modern building has become known by the name of skyscraper furniture." In Frankl's later *Machine-Made Leisure* (New York and London: Harper and Brothers, 1932), p. 140, he rejected the skyscraper, referring to it as "a passing fad." He categorized the Empire State Building as "a tombstone on the grave of an era that built it."

23. Frankl, *New Dimensions*, pp. 44, 54–55.

24. Ibid., p. 58.

25. Ibid., p. 61.

26. Following the art deco aesthetic, Frankl often used expensive colored woods. One of his favorite materials was California redwood juxtaposed with black lacquered surfaces.

27. Three photographs entitled *New York* by Caesar Zwaska were illustrated in the *Little Review* 12 (Spring–Summer 1926), n.p. Ira Martin's images accompanied an article entitled "More Topless Towers for New York," *Vanity Fair* 33 (November 1929): 86–87. See "No Limit in Sight for Future Skyscrapers," *New York Times*, 22 July 1923, sec. 7, p. 5.

Afterword

1. Theodore James, Jr., *The Empire State Building* (New York: Harper and Row, 1975).

2. Jonathan Goldman, *The Empire State Building Book* (New York: St. Martin's Press, 1980), p. 46.

3. "Bull Market Architecture," *New Republic* 68 (8 July 1931): 192.

4. Edmund Wilson, "Progress and Poverty," *New Republic* 68 (20 May 1931): 14.

5. Alfred E. Smith, quoted in James, *The Empire State Building*, p. 100.

6. Ibid.

7. This was reported in "Sky Boys Who 'Rode the Ball' on Empire State," *Literary Digest* 109 (23 May 1931): 30.

8. Lewis W. Hine, *Men at Work* (New York: The Macmillan Co., 1932; reprint ed., New York: Dover Publications and Rochester: International Museum of Photography at George Eastman House, 1977), n.p.

9. Goldman, *The Empire State Building Book*, p. 73; "Sky Boys Who 'Rode the Ball' on Empire State," p. 30.

10. Hine, *Men at Work*, n.p.

11. F. Scott Fitzgerald, "My Lost City," in *The Crack-up*, ed. Edmund Wilson (New York: New Directions, 1945; reprint ed., 1956), pp. 32–33.

Bibliography

Published Sources

Books

Adams, Adeline. *Childe Hassam*. New York: American Academy of Arts and Letters, 1938.

Adams, Henry. *The Education of Henry Adams*. Cambridge: The Riverside Press, 1918.

Adams, James Truslow. *Our Business Civilization*. New York: Albert and Charles Boni, 1929.

Adams, Thomas. *The Regional Plan of New York and Its Environs*. Vol. 2, The Building of the City. New York: Regional Plan of New York and Its Environs, 1931.

Addington, H. Bruce. *Above the Clouds and Old New York*. Baltimore: Hugh McAtamney, 1913.

Ade, George. *Stories of the Streets and of the Town*. With illustrations by John McCutcheon. Chicago: The Caxton Club, 1941.

Allen, Frederick Lewis. *Only Yesterday: An Informal History of the Nineteen-Twenties*. New York: Harper and Row, 1931.

America and Lewis Hine. Foreword by Walter Rosenblum. Essay by Alan Trachtenberg. Biographical notes by Naomi Rosenblum. New York: Aperture, Inc., 1977.

Apollonio, Umbro, ed. *Futurist Manifestos*. Translated by Robert Brain, R.W. Flint, J.C. Higgitt, Caroline Tisdall. New York: The Viking Press, 1973.

Archer, William. *America Today*. New York: Charles Scribner's Sons, 1899.

Arnold, Mathew. *The Complete Prose of Mathew Arnold*. Edited by R.H. Super. Vol. 10. Ann Arbor: Michigan University Press, 1974.

Art and Industry. Foreword by Richard Wolfgang Schmidt. New York: Albert and Charles Boni, 1923.

Baedeker, Karl. *The United States Handbook For Travellers*. Fourth revised edition. Leipzig: Karl Baedeker; New York: Charles Scribner's Sons, 1909.

Bailey, V.H. *Skyscrapers of New York*. New York: W.E. Rudge, 1928.

Banham, Reyner. *Theory and Design in the First Machine Age*. New York: Praeger, 1970.

Baritz, Loren, ed. *The Culture of the Twenties*. New York: Bobbs-Merrill Co., 1970.

Barr, Feree. *The Modern Office Building*. New York: 231 Broadway, 1896.

Baudelaire, Charles. *The Mirror of Art*. Translated by Jonathan Mayne. London: Phaidon Press, 1955.

Baur, John I.H. *Joseph Stella*. New York: Praeger, 1971.

Beard, Charles, ed. *Whither Mankind*. New York: Longmans, Green and Co., 1928.

Beard, Charles A., and Beard, Mary R. *The Rise of American Civilization*. 2 vols. New York: The Macmillan Co., 1927.

Beaton, Cecil, and Buckland, Gail. *The Magic Image: The Genius of Photography from 1839 to the Present Day*. Boston: Little, Brown and Co., 1975.

Berger, John. *Ways of Seeing*. New York: The Viking Press, 1972.

Blesh, Rudi. *Shining Trumpets: A History of Jazz*. New York: Alfred A. Knopf, 1946.

Bletter, Rosemarie Haag, and Robinson, Cervin. *Skyscraper Style: Art Deco New York*. New York: Oxford University Press, 1975.

Borden, Mary. *Flamingo*. New York: Doubleday and Page, 1927.

Bourget, Paul. *Outre-Mer*. Translated by James Gordon Bennett. Massachusetts: Norwood Press, 1894.

Bourke-White, Margaret. *Portrait of Myself*. New York: Simon and Schuster, 1963.

Braider, Donald. *George Bellows and the Ashcan School of Painting*. New York: Doubleday, Page and Co., 1971.

Bremner, Robert H. *From the Depths*. New York: New York University Press, 1956.

Brooks, Van Wyck. *America's Coming-of-Age*. New York: B.W. Huebsch, 1915.

_____. *John Sloan: A Painter's Life*. New York: E.P. Dutton, 1955.

_____. *The Wine of the Puritans*. New York: Mitchel Kennerly, 1909.

Brosseau, Ray, and Andrist, Ralph. *Looking Forward, 1895–1905*. New York: American Heritage Press, 1970.

Brown, Milton. *American Art from the Armory Show to the Depression*. New Jersey: Princeton University Press, 1955.

_____. *The Story of the Armory Show*. Washington, D.C.: Joseph Hirshborn Foundation, 1963.

Brown, Theodore M. *Margaret Bourke-White*. Ithaca, New York: Andrew Dickson White Museum of Art, 1972.

Bry, Doris. *Alfred Stieglitz: Photographer*. Boston: Museum of Fine Arts, 1965.

Bry, Doris, and Goodrich, Lloyd. *Georgia O'Keeffe*. New York: Whitney Museum of American Art, 1970.

Buchard, John, and Bush-Brown, Albert. *The Architecture of America*. Boston: Little, Brown and Co., 1961.

Caffin, Charles. *Photography as a Fine Art*. New York: Doubleday, Page and Co., 1901; reprint ed., New York: American Photographic Books Co., 1972.

_____. *The Story of American Painting*. New York: Frederick A. Stokes, 1907.

Callahan, Sean, ed. *The Photographs of Margaret Bourke-White*. New York: Bonanza Books, 1972.

Callow, Alexander B., ed. *American Urban History*. New York: Oxford University Press, 1969.

Camfield, William A. *Francis Picabia*. Princeton, New Jersey: Princeton University Press, 1979.

Canfield, Mary Cass. *Grotesques and Other Reflections*. New York: Harper, 1927.

Carter, Paul Allen. *The Twenties in America*. London: Routledge and Kegan Paul, 1968.

Chase, W. Parker. *New York—The Wonder City*. New York: Wonder City Publishing Co., 1931.

Cheney, Sheldon. *The New World Architecture*. New York: Tudor Publishing Co., 1930.

Chudacoff, Howard P. *The Evolution of American Urban Society*. New Jersey: Prentice-Hall, Inc., 1975.

Clark, William Clifford, and Kingston, J.L. *The Skyscraper*. New York: American Institute of Steel Construction, 1930.

Classic Photographs of New York City, Views of Lower Manhattan. New York: Eakins Press Foundation, 1975.

Coburn, Alvin Langdon. "The Future of Pictorial Photography." In *Photograms of the Year 1916*. London: Hazell, Watson and Viney Ltd., 1916.

_____. *New York*. With a foreword by Herbert George Wells. London: Duckworth Press, 1910.

Cochran, Edwin A. *The Cathedral of Commerce*. New York: Woolworth Building, 1916.

Coke, Van Deren. "The Cubist Photographs of Paul Strand and Morton Schamberg." In *One Hundred Years of Photographic History: Essays in Honor of Beaumont Newhall*. Albuquerque: University of New Mexico Press, 1975.

Commager, Henry Steele. *The American Mind*. New Haven: Yale University Press, 1950.

Condit, Carl W. *The Chicago School of Architecture*. Chicago: Chicago University Press, 1964.

_____. *The Rise of the Skyscraper*. Chicago: Chicago University Press, 1952.

Cork, Richard. *Vorticism and Abstract Art in the First Machine Age*. 2 vols. Berkeley and Los Angeles: University of California Press, 1976.

Cowley, Malcom. *Exile's Return*. New York: W.W. Norton and Co., 1934.

Cummings, E.E. *Complete Poems, 1913-1962*. New York: Harcourt, Brace and Co., 1972.

De Casseres, Benjamin. *Mirrors of New York*. New York: Joseph Lawrence, 1925.

De Zayas, Marius, and Haviland, Paul. *A Study of the Modern Evolution of Plastic Expression*. New York: 291, 1913.

d'Harnoncourt, Anne, and McShine, Kynaston, eds. *Marcel Duchamp*. New York: Museum of Modern Art, 1973.

Dijkstra, Bram. *The Hieroglyphs of the New Speech: Cubism, Stieglitz, and the Early Poetry of William Carlos Williams*. Princeton: Princeton University Press, 1969.

Dinner Given to Cass Gilbert Architect by Frank W. Woolworth. New York: Hugh McAtamney, 1913.

Dos Passos, John. *Manhattan Transfer*. New York: Houghton, Mifflin Co., 1925.

Doty, Robert. *Photo-Secession: Photography as a Fine Art*. Rochester: International Museum of Photography at George Eastman House, 1960.

Dreiser, Theodore. *The Bulwark*. Garden City, New York: Doubleday and Co., Inc., 1946.

_____. *The Financier*. New York: Harper, 1912.

_____. *My City*. New York: Horace Liveright, 1929.

_____. *The Titan*. New York: John Lane Co., 1914.

Drexler, Arthur. *The Architecture of the Ecole des Beaux-Arts*. New York: Museum of Modern Art, 1977.

Duchamp, Marcel. *Salt Seller: The Writings of Marcel Duchamp [Marchand du Sel]*. Edited by Michel Sanouillet and Elmer Peterson. New York: Oxford University Press, 1973.

Edgell, G.H. *The American Architecture of Today*. New York: Charles Scribner's Sons, 1928.

Editors of Time-Life Books. *This Fabulous Century, 1900-1910*. New York: Time-Life Books, 1969.

Edward Weston: Fifty Years. With an illustrated biography by Ben Maddow. New York: Aperture, Inc., 1973.

Ferriss, Hugh. *The Metropolis of Tomorrow*. New York: Ives Washburn, 1929.

_____. *Power in Building*. New York: Columbia University Press, 1953.

_____. *Ten Drawings—(Showing Notable Architectural and Engineering Construction Wherein Pennsylvania Cement Was Used)*. New York: Pennsylvania Cement Co., 1917.

Fitzgerald, Francis Scott. *The Crack-up*. Edited by Edmund Wilson. New York: Charles Scribner; reprint ed., New York: New Directions, 1956.

Fitzgerald, Richard. *Art and Politics: Cartoonists of the Masses and Liberator*. Westport, Connecticut: Greenwood Press, 1973.

Flanner, Janet. *The Cubical City*. New York: Putnam, 1926; reprint ed., Southern Illinois University Press, 1974.

Ford, Henry. *My Life and Work*. New York: Doubleday, Page and Co., 1922.

Frank, Waldo. *Our America*. New York: Boni and Liveright, Inc., 1919.

_____. *The Re-discovery of America*. New York: Charles Scribner's Sons, 1929.

Frank, Waldo; Mumford, Lewis; Norman, Dorothy; Rosenfeld, Paul; Rugg, Harold, eds. *America and Alfred Stieglitz: A Collective Portrait*. Garden City, New York: The Literary Guild, 1934.

Frankl, Paul. *Machine-Made Leisure*. New York and London: Harper and Bros., 1932.

_____. *New Dimensions*. New York: Payson and Clarke Ltd., 1928.

Friedman, Martin. *Charles Sheeler*. New York: Watson-Guptill, 1975.

Fuller, Henry. *The Cliff-Dwellers*. New York: Harper and Bros., 1893.

Gelfant, Blanche Housman. *The American City Novel*. Norman: University of Oklahoma Press, 1954.

Gershwin, George. "The Composer in the Machine Age." In Oliver M. Sayler, ed., *Revolt in the Arts*. New York: Brentano's, 1930.

Giedion, Sigfried. *Space, Time and Architecture*. Cambridge: Harvard University Press, 1941.

Gilpin, William. *Three Essays on the Picturesque*. London: R. Blamire, 1792.

Ginestier, Paul. *The Poet and the Machine*. Translated by Martin B. Friedman. Chapel Hill: The University of North Carolina Press, 1961.

Girder, John H., M.D. *Newyorkitis*. New York: The Grafton Press, 1901.

Glaab, Charles N., and Brown, Theodore A. *A History of Urban America*. New York: Macmillan Publishing Co., 1976.

Glimpses of New York. New York: The New York Edison Co., 1911.

Goldberger, Paul. *The Skyscraper*. New York: Alfred A. Knopf, 1981.

Golding, John. *Marcel Duchamp: The Bride Stripped Bare by Her Bachelors, Even*. London: Penguin Press, 1973.

Goldman, Jonathan. *The Empire State Building Book*. New York: St. Martin's Press, 1980.

Goodman, Paul, and Gatell, Frank Otto. *America in the Twenties*. New York: Holt, Rinehart and Winston, 1972.

Gordon, John. *New York New York: The City as Seen by Masters of Art and Literature*. New York: Shorecrest, Inc., 1965.

Gray, Cleve, ed. *John Marin by John Marin*. New York: Holt, Rinehart and Winston, 1977.

Green, Jonathan. *Camera Work: A Critical Anthology*. New York: Aperture Inc., 1973.

Gutman, Judith Mara. *Lewis W. Hine, 1874–1910*. New York: Grossman Publishers, 1974.

_____. *Lewis W. Hine and the American Social Conscience*. New York: Walker Publishing Co., 1967.

Handbook of the Complete Etchings and Drypoints of Childe Hassam. Introduction by Paula Eliosoph. New York: The Leonard Clayton Gallery, 1933.

Harrison, Birge. *Landscape Painting*. New York: Charles Scribner's Sons, 1909.

Henderson, Linda Dalrymple. *The Fourth Dimension and Non-Euclidean Geometry in Modern Art*. Princeton: Princeton University Press, 1983.

Henri, Robert. *The Art Spirit*. New York: J.B. Lippincott Co., 1923; reprint ed., Philadelphia: J.B. Lippincott Co., 1960.

Hine, Lewis W. *Men at Work, Photographic Studies of Modern Men and Machines*. New York: The Macmillan Co., 1932; reprint ed., New York: Dover Publications, Inc. and Rochester: The International Museum of Photography at George Eastman House, 1977.

Hitchcock, Henry Russell, ed. *The Rise of an American Architecture*. New York: Praeger, 1970.

Hoffman, Katherine. *An Enduring Spirit: The Art of Georgia O'Keeffe*. Metuchen, New Jersey: Scarecrow Press, 1984.

Homer, William Innes. *Alfred Stieglitz and the American Avant-Garde*. Boston: New York Graphic Society, 1977.

_____. *Robert Henri and His Circle*. Ithaca, New York: Cornell University Press, 1969.

Hoopes, Donelson F. *Childe Hassam*. New York: Watson-Guptill Publications, 1979.

Howells, William Dean. *Impressions and Experiences*. New York, 1896; reprint ed., Freeport, New York: Books for Library Press, 1972.

_____. *Letters of an Altrurian Traveller*. Introduction by Clara M. and Rudolf Kirk. 1893–1894; reprint ed., Gainesville, Florida: Scholar's Facsimile Reprints, 1961.

Hughes, Rupert. *The Real New York*. New York: The Smart Set Publishing Co., 1904.

Hussey, Christopher. *The Picturesque*. London: Frank Cass and Co. Ltd., 1927; reprint ed., Hamden, Connecticut: The Shoe String Press, 1967.

The International Competition for a New Administration Building for the Chicago Tribune. Chicago: The Tribune Co., 1923.

Jaffe, Irma. *Joseph Stella*. Cambridge: Harvard University Press, 1970.

James, Henry. *The American Scene*. New York: Harper and Bros., 1907.

James, Theodore, Jr. *The Empire State Building*. New York: Harper and Row, 1975.

Jones, Howard Mumford. *The Age of Energy: Varieties of the American Experience, 1865–1915*. New York: The Viking Press, 1970.

Jones, Robert Edmond. "Toward an American Ballet." In Sayler, Oliver, ed., *Revolt in the Arts*. New York: Brentano's, 1930.

Keppel, Frederick. *Mr. Pennell's Etchings of N.Y. "Skyscrapers"*. New York: Frederick Keppel and Co., 1905.

Kimball, Fiske. *American Architecture*. Indianapolis: The Bobbs-Merrill Co., 1928.

King, Moses. *King's Views of New York, 1896–1915 and Brooklyn, 1905*. Boston 1908; reprint ed., New York: Arno Press, 1977.

Klingender, Francis. *Art and the Industrial Revolution*. London: Adams and MacKay Ltd., 1947; reprint ed., New York: Schocken, 1970.

Kolodin, Irving. *The Story of the Metropolitan Opera, 1883–1950*. New York: Alfred A. Knopf, 1953.

Koolhaas, Rem. *Delirious New York*. New York: Oxford University Press, 1978.

Kopman, B. A. *Walkowitz*. Paris: Le Triangle, n.d.

Kouwenhoven, John Atlee. *The Columbia Historical Portrait of New York*. New York: Doubleday and Co., 1953.

_____. *Made in America*. New York: Doubleday and Co., Inc., 1949.

Kreymborg, Alfred. *Troubador*. 1925; reprint ed., New York: Sagamore Press, 1957.

Kuh, Katherine. *The Artist's Voice*. New York: Harper and Row, 1960.

Lamb, Martha J. *Wall Street in History*. New York: Funk and Wagnalls, 1883.

Leich, Jean Ferriss. *Architectural Visions: The Drawings of Hugh Ferriss*. With essays by Paul Goldberger and a foreword by Adolf Placzek. New York: Whitney Library of Design, 1980.

Leonard, Sandra E. *Henri Rousseau and Max Weber*. New York: Richard L. Feigen Co., 1970.

Lewis, Sinclair. *Babbitt*. New York: Harcourt, Brace and World, 1922.

Links, J.G. *Townscape Painting and Drawing*. New York: Harper and Row, 1972.

Lisle, Laurie. *Portrait of an Artist: A Biography of Georgia O'Keeffe*. New York: Seaview Books, 1980.

Lockwood, Charles. *Manhattan Moves Uptown*. Boston: Houghton Mifflin Co., 1976.

Longwell, Dennis. *Steichen: The Master Prints, 1895–1914, The Symbolist Period*. New York: Museum of Modern Art, 1978.

Lowe, Sue Davidson. *Stieglitz: A Memoir/Biography*. New York: Farrar, Straus, Giroux, 1983.

Lowell, Amy. *Complete Poetical Works of Amy Lowell*. New York: Houghton Mifflin Co., 1955.

Lynd, Robert S. and Helen M. *Middletown*. New York: Harcourt, Brace and Co., 1929.

MacDonald, Gordon D. *Office Building Construction Manhattan, 1901-1953*. New York: The Real Estate Board of New York, 1953.

McKelvey, Blake. *Emergence of Metropolitan America*. Rutgers, New Jersey: Rutgers University Press, 1965.

Margolis, Marianne Fulton, ed. *Alfred Stieglitz: Camera Work*. New York: Dover Publications, Inc., 1978.

Marx, Leo. *The Machine in the Garden*. London: Oxford University Press, 1964.

Master Builders of the World's Greatest Structure [Woolworth Building]. New York: Hugh McAtamney and Co., 1913.

Max Weber. New York: American Artists' Group, 1945.

May, Henry. *The Discontent of the Intellectuals*. Chicago: Rand, McNally, 1963.

Mayer, Grace M. *Once Upon a City*. With a foreword by Edward Steichen. New York: The Macmillan Co., 1958.

Miller, Zane. *The Urbanization of Modern America*. New York: Harcourt, Brace and Co., 1973.

Morgan, Alfred. *The Story of Skyscrapers*. New York: Farrar and Rinehart, Inc., 1934.

Morgan, Charles. *George Bellows, Painter of America*. New York: Reynal and Co., 1965.

Motherwell, Robert. *Dada Painters and Poets*. New York: Museum of Modern Art, 1951.

Mott, Frank Luther. *A History of American Magazines*. Vols. 4-5. Cambridge: Harvard University Press, 1957, 1968.

Mowry, George, ed. *The Twenties: Fords Flappers and Fanatics*. Englewood Cliffs, New Jersey: Prentice-Hall, Inc., 1963.

Mujica, Francisco. *History of the Skyscraper*. New York and Paris: Archeology and Architecture Press, 1929; reprint ed., New York: Da Capo Press, 1977.

Mumford, Lewis. *The Culture of Cities*. New York: Harcourt, Brace and Co., 1938.

_____. *The Golden Day*. New York: Horace, Liveright, 1926.

_____. *Sticks and Bones*. New York: Boni and Liveright, 1924.

Myers, Jerome. *An Artist in Manhattan*. New York: American Artists' Group, 1940.

New York. A series of wood engravings by Rudolph Ruzicka and prose impressions by Prichard Eaton. New York: Grolier Club, 1915.

Newhall, Nancy, ed. *Edward Weston: The Flame of Recognition*. New York: Aperture, 1971.

Norman, Dorothy. *Alfred Stieglitz: An American Seer*. New York: Random House, 1960.

_____. *Alfred Stieglitz: Introduction to an American Seer*. New York: Duell, Sloan and Pearce, 1960.

_____, ed. *The Selected Writings of John Marin*. New York: Pellegrini and Cudahy, 1949.

Norris, Frank. *The Pit: A Story of Chicago*. New York: The Curtis Publishing Co., 1902; reprint ed., New York: Grove Press, 1956.

Novack, Barbara. *American Painting of the Nineteenth Century*. New York: Praeger, 1969.

O'Keeffe, Georgia. *Georgia O'Keeffe*. New York: Viking Press, 1976.

Papadaki, Stamo. *Le Corbusier*. New York: The Macmillan Co., 1948.

Park, Edwin Avery. *New Backgrounds for a New Age*. New York: Harcourt, Brace and Co., 1927.

Paul Strand: A Retrospective Monograph, The Years 1915-1968. New York: Aperture, Inc., 1971.

Payne, Will. *The Money Captain*. Chicago and New York: Herbert S. Stone, 1908.

Pehnt, Wolfgang. *Expressionist Architecture*. New York: Praeger, 1973.

Pells, Richard. *Radical Visions and American Dreams*. New York: Harper and Row, 1973.

Pendleton, Ralph, ed. *The Theatre of Robert Edmond Jones*. Middletown, Connecticut: Wesleyan University Press, 1958.

Pennell, Elizabeth Robins. *The Life and Letters of Joseph Pennell*. 2 vols. Boston: Little, Brown and Co., 1929.

Pennell, Joseph. *The Adventures of an Illustrator*. Boston: Little, Brown and Co., 1925.

_____. *The Glory of New York*. With an introduction by Elizabeth Robins Pennell. New York: William Rudge, 1927.

_____. *The Great New York*. Boston: Le Roy Phillips, 1912.

_____. *Joseph Pennell's Pictures of the Wonder of Work*. New York: J.B. Lippincott Co., 1916.

Penrose, Roland. *Man Ray*. London: Thames and Hudson, 1975.

Perlman, Bernard B. *The Immortal Eight*. New York: Exposition Press, 1962.

Poe, Edgar Allen. *Poems*. Chicago: W.B. Conkey, ca. 1890s.

Price, Uvedale. *Essays on the Picturesque*. Vol. 2. London: Hereford, 1798.

Ray, Man. *Self Portrait*. Boston: Little, Brown and Co., 1963.

Reich, Sheldon. *John Marin: A Stylistic Analysis and a Catalogue Raisonné*. 2 vols. Tucson: University of Arizona Press, 1970.

Ringel, Fred, ed. *America as Americans See It*. New York: Harcourt and Brace, 1932.

Rockwell, Rufus. *New York Old and New*. 2 vols. Philadelphia: J.B. Lippincott Co., 1909.

Rosenblum, Robert. *Modern Painting and the Northern Romantic Tradition*. New York: Harper and Row, 1975.

Rourke, Constance. *Charles Sheeler: Artist in the American Tradition*. New York: Harcourt, Brace and Co., 1938.

Ruckley, Samuel B. *Rebuilding Manhattan: A Study of New Office Construction*. New York: The Real Estate Board of New York, 1972.

Sandburg, Carl. *The Complete Poems*. New York: Harcourt, Brace, Jovanovich, 1969.

Sanouillet, Michel. *Francis Picabia et "391"*. 2 vols. Paris: Eric Losfeld, 1966.

Santayana, George. *The Genteel Tradition, Nine Essays by George Santayana*. Edited by Douglas Wilson. Cambridge: Harvard University Press, 1967.

Schapiro, Meyer. "Rebellion in Art." In Daniel Aaron, ed., *America in Crisis*. New York: Alfred A. Knopf, Inc., 1952.

Scharf, Aaron. *Art and Photography*. London: The Penguin Press, 1968.

Schuyler, Montgomery. *American Architecture and Other Writings*. New York: Atheneum, 1964.

_____. *The Woolworth Building*. New York: Hugh McAtamney, 1913.

Schwartz, Arturo. *The Complete Works of Marcel Duchamp*. New York: Harry N. Abrams, 1969.

_____. *Man Ray*. New York: Rizzoli, 1977.

_____. *New York Dada*. Munich: Prestel-Verlag, 1975.

Scott, David. *John Sloan*. New York: Watson-Guptill, 1975.

Scully, Vincent. *American Architecture and Urbanism*. New York: Praeger Publishers, Inc., 1969.

Seligmann, Herbert, ed. *Alfred Stieglitz Talking: Notes on Some of his Conversations, 1925-1931*. New Haven: Yale University Press, 1966.

Semsch, Otto F., ed. *A History of the Singer Building*. New York: Shumway and Beattle, 1908.

Sherman, Claire Richter, and Holcomb, Adele M., eds. *Women as Interpreters of the Visual Arts, 1820-1979*. Westport, Connecticut and London: Greenwood Press, 1981.

The Skyscraper from Fortune. New York: American Institute of Steel Construction, Inc., 1930.

Sloan, John. *The Gist of Art*. New York: American Artists' Group, 1939.

_____. *John Sloan's New York Scene*. New York: Harper and Row, 1965.

Slonimsky, Nicholas. *Music Since 1900*. Fourth edition. New York: C. Scribner's, 1971.

Smith, F. Hopkinson. *Charcoals of New and Old New York*. New York: Doubleday, Page and Co., 1912.

Soule, George Henry. *Prosperity Decade, 1917-1929*. New York: Holt, Rinehart and Winston, 1947.

Spewack, Samuel. *The Skyscraper Murder*. New York: The Macauley Co., 1928.

Startett, William A. *Skyscrapers and the Men Who Build Them*. New York: Scribner's, 1928.

Stearns, Harold, ed. *Civilization in the United States*. New York: Harcourt, Brace and Co., 1922.

Stearns, Marshall W. *The Story of Jazz*. New York: Oxford University Press, 1956.

Steichen, Edward. *A Life in Photography*. New York: Doubleday and Co., Inc., 1963.

Stieglitz, Alfred. "The Photo-Secession." In *Bausch and Lomb Lens Souvenir*. Rochester, New York: Bausch and Lomb Optical Co., 1903.

_____. *Picturesque Bits of New York and Other Studies*. New York: R.H. Russell, 1897.

_____. "Simplicity in Composition." In *The Modern Way in Picture Making*. Rochester, New York: Eastman Kodak Co., 1905.

Still, Bayrd. *Mirror for Gotham*. New York: New York University Press, 1956.

Strauss, Anselm. *The American City: A Sourcebook of Imagery*. Chicago: Aldine, 1968.

_____. *Images of the American City*. New York: The Free Press of Glencoe, 1961.

Sullivan, Louis. *Kindergarten Chats*. 1901-1902; reprint ed., New York: George Wittenborn, Inc., 1947.

Tallmadge, Thomas E. *The Story of Architecture in America*. New York: Norton, 1927.

Tashjian, Dickran. *Skyscraper Primitives: Dada and the American Avant-Garde*. Middletown, Connecticut: Wesleyan University Press, 1975.

Templeton, William D. *The Life and Work of William Gilpin*. Urbana, Illinois: University of Illinois Press, 1939.

Thorton, Gene. *Masters of the Camera: Stieglitz, Steichen and Their Successors*. New York: Holt, Rinehart and Winston, 1976.

Tomkins, Calvin. *Paul Strand: Sixty Years of Photographs*. New York: Aperture, Inc., 1976.

Trachtenberg, Alan. *Brooklyn Bridge: Fact and Symbol*. New York: Oxford University Press, 1965.

_____. *Democratic Vistas*. New York: George Braziller, 1970.

Trachtenberg, Alan; Neill, Peter; Bunnell, Peter, eds. *The City: American Experience*. New York: Oxford University Press, 1971.

Van Dyke, John C. *The New New York*. New York: The Macmillan Co., 1909.

Walkowitz, Abraham. *Barns and Coal Mines Around Girard, Kansas*. Introduction by E. Haldeman-Julius. Kansas: Haldeman-Julius Publications, 1947.

_____. *A Demonstration of Objective, Abstract, and Non-Objective Art*. Kansas: Haldeman-Julius Publications, 1948.

_____. *Improvisations of New York: A Symphony in Lines*. Kansas: Haldeman-Julius Publications, 1948.

Weber, Max. *Cubist Poems*. London: Elkin Mathews, 1914.

_____. *Essays on Art*. New York: William Edwin Rudge, 1916.

Weimer, David R. *The City as Metaphor*. New York: Random House, 1966.

Wells, Herbert George. *The Door in the Wall*. With photographs by Alvin Langdon Coburn. New York and London: Mitchel Kennerly, 1911.

_____. *The Future in America*. New York: Harper and Brothers, 1906.

_____. *Modern Utopia*. New York: Charles Scribner's Sons, 1904.

Werner, Alfred. *Max Weber*. New York: Harry Abrams, 1975.

Wertheim, Arthur Frank. *The New York Little Renaissance, 1908-1917*. New York: New York University Press, 1976.

West, Thomas Reed. *Flesh of Steel: Literature and the Machine in American Culture*. Nashville: Vanderbilt University Press, 1967.

White, Morton and White, Lucia. *The Intellectual Versus the City*. Cambridge: Harvard University and M.I.T. Press, 1962.

White, Norval, and Willensky, Elliot. *AIA Guide to New York City*. New York: Collier Books, 1978.

Whiteman, Paul. *Jazz*. New York: J.H. Sears and Co., Inc., 1926.

Whitman, Walt. *Democratic Vistas*. London: The Walter Scott Publishing Co., 1873; reprint ed., St. Clair Shores, Michigan: Scholarly Press, 1970.

Williams, Jesse Lynch. *New York Sketches*. New York: Charles Scribner's Sons, 1902.

Williams, William Carlos. *The Autobiography of William Carlos Williams*. New York: Random House, 1948.

Wolfe, Gerald R. *New York: A Guide to the Metropolis*. New York: New York University Press, 1975.

Wuerth, Louis. *Catalogue of the Complete Etchings of Joseph Pennell*. Introduction by Elizabeth Robins Pennell. Boston: Little, Brown and Co., 1931.

Yale University Art Gallery. *Collection of the Société Anonyme*. New Haven: Yale University Press, 1941.

Young, Mahroni Sharp. *The Eight*. New York: Watson-Guptill, 1973.

Zigrosser, Carl. *Childe Hassam*. New York: Keppel and Co., 1916.

_____. *The Complete Etchings of John Marin*. Philadelphia: Philadelphia Museum of Art, 1969.

Articles

Addington, Sarah. "Interview with M. and Mme. Gleizes." *New York Tribune*, 9 October 1915, p. 7.

Agee, William. "New York Dada, 1910-1930." *Art News Annual* 34 (1968): 105-13.

Agha, M.F. "Ralph Steiner." *Creative Art* 10 (January 1932): 35-40.

Aisen, Maurice. "The Latest Evolution of Art and Picabia." *Camera Work*, special no. (June 1913): 14-21.

"Alfred Stieglitz, Artist and His Search for the Human Soul." *New York Herald*, 8 March 1908, sec. 3, p. 5.

"Alvin Langdon Coburn: Artist-Photographer by Himself." *Pall Mall Magazine* 51 (June 1913): 757-63.

"America as a Nation of Artists and Poets." *Current Literature* 41 (August 1906): 173-76.

"The American Skyscraper, the Giant in Architecture: Its Purpose, Beauty and Development." *The Craftsman* 24 (April 1913): 3-10.

Anderson, James. "The Highest Building in the World." *Metropolitan Magazine* 27 (December 1907): 386-89.

Anderson, Sherwood. "New York." *Vanity Fair* 28 (July 1927): 33, 90.

Antheil, George. "American Folk Music." *Forum* 80 (December 1928): 957-58.

"The Appeal of Primitive Jazz." *Literary Digest* 55 (25 August 1917): 28-29.

"Architectural Competition Drawings." *Bulletin of the Minneapolis Institute of Art* 12 (March 1923): 22.

"Art Critic and the Tall Building." *Scientific American* 80 (28 January 1899): 50.

"Artistic Aspects of the Skyscraper." *Current Opinion* 55 (April 1913): 321–23.

"Artistic Terra Cotta Effects." *New York Times*, 28 July 1912, sec. 8, p. 2.

Austin Fred. "Skyscrapers." *Dance Magazine* 5 (April 1926): 24–25, 58.

Baigell, Matthew. "Notes on Realistic Painting and Photography." *Arts* 54 (November 1979): 141–43.

Baur, John I.H. "The Machine and the Subconscious: Dada in America." *Magazine of Art* 44 (October 1951): 233–37.

"Beauty in the Skyscraper: The Shelton Hotel." *Vanity Fair* 23 (October 1924): 51.

Benson, E.M. "John Marin: The Man and His Work." *American Magazine of Art* 27 (October 1935): 597–611, 632–33, and (November 1935): 655–70.

Bergson, Henri. Excerpt from *Laughter. Camera Work*, no. 36 (October 1911): 20–21.

"Berlin Calls Jazz American Folk Music." *New York Times*, 10 January 1925, sec. 2, p. 7.

"Berlin Opera Mingles Auto Horn, Films, Jazz." *New York Times*, 3 March 1927, p. 23.

Bishop, John Peale. "The Painter and the Dynamo." *Vanity Fair* 20 (August 1923): 57, 92.

Blackshaw, Randall. "The New New York." *Century* 44 (August 1902): 493–513.

Bluemner, Oscar. "Kandinsky and Walkowitz." *Camera Work*, no. 44 (March 1914): 37.

Bohn, Willard. "In Pursuit of the Fourth Dimension: Guillaume Apollinaire and Max Weber." *Arts* 54 (June 1980): 166–69.

Borgmeyer, Charles Louis. "Birge Harrison—Poet Painter." *Fine Arts Journal* 29 (October 1913): 583–606.

Bossom, Alfred. "New Beauty in the Skyscraper." *Literary Digest* 93 (May 1927): 26–27.

_____. "New Styles in American Architecture." *The World's Work* 55 (June 1928): 189–95.

Brown, Frank Chouteau. "A New Note in Architectural Rendering: The Work of Mr. Hugh Ferriss." *Architectural Review* 7 (August 1918): 21–25.

Brown, Milton. "Cubist-Realism, An American Style." *Marsyas* 3 (1943): 139–58.

Bryant, Louise. "John Storrs." *The Masses* (October 1917): 21.

Buffet, Gabrielle. "Modern Art and the Public." *Camera Work*, special no. (June 1913): 15–17.

"Buildings Still in Blue-Print May Be Obsolete." *Fortune* 2 (April 1930): 155.

"Bull Market Architecture," *New Republic* 67 (8 July 1931): 192–93.

Burnham, Daniel. "The Flatiron from the Southeast Corner of 22nd and Broadway, New York." *American Architectural and Building News*, 27 September 1902, p. 102.

Caffin, Charles. "Municipal Art." *Harper's Monthly* 100 (April 1900): 655–56.

Camfield, William. "The Machinist Style of Francis Picabia." *Art Bulletin* 48 (September–December 1966): 28–51.

Carrington, Fitzroy. "Joseph Pennell and the Wonder of Work." *Art and Progress* 4 (November 1912): 766–71.

Carter, Irving. "Jazz Brings First Dance of the City." *New York Times Magazine*, 14 June 1925, sec. 4, p. 9.

"A Census of Skyscrapers." *American City* 41 (September 1929): 130.

"The *Chicago Tribune* Building." *American Magazine of Art* 14 (February 1923): 72–74.

Chotzinoff, Samuel. "Jazz: A Brief History." *Vanity Fair* 20 (June 1923): 69, 104, 106.

Churchill, Henry S. "The New Architecture." *Nation* 117 (14 November 1923): 552–53.

Coady, Robert J. "American Art." *The Soil* 1 (December 1916): 3–4.

_____. "American Art." *The Soil* 1 (January 1917): 54.

Coburn, Alvin Langdon. "Contrasts." *Metropolitan Magazine* 26 (March 1908): n.p.

_____. "Is the Photographer the Best Judge of His Own Work?" *Photographic News* 51 (February 1907): 83–84.

_____. "The Relation of Time to Art." *Camera Work*, no. 36 (October 1911): 72–73.

_____. "Some Photographic Impressions of New York." *Metropolitan Magazine* 23 (February 1906): n.p.

"Cook-Number" (issue on artist Howard Cook). *The Checkerboard*. New York: The Weyhe Gallery, 1934.

Cooper, Colin Campbell. "Skyscrapers and How To Build Them in Paint." *Palette and Bench* 1 (1909): 90–92, 106–8.

Corbett, Harvey Wiley. "The Birth and Development of the Tall Building." *American Architect* 129 (5 January 1926): 37–40.

_____. "Different Levels for Foot, Wheel and Rail." *American City* 31 (July 1924): 2–6.

_____. "High Buildings on Narrow Streets." *American Architect* 119 (8 June 1921): 603–8.

_____. "The Influence of Zoning on New York's Skyline." *American Architect* 123 (5 January 1923): 1–4.

_____. "The Problem of Traffic Congestion, and a Solution." *Architectural Forum* 46 (March 1927): 201–8.

_____. "Zoning and the Envelope of the Building." *Pencil Points* 4 (April 1923): 13–18.

Corbett, Harvey Wiley, and Curran, Henry H. "Skyscrapers and Traffic Congestion." *American Architect* 131 (27 March 1927): 386–88.

Corbin, John. "The Twentieth Century City." *Scribner's* 33 (March 1903): 259–72.

Corn, Wanda. "Apostles of the New American Art: Waldo Frank and Paul Rosenfeld." *Arts* 54 (February 1980): 154–58.

_____. "The New New York." *Art in America* 61 (July–August 1973): 58–65.

Cravan, Arthur. "Oscar Wilde is Alive." *The Soil* 1 (April 1917): 146.

_____. "Poem on New York." *The Soil* 1 (December 1971): 36.

Creative Arts 9 (August 1931): entire issue.

Croly, Herbert. "Architectural Counterpoint" (review of the 1926 ballet *Skyscrapers* in Notes and Comments). *Architectural Record* 59 (May 1926): 489–90.

_____. "A New Dimension in Architectural Effects." *Architectural Record* 57 (January 1925): 93–94.

"Cubist Architecture in New York." *Vanity Fair* 15 (January 1921): 72.

"Cubistic Phases of New York." With photographs by Ralph Steiner. *Vanity Fair* 29 (April 1928): 58.

Curran, Henry H. "St. Nicholas, Smoke, and Skyscrapers." *American City* 36 (January 1927): 68.

Cusack, T. "Architectural Photography." *American Amateur Photographer* 5 (September 1893): 447–55.

Cushing, Charles Phelps. "Frozen Jazz." *The World's Work* (May 1929): 50–51.

Davidson, Abraham. "John Storrs, Early Sculptor of the Machine Age." *Artforum* 13 (November 1974): 41–45.

_____. Reviw of Dickran Tashjian's *Skyscraper Primitives*. *Art Bulletin* 61 (February 1980): 143–46.

Dean, Elizabeth. "Georgia O'Keeffe's Radiator Building: Icon of Glamorous Gotham." *Revue Française D'Etudes Américaines*, no. 11 (April 1981), pp. 81–92.

"Debunking Jazz." *Literary Digest* 92 (26 March 1927): 26–27.

De Casseres, Benjamin. "American Indifference." *Camera Work*, no. 28 (October 1909): 24.

_____. "The Physiognomy of the New Yorker." *Camera Work*, no. 29 (January 1910): 35.

Delano, Frank. "Skyscrapers." *American City* 34 (January 1926): 1–9.

"The Descent of Jazz Upon Opera" (review of ballet *Skyscrapers*). *Literary Digest* 88 (13 March 1926): 24–25.

Desmond, H.W. "A Rational Skyscraper." *Architectural Record* 15 (March 1904): 275–84.

De Zayas, Marius. "Modern Art: Theories and Representation." *Camera Work*, no. 44 (October 1913): 13–19.

_____. Statement in *291*, nos. 5–6 (July–August 1915), p. 5.

Downes, Olin. "Concerning 'Modern American Music.'" *New York Times*, 23 November 1924, sec. 8, p. 6.

"Downtown in the Banking District of New York." With a drawing by Arnold Ronnebeck and a poem by George S. Chappell. *Vanity Fair* 24 (July 1925): 58.

Dreiser, Theodore. "The Camera Club of New York." *Ainslee's Magazine* 4 (October 1899): 324–35.

_____. "A Master of Photography." *Success* 2 (10 June 1889): 471.

_____. "A Remarkable Art: The New Pictorial Photography." *The Great Round World* 19 (3 May 1902): 430–34.

Duchamp, Marcel. "A Complete Reversal of Art Opinions." *Arts and Decoration* 5 (September 1915): 427–28, 442.

_____. "The Iconoclastic Opinions of Marcel Duchamp." *Current Opinion* 59 (November 1915): 346–47.

_____. Interview with Otto Hahn. *Art and Artists* 1 (July 1966): 7–11.

Duer, Edward Rush. "The Skyscraper in New York." *Architectural Forum* 44 (February 1926): 105–8.

Editorial Comment. *Camera Work*, no. 4 (October 1903): 25.

Editors. "The Pictures in This Number." *Camera Work*, no. 7 (January 1903): 63.

"The Effort to Take Jazz Seriously." *Literary Digest* 81 (26 April 1924): 29–30.

Eken, Andrew J. "The Ultimate in Skyscrapers?" *Scientific American* (May 1931): 318–20.

Epstein, Jean. "The New Conditions of Literary Phenomena." *Broom* 2 (April 1922): 3–10.

"The Etcher of the City" (review of the work of Joseph Pennell). *Outlook* 96 (24 December 1910): 912–13.

"The European Art-Invasion." *Literary Digest* 51 (27 November 1915): 1224–27.

"The Exhibition of Competitive Drawings for the *Chicago Tribune* Tower." *Academy Notes* 18 (January–June 1923): 66–67.

Feree, Barr. "The Art of High Building." *Architectural Record* 15 (May 1904): 445–66.

_____. "The High Building and Its Art." *Scribner's* 15 (March 1894): 297–318.

Ferriss, Hugh. "American Capitals of Industry." *Harper's Monthly* 139 (July 1919): 217–24.

_____. "Architectural Tendencies of Today." *Vanity Fair* 21 (February 1924): 44–45.

_____. "Civic Architecture of the Immediate Future." *Arts and Decoration* 18 (November 1922): 12–13.

_____. "Daily News Building, New York." *American Architect* 135 (5 May 1929): 588.

_____. "How Hugh Ferris Draws." *American Architect* 140 (July 1931): 30–33.

_____. "The New Architecture." *New York Times*, 19 March 1922, sec. 3, pp. 7, 9, 27.

_____. "The New New York." *Vanity Fair* 25 (December 1925): 66–67.

_____. "New Theatre Guild Playhouse." *Vanity Fair* 22 (August 1924): 32.

_____. "New York of the Future." *Vanity Fair* 27 (September 1926): 84.

_____. "The Sesqui-Centennial at Philadelphia." *Vanity Fair* 26 (July 1926): 46–47.

"55-Story Building in Lower Broadway." *New York Times*, 20 January 1911, p. 5.

"55-Story Building Opens in a Flash." *New York Times*, 25 April 1913, p. 20.

"57-Story Tower Flooded on a Test." *New York Times*, 9 June 1913, p. 18.

"The Fight for Recognition." *Camera Work*, no. 30 (April 1910): 21–22.

"Flag to Fly 830 Feet Up." *New York Times*, 30 June 1912, p. 10.

"The Flat Iron Building." *Architects' and Builders' Magazine* 3 (August 1902): 391–96.

"Flatiron Building Wind." *New York Times*, 6 February 1903, p. 8.

"The 'Flatiron' or Fuller Building." *Architectural Record* 12 (October 1902): 528–36.

"Flatiron's Fallen Stone." *New York Times*, 11 September 1903, p. 14.

"Folk Music of the Machine Age." *Literary Digest* 92 (26 March 1927): 27.

"A Foreign Artist Among New York Skyscrapers." *Vanity Fair* 24 (April 1925): 56.

"Foundation Work for Big Building." *New York Times*, 28 May 1911, sec. 8, p. 2.

Frank, Waldo. "Jazz and Folk Art." *New Republic* 49 (1 December 1926): 42–43.

Frankl, Paul. "Just What is This Modernistic Movement?" *Arts and Decoration* 29 (May 1928): 56–57ff.

_____. "Logic in Modernistic Decoration." *Arts and Decoration* 29 (June 1928): 54–55ff.

_____. "Why We Accept Modernistic Furniture." *Arts and Decoration* 29 (June 1928): 58–59ff.

"French Artists Spur on American Art." *New York Tribune*, 24 October 1915, sec. 4, p. 2.

French, Herbert. "The Measure of Greatness." *Camera Work*, no. 27 (July 1909): 45.

"From the Singer Tower." *New York Times*, 24 June 1908, p. 1.

Fuguet, Dallet. "Notes by the Way: The Man Behind the Camera." *Camera Work*, no. 2 (April 1903): 52.

Fuller, Eunice Barnard. "Jazz is Linked to the Factory Wheel." *New York Times Magazine*, 30 December 1928, p. 4–5.

Fuller, Henry B. "Chicago's Book of Days." With drawings by Albert Fleury. *Outlook* 69 (5 October 1901): 288–99.

"Furious Gales Lash City and Harbor." *New York Times*, 17 September 1903, p. 1.

"The Future Architectural Development of New York." With drawings by Dobuzhinsky. *Vanity Fair* 22 (April 1924): 57.

Gilbert, Cass. "The Woolworth Building." *Architects' and Builders' Magazine* 12 (November 1911): 670–71.

Gilder, Joseph B. "The City of Dreadful Heights." *Putnam's Monthly* 5 (November 1908): 131–43.

"Girls Ban Jazz, Petting, Cigarettes." *New York Times*, 18 February 1922, p. 2.

Gordon, F.C. "The Sky-scraper." *American Architect and Building News* 46 (8 December 1894): 100–101.

Gorky, Maxim. "The City of Mammon: My Impressions of America." *Appleton's Magazine* 8 (August 1906): 176–82.

_____. "The Music of the Degenerate." *Dial* 85 (December 1928): 480–84.

Gosliner, L.S. "Paul Frankl" (biographical sketch). *Arts and Architecture* 51 (March 1937): 7.

Graham, Charles. "Panorama of the New York Skyline." *New York Journal* (3 May 1894): 20.

Graves, Louis. "The New Zoning Ordinance in New York City." *Architectural Forum* 26 (January 1917): 1–6.

Hamilton, George Heard. "John Covert: Early American Modern." *Journal* 12 (Fall 1952): 37–42.

Hand, John Oliver. "Futurism in America, 1909–14." *Art Journal* 41 (Winter 1981): 337–42.

Hartmann, Sadakichi. "Aesthetic Activity in Photography." *Brush and Pencil* 14 (April 1904): 24–40.

_____. "An Art Critic's Estimate of Alfred Stieglitz." *Photographic Times* 30 (June 1898): 257–62.

_____. "To the Flatiron." *Camera Work*, no. 4 (October 1903): 40.

_____. "The 'Flat-Iron' Building: An Esthetical Dissertation." *Camera Work*, no. 4 (October 1903): 36–40.

_____. "The Photo-Secession." *The Craftsman* 6 (April 1904): 30–37.

_____. "A Plea for the Picturesqueness of New York." *Camera Notes* (October 1900): 91–97.

_____. "Structural Units." *Camera Work*, no. 36 (October 1911): 17–18.

Hassam, Childe. "New York the Beauty City." *New York Sun*, 23 February 1913, p. 16.

Haviland, Paul. "The Home of the Golden Disk." *Camera Work*, no. 25 (January 1909): 21–28.

Hayden, Dolores. "Skyscraper Seduction: Skyscraper Rape." *Heresies* 1 (May 1977): 108–15.

Heap, Jane. "Machine Age Exposition" (announcement). *Little Review* 11 (Spring 1925): 22–24.

_____. "Notes on the Machine Age Exposition." *Little Review* 12 (May 1929): 63.

"The Heart of New York: A Skeleton Portrait." *Vanity Fair* 24 (August 1925): 30.

Henderson, Linda Dalrymple. "Mabel Dodge, Gertrude Stein, and Max Weber: A Four-Dimensional Trio." *Arts* 57 (September 1982): 106–11.

_____. "A New Facet of Cubism: 'The Fourth Dimension' and 'Non-Euclidean Geometry' Reinterpreted." *Art Quarterly* 34 (Winter 1971): 410–33.

Henri, Robert. "The New York Exhibition of Independent Artists." *The Craftsman* 18 (May 1910): 160–72.

Heydecker, Wayne. "Up in the Air." *American City* 38 (February 1928): 124–25.

"High Building Contract Let." *New York Times*, 20 April 1911, sec. 8, p. 2.

"High Buildings" (in The Field of Art). *Scribner's* 19 (January 1896): 127–28.

"High Winds Upset Woman and a Horse." *New York Times*, 15 April 1903, p. 2.

"Higher Buildings an Absurdity?" *Literary Digest* 92 (22 January 1927): 25.

Hitchcock, Henry-Russell. "Some American Interiors of the Moderne Style." *Architectural Record* 64 (September 1928): 236.

Hoeber, Arthur. "A 'Twin' Exhibition – Alexander and Birge Harrison at the Albright Art Gallery." *Academy Notes* (October 1913): 153–71.

Homer, William Innes. "The Exhibition of 'The Eight': Its History and Significance." *American Art Journal* 1 (Spring 1969): 53–64.

_____. "Picabia's *Jeune fille, américaine dans l'état de nudité* and Her Friends." *Art Bulletin* 57 (March 1975): 110–14.

Horwood, Henry Alexander. "New Skyscrapers for New York." *Metropolitan Magazine* 25 (January 1907): 461–70.

Howe, Willis E. "The Work of Colin C. Cooper, Artist." *Brush and Pencil* 18 (August 1906): 72–78.

Howells, William Dean. "Certain of the Chicago School of Fiction." *North American Review* 176 (May 1903): 739–43.

Hussy, Christopher. "The Picturesque." In *Encyclopedia of World Art*. Vol. 11. New York: McGraw Hill, 1966, pp. 335–42.

"The Iconoclastic Opinions of M. Marcel Duchamps [sic] Concerning Art and America." *Current Opinion* 59 (November 1915): 346–47.

Irving, Carter. "Jazz Brings First Dance of the City." *New York Times*, 14 June 1925, sec. 4, p. 9.

"Is Jazz Our National Anthem?" *New York Times*, 30 January 1922, sec. 2, p. 3.

"Is the Skyscraper a Mistake?" *Review of Reviews* 76 (September 1927): 313–14.

Jaffe, Irma B. "Joseph Stella and Hart Crane: The Brooklyn Bridge." *American Art Journal* 1 (Fall 1969): 98–107.

James, Henry. "Is the Skyscraper a Public Nuisance?" *The World's Work* 54 (May 1927): 67–76.

"Jazz." *Opportunity* 3 (May 1925): 132–33.

"Jazz." *Outlook* 136 (5 March 1924): 381–82.

"Jazz: A State of Mind." *New York Times*, 2 April 1925, p. 23.

"Jazz Is Compared to Comic Cartoon." *New York Times*, 18 February 1927, p. 24.

J.B. "The Woolworth." *The Soil* 1 (January 1917): 61–65.

Johns, Orrick. "Broadway's Towering House of Prayer." With illustrations by Hugh Ferriss. *New York Times Magazine*, 29 March 1925, p. 4.

——. "The Excelsior of Architecture." With illustrations by Hugh Ferriss. *New York Times Magazine*, 20 July 1924, p. 3.

——. "Our Billion Dollar Building Year." *New York Times*, 14 September 1924, sec. 1, p. 7.

Jones, Hinton. "Insists Jazz Is No Product of Machine Age But Negroic." *New York Times*, 20 March 1927, sec. 9, p. 16.

Josephson, Matthew. "Made in America." *Broom* 2 (June 1922): 266–70.

Kasebier, Gertrude. "Studies in Photography." *Photographic Times* 30 (June 1898): 270.

Keiley, Joseph. "Landscape A Reverie." *Camera Work*, no. 4 (October 1903): 45–46.

Keller, Ulrich. "An Art Historical View of Paul Strand." *Image* 17 (December 1974): 1–11.

Kent, H.H. "*Chicago Tribune* Competition." *Architectural Record* 53 (April 1923): 378–79.

Keppel, Frederick. "Joseph Pennell: Etcher, Illustrator, Author." *Outlook* 81 (23 September 1905): 172–83.

Klein, Michael. "John Covert's Time: Cubism, Duchamp, Einstein—A Quasi-Scientific Fantasy." *Art Journal* 33 (Summer 1974): 314–20.

Knowlton, Clarke, "The *Chicago Tribune* Competition." *Nation* 116 (4 April 1923): 388–89.

Kolisch, Mitzi. "Jazz in High Places." *The Independent* 116 (10 April 1926): 424.

Kramer, Hilton. "The American Precisionists." *Arts* 35 (March 1961): 32–37.

Kreymborg, Alfred. "Stieglitz and '291.' " *The Morning Telegraph*, 14 June 1914, sec. 2, p. 1.

Kuspit, Donald B. "Individual and Mass Identity in Urban Art: The New York Case." *Art in America* 65 (September–October 1977): 67–77.

La Farge, C. Grant. "The New Sky-line." *American Mercury* 1 (January 1924): 89–91.

Lane, M.A. "High Buildings in Chicago." *Harper's Weekly* 35 (31 October 1891): 853–54.

Laurvik, J. Nilsen. "Alfred Stieglitz, Pictorial Photographer." *International Studio* 44 (August 1911): 21–27.

Lay, Charles Downing. "New Architecture in New York." *Arts* 4 (August 1923): 67–86.

Le Galliene, Richard. "Brooklyn Bridge at Dawn." With photographs by Alvin Langdon Coburn. *Metropolitan Magazine* 23 (February 1905): 526–28.

Léger, Fernand. "The Esthetics of the Machine." Parts 1 and 2. *Little Review* 9 (Spring 1923): 45–49, and 10 (Fall–Winter 1924): 55–58.

Leonard, Neil. "Alfred Stieglitz and Realism." *Art Quarterly* 29, nos. 3–4 (1966): 277–86.

Loeb, Harold. "The Mysticism of Money." *Broom* 3 (September 1922): 115–29.

Lozowick, Louis. " 'Gas': A Theatrical Experiment." *Little Review* 11 (Winter 1926): 58–60.

——. "Tatlin's Monument to the Third International." *Broom* 3 (October 1922): 232–34.

MacCameron, Robert. "Change in Our Skyline Foretells a New Art." *New York Times*, 5 January 1913, p. 14.

MacGowan, Kenneth. "Robert Edmond Jones." *Theatre Arts* 7 (November 1925): 720–28.

McMay, A.B. "A Defense of Jazz." *New York Times*, 18 September 1926, p. 14.

"Manhattan—'The Proud and Passionate City.' " *Vanity Fair* 18 (April 1922): 51.

"Manhattan's Building Peak Shifts." *New York Times*, 3 February 1929, sec. 2, p. 1.

"Man's Mightiest Monument," *Popular Mechanics Magazine* 54 (December 1930): 920–24.

Marin, John. Statement. *Camera Work*, nos. 42–43 (April–June 1913): 18.

May, Earl Chapin. "Where Jazz Comes From." *Popular Mechanics* 45 (January 1926): 97–102.

May, Henry F. "Shifting Perspectives on the Twenties." *Mississippi Valley Historical Review* 43 (December 1956): 405–21.

Mayo, Earl. "Modern Cliff-Dwellers." *Metropolitan Magazine* 24 (June 1906): 310–17.

Mead, Lucia Ames. "What the American Woman Thinks: A Towering Menace." *Woman Citizen* 10 (November 1925): 22–23.

Meyer, Annie Nathan. "A City Picture, Mr. Hassam's Latest Painting of New York." *Art and Progress* 11 (March 1911): 137-39.

"Mr Coburn's New York Photographs." *The Craftsman* 19 (February 1911): 464-68.

"More Skyscrapers Heard From." *American City* 41 (October 1929): 163.

"More Topless Towers for New York." *Vanity Fair* 31 (November 1929): 86-87.

Mumford, Lewis. "American Architecture: The Realization of Industrialism." *Freeman* (27 February 1924): 584-86.

_____. "Architecture and the Machine." *American Mercury* 3 (September 1924): 77-80.

_____. "Botched Cities." *American Mercury* 18 (October 1929): 143-50.

_____. "High Buildings—An American View." *American Architect* 126 (5 November 1924): 423-24.

_____. "The Intolerable City." *Harper's Monthly* 152 (February 1926): 283-93.

_____. "Is the Skyscraper Tolerable?" *Architecture* 55 (February 1927): 67-69.

_____. "New York vs. Chicago in Architecture." *Architecture* 56 (November 1927): 241-44.

_____. "The Sacred City" (review of the 1925 Wanamaker show). *New Republic* 45 (27 January 1926): 270-74.

_____. "Towers." *American Mercury* 4 (February 1925): 193-96.

Munson, Gorham B. "The Skyscraper Primitives." *The Guardian* 1 (March 1925): 164-75.

"Must the Sky-Scraper Go?" *Literary Digest* 90 (14 August 1926): 23.

"Must We Come to This?" *American City* 36 (June 1927): 801-5.

Nauman, Francis. "The New York Dada Movement: Better Late Than Never." *Arts* 54 (February 1980): 143-46.

"New Beauty in the Skyscraper." *Literary Digest* 93 (21 May 1927): 26-27.

"No Limit in Sight for Future Skyscrapers." *New York Times*, 22 July 1923, sec. 7, p. 5.

Noble, Hollister. "Jazz Feels Surge of a Higher Order." *New York Times Magazine*, 15 March 1925, sec. 4, p. 9.

Norman, Dorothy, ed. "From the Writings and Conversations of Alfred Stieglitz." *Twice a Year*, no. 1 (Fall-Winter 1938), pp. 77ff.

"Obituary" (Paul Frankl). *Interiors* 117 (April 1958): 156.

Oliver, Maude I.G. "A Chicago Painter: The Work of Albert Fleury." *International Studio* 22 (March 1904): 21-23.

"100-Story Building Entirely Possible." *New York Times*, 20 October 1912, sec. 3, p. 4.

"Our Illustrations." *Camera Work*, no. 4 (October 1903): 25.

"Pageant of New York: The Titan City, in a Tercentenary Pictorial Exhibition." *Art News* 31 (October 1925): 10.

"Painter's Motifs in New York City" (in The Field of Art). *Scribner's* 20 (July 1896): 127-28.

"The Painter's New Rival: An Interview with Alvin Langdon Coburn." *American Photographer* 2 (January 1908): 13-19.

"Paintings by Birge Harrison." *Academy Notes* 4 (January 1909): 113-16.

"Paintings by Max Weber." *The Newark Museum—Art, Science, Technology, History* 3 (July 1913): 1-6.

Parker, Robert Allerton. "The Art of the Camera: An Experimental 'Movie.'" *Arts and Decoration* 15 (Octboer 1921): 369, 414-15.

_____. "The Classical Vision of Charles Sheeler." *International Studio* 84 (May 1926): 68-72.

Peattie, Elia W. "The Artistic Side of Chicago." *Atlantic Monthly* 84 (December 1899): 828-34.

Pennell, Joseph. "My View of the Wonder of Work." *American Architect* 109 (31 May 1916): 363-66.

_____. "My Views of the 'Wonder of Work.'" *The Builder* 110 (21 April 1916): 292-94.

_____. "The Wonder of Work." *Scribner's* 58 (December 1915): 775-78.

_____. "The Wonder of Work on the Panama Canal." *International Studio* 48 (December 1912): 132–42.

"Picabia, Art Rebel, Here to Teach New Movement." *New York Times*, 16 February 1913, sec. 5, p. 9.

Picabia, Francis. "How New York Looks to Me." *New York American*, 30 March 1912, magazine sec., p. 11.

_____. "A Post-Cubist's Impression of New York." *New York Tribune*, 9 March 1913, sec. 2, p. 1.

Pickering, Ruth. "The Economic Interpretation of Jazz." *New Republic* 26 (11 May 1921): 323–24.

Pincus-Witten, Robert. "Man-Ray: The Homonymic Pun and the American Vernacular." *Art Forum* 13 (April 1975): 54–59.

Pond, DeWitt Clinton. "Art and the Skyscraper." *Scribner's* 74 (October 1923): 508–12.

Poole, Ernest. "Cowboys of the Skies." *Everybody's Magazine* 19 (November 1908): 641–53.

"A Post Cubist's Impression of New York." *New York Tribune*, 3 March 1915, sec. 2, p. 1.

Powell, Earl A. III. "The Picturesque." *Arts* 52 (March 1978): 110–17.

"Primitive Savage Animalism, Preacher's Analysis of Jazz." *New York Times*, 3 March 1922, p. 15.

Ray, David H. "The Skyscraper of the Future." *Scientific American Supplement* 75 (8 March 1913): 148–50.

Reich, Sheldon. "Abraham Walkowitz: Pioneer of American Modernism." *American Art Journal* 3 (Spring 1971): 72–82.

Robbins, Daniel. "From Cubism to Abstract Art: The Evolution of the Work of Gleizes and Delaunay." *Baltimore Museum of Art News* 25 (Spring 1962): 9–21.

_____. "John Marin: Paintings of New York, 1912." *American Art Journal* 1 (Spring 1969): 43–52.

_____. "From Symbolism to Cubism: The Abbaye Créteil." *Art Journal* 33 (Winter 1963–1964): 11–16.

Roberts, Mary Fanton [Giles Edgerton]. "How New York has Redeemed Herself from Ugliness—An Artist's Revelation of the Beauty of the Skyscraper." *The Craftsman* 15 (January 1907): 458–71.

_____. "Photography as One of the Fine Arts; The Camera Pictures of Alvin Langdon Coburn as a Vindication of the Statement." *The Craftsman* 15 (July 1907): 394–403.

Rood, Roland. "The Origin of the Poetical Feeling in Landscape." *Camera Work*, no. 11 (July 1905): 21–25.

Rosenfeld, Paul. "Musical Chronicle." *Dial* 75 (November 1923): 518–20.

Rubenfeld, Richard. "Stefan Hirsch: Pioneer Precisionist." *Arts* 54 (November 1979): 96–97.

Sadakichi Hartmann Newsletter 1–5 (1970–1974).

Saltus, Edgar. "New York from the Flatiron." *Munsey's Magazine* 33 (July 1905): 381–90.

Sawin, Martica. "Abraham Walkowitz, Artist." *Arts* 38 (March 1964): 42–45.

"Say Autos and Jazz Ruin American Youth." *New York Times*, 11 October 1924, p. 16.

Schauffler, Robert Haven. "Who Invented Jazz?" *Collier's* 75 (3 January 1925): 38.

Schuyler, Montgomery. "The Skyline of New York, 1881–1897." With drawings by Fred Pansing. *Harper's Weekly* 41 (20 March 1897): 292–93, 295.

_____. "The Towers of Manhattan and Notes on the Woolworth Building." *Architectural Record* 33 (February 1913): 98–122.

Scott, Temple. "Fifth Avenue and the Boulevard St. Michel." *Forum* 44 (July–December 1910): 665–83.

_____. "The Terrible Truthfulness of Mr. Shaw." *Camera Work*, no. 29 (January 1910): 17–20.

Seldes, Gilbert. "Thompson's Panorama, The Woolworth Building, and Do It Again." *Vanity Fair* 23 (December 1924): 39, 108, 118.

Sexton, R.W. "Unifying Architecture in America." *International Studio* 83 (February 1926): 41–45.

Shaw, George Bernard. "Coburn The Camerist." *Metropolitan Magazine* 24 (May 1906): 236–40.

Singer, H.W. "New American Etchings by Pennell." *International Studio* 38 (July 1909): 22–28.

"The Singer Building." *Architects' and Builders' Magazine* 9 (July 1907): 429–44.

"Sky Boys Who 'Rode the Ball' on the Empire State," *Literary Digest* 109 (23 May 1931): 30–32.

"The Skyscraper: Babel or Boon?" With Essays by Harvey Wiley Corbett and Henry H. Curran. *New York Times Magazine*, 5 December 1926, pp. 1–2.

"Skyscrapers" (review). *Outlook* 142 (3 March 1926): 314–15.

"Skyscrapers" (four designs); "Skyscrapers" (two designs). *Theatre Arts Monthly* 10 (March 1926): 147–53; 189–90.

"Skyscrapers by J.A. Carpenter at the Met." *New York Times*, 30 December 1926, p. 23.

"Skyscrapers by J.A. Carpenter Will Have Premiere at Met." *New York Times*, 8 February 1926, p. 25.

Solon, Leon V. "The Titan City Exhibition." *Architectural Record* 59 (January 1926): 92–94.

Spaeth, Sigmund. "Jazz Is Not Music." *Forum* 80 (August 1928): 267–71.

Stapley, Mildred, "The City of Towers." *Harper's Monthly* 123 (October 1911): 697–706.

"Stately Mansions" (the *Chicago Tribune* Competition). *Freeman* 7 (14 March 1923): 4–5.

Steffens, J. Lincoln. "The Modern Business Building." *Scribner's* 23 (July 1897): 37–61.

Steiner, Ralph. "Dramatic Photography, Four Studies." *Theatre Arts* 14 (January 1930): 77–80.

Stella, Joseph. "The Brooklyn Bridge (A page of my life)." *transition*, nos. 16–17 (June 1929): pp. 86–88.

———. "Discovery of America: Autobiographical Notes." *Art News* originally published in 1946 (October 1960): 41–42, 64–67.

———. "On Painting." *Broom* 1 (December 1921): 119–23.

Stewart, Patrick. "The European Art Invasion." *Arts* 51 (May 1977): 108–12.

Stieglitz, Alfred. "The First Great Clinic to Revitalize Art." *New York American*, 26 January 1913, sec. CE, p. 5.

———. "I Photograph the Flatiron — 1902" (in Six Happenings). *Twice a Year*, nos. 14–15 (Fall-Winter 1946): 188–91.

———. "Photographs by Paul Strand." *Camera Work*, no. 48 (October 1916): 11–12.

———. "Pictorial Photography." *Scribner's* 26 (November 1899): 528–37.

———. "A Plea for Art: Photography in America." *Photographic Mosaics* 28 (1892): 135–37.

Stone, Melville E. "Chicago." *Scribner's* 17 (June 1895): 665–71.

Storrs, John. "Museum of Artists." *Little Review* 9 (Winter 1922): 63.

Strand, Paul. "Alfred Stieglitz and a Machine." *Manuscripts*, no. 2 (March 1922), pp. 6–7.

———. "Photography and the New God." *Broom* 3 (November 1922): 252–58.

Studebaker, J.W. "The Age of Jazz." *Journal of Education* 109 (21 January 1929): 68.

"Sues 'Flatiron' Owners, Clothier Says Winds Deflected by Big Building Wrought Havoc." *New York Times*, 23 January 1903, p. 3:4.

Sullivan, Louis. "*Chicago Tribune* Competition." *Architectural Record* 53 (February 1923): 151–57.

Thompson, Jan. "Picabia and His Influence on American Art, 1913-1917." *Art Journal* 19 (Fall 1979): 14–21.

"Thunderbolt Hits the France in Bay—Woolworth Tower Hit." *New York Times*, 13 December 1912, p. 12.

"Took Poison in Flatiron." *New York Times*, 12 September 1904, p. 14.

"Tower 1000 Feet High." *New York Times*, 19 July 1908, p. 1.

"Towered Cities." *Living Age* 42 (2 January 1909): 45–47.

"Towers of Babel." *New York Times*, 7 March 1920, sec. 2, p. 2.

Towne, Francis E. "Albert Fleury, Painter." *Brush and Pencil* 12 (June 1903): 201–8.

Traks, John. "Birge Harrison." *Scribner's* 42 (November 1907): 576–84.

"Two Examples of Rendering by Hugh Ferriss." *American Architect* 120 (23 November 1921): 401, 413–14.

"2,000,000 Broadway Building." *New York Times*, 1 July 1910, sec. 6, p. 9.

"Upward Movement in Chicago." *Atlantic Monthly* 80 (October 1897): 34–47.

Van Rensselaer, Marianna Griswold. "Picturesque New York." *Century* 45 (December 1892): 164–75.

_____. "Places in New York." *Century* 53 (February 1897): 501–16.

"Vanity Fair's New Home—The Graybar Building." *Vanity Fair* 27 (March 1927): 77.

"Visits Woolworth Tower." *New York Times*, 20 October 1912, sec. 3, p. 6.

Walker, C. Howard. "America's Titanic Strength Expressed in Architecture." *Current History Monthly* 21 (January 1925): 550–55.

"Walkowitz, Abraham. New York. Interview with Abram Lerner and Bartlett Cowdrey, December 8 and December 22, 1958." *Archives of American Journal* 9 (January 1969): 10–16.

Walsh, George Ethelbert. "Modern Towers of Babel in New York." *Harper's Weekly* 51 (12 January 1907): 68–69.

Walt, Adrienne. "Guy Wiggins: American Impressionist." *American Art Review* 4 (December 1977): 100–13.

Ward, Clarence. "The Woolworth Building in New York City." *American Magazine of Art* 8 (December 1916): 54–60.

Ware, Alice Holdship. "Skyscrapers." *Survey* 56 (1 April 1926): 35–37.

Weber, Max. "Chinese Dolls and Modern Colorists." *Camera Work*, no. 31 (July 1910): 51.

_____. "The Filling of Space." *Platinum Print* 1 (December 1913): 6.

_____. "The Fourth Dimension from a Plastic Point of View." *Camera Work*, no. 31 (July 1910): 25.

_____. "The Workmass." *New York Evening Sun*, 5 September 1914, n.p.

_____. "Xochipolli, Lord of Flowers." *Camera Work*, no. 33 (January 1911): 34.

Wells, Herbert George. "Mr. Coburn's New York Photographs." *The Craftsman* 19 (February 1911): 464–68.

White, Israel. "Child Hassam—A Puritan." *International Studio* 45 (December 1911): 29–34.

Whiteman, Paul. "In Defense of Jazz and Its Makers." *New York Times Magazine*, 13 March 1927, p. 21.

Williams, Jesse Lynch. "The Waterfront of New York." With illustrations by Henry McCarter, W.R. Leigh, Jules Guerin, Shipley, Charles Hinton, E.C. Peixotto. *Scribner's* 26 (October 1899): 385–99.

Wilson, Edmund. "Progress and Poverty." *New Republic* 67 (20 May 1931): 13–16.

"Wind Causes Boys Death—Blows Him Under an Automobile Near Flatiron Building." *New York Times*, 6 February 1903, p. 1.

"Wonder of Work on Panama Canal by Joseph Pennell." *International Studio* 48 (December 1912): 132–42.

"Woolworth Building on Broadway Will Eclipse Singer Tower in Height." *New York Times*, 13 November 1910, sec. 8, p. 1.

"Woolworth Building Will Be World's Greatest Skyscraper." *New York Times*, 7 May 1911, sec. 8, p. 3.

Wright, Frank Lloyd. "The Architect and the Machine." *Architectural Record* 61 (May 1927): 394-96.

Yeh, Susan Fillin. "Charles Sheeler's 1923 'Self Portrait.' " *Arts* 52 (January 1978): 106-9.

_____. "Charles Sheeler's 'Upper Deck.' " *Arts* 50 (January 1979): 90-94.

Young, James C. "Titanic Forces Rear Up a New Skyline." *New York Times*, 15 November 1925, sec. 4, p. 6.

Zilczer, Judith K. "The Armory Show and the American Avant-Garde: A Reevaluation." *Arts* 53 (September 1978): 126-30.

_____. "Robert Coady, Forgotten Spokesman of Avant-Garde Art in America." *American Art Review* 2 (September–October 1975): 77-89.

Exhibition Catalogues and Books from Exhibitions

Abraham Walkowitz and Alfred Stieglitz: The "291" Years—1912-1917. Exhibition, 1 June-26 June 1976. New York: Zabriskie Gallery.

Abraham Walkowitz (1880-1965): 50 Early Works. New York: Bernard Danenberg Galleries, 1971.

Abraham Walkowitz: 50 Early Works. Exhibition, 23 February-13 March 1971. New York: Bernard Danenberg Galleries.

Abraham Walkowitz: The Early Years, 1895-1925. Exhibition, 9 January-3 February 1973. New York: Zabriskie Gallery.

Abraham Walkowitz: Works on Paper. Exhibition, 1 November-28 December 1975. Memphis, Tennessee: Brooks Memorial Art Gallery.

Ades, Dawn. *Dada and Surrealism Reviewed*. London: Arts Council of Great Britain, 1978.

Albert Fleury. Exhibition, November 1900. Detroit: Detroit Museum of Art.

Albert Gleizes and the Section D'Or. With an essay by Daniel Robbins. Exhibition, 28 October-5 December 1964. New York: Leonard Hutton Galleries.

Alvin Langdon Coburn, 1882-1966. With an essay by Paul Blatchford. Rochester: The International Museum of Photography at George Eastman House, 1966.

Alvin Langdon Coburn, 1882-1966. Exhibition of Photographs from the International Museum of Photography, at George Eastman House, Rochester. London: The Arts Council of Great Britain and Paul Blatchforth, 1978.

Amerika: Traum und Depression. Berlin: Akademie der Künste, 1981.

Bermingham, Peter. *American Art in the Barbizon Mood*. Washington, D.C.: Smithsonian Institution Press, 1975.

The Brooklyn Institute of Arts and Sciences. *The American Renaissance, 1876-1917*. New York: Pantheon Books, 1976.

The Brooklyn Museum. *The Great East River Bridge, 1883-1893*. New York: Harry N. Abrams, 1983.

Buildings: Architecture in American Modernism. Exhibition, 29 October-29 November 1980. New York: Hirschl and Adler Galleries.

Cahill, Holger. *Max Weber*. New York: The Downtown Gallery, 1930.

Catalogue of a Collection of Paintings by Birge Harrison. Exhibition, 15 December 1907-10 January 1908. Buffalo, New York: Buffalo Fine Arts Academy.

Catalogue of Exhibition of Paintings and Drawings by Max Weber. Exhibition, 1 February-13 February 1915. New York: The Print Gallery.

Catalogue of Paintings by Stefan Hirsch. Introduction by Stephan Bourgeois. 26 February-19 March 1927. New York: Bourgeois Galleries.

Childe Hassam. With a prefatory note by J. Alden Weir and a catalogue by Carl Zigrosser. New York: Frederick Keppel and Co., 1916.

Childe Hassam (checklist). Exhibition, 7 November 1959–3 December 1960. New York: Babcock Galleries.

Childe Hassam as a Printmaker. Exhibition, 28 July–11 September 1977. Introduction by David W. Kiehl. New York: Metropolitan Museum of Art.

Childe Hassam, 1859–1935. Exhibition, 18 February–7 March 1964. New York: Hirschl and Adler Galleries.

Coburn, Alvin Langdon. *New York From Its Pinnacles.* Exhibition. London: Goupil Gallery, 1913.

Corn, Wanda. *The Color of Mood: American Tonalism, 1880–1910.* San Francisco: M.H. DeYoung Museum, 1972.

Curry, Larry. *John Marin, 1870–1953.* Los Angeles: Los Angeles County Museum of Art, 1970.

Doezema, Marianne. *American Realism and the Industrial Age.* Cleveland: Cleveland Museum of Art, in cooperation with Indiana University Press, 1980.

Drawings of the Future City by Hugh Ferriss. Exhibition, 13 April–25 April, 1925. New York: The Anderson Galleries.

Dreier, Katherine. *Joseph Stella.* New York: Société Anonyme, 1923.

Exhibition of Paintings and Sculpture of Max Weber. Exhibition, 14 December–30 December 1915. New York: Montross Gallery.

Exhibition of Paintings by Birge Harrison. Exhibition, 1 January–20 January, 1907. Chicago: The Art Institute of Chicago.

Exhibition of Paintings by Birge Harrison. Exhibition, 7 March–22 March 1908. Philadelphia: Pennsylvania Academy of Fine Arts.

Exhibition of Paintings by Birge Harrison, N.A. Exhibition, 1 March–26 March 1911. Indianapolis: John Herron Art Institute.

Exhibition of Paintings, Sketches and Drawings by Kenneth Frazier, Birge Harrison, William H. Hyde and Allen Tucker. Exhibition, 17 February–1 March 1909. New York: The Century Club.

Exhibition of Paintings, Watercolors, Drawings, Etchings, Lithographs, Photographs and Old Prints of New York (checklist). Exhibition, 19 May–15 June 1923. New York: Wanamaker Gallery of Modern Decorative Art.

Exhibition of Works by Chicago Artists. Exhibition, 31 January–24 February 1901. Chicago: The Art Institute of Chicago.

Exposition de Dessins et Gravures de Louis Lozowick. Exhibition, 11 July–25 July 1928. Paris: Galerie Zak.

Farmer, Jane. *The Image of Urban Optimism.* Travelling exhibition. Washington, D.C.: Smithsonian Institution, 1977.

Fifty Years of Painting by Max Weber. Exhibition, 15 April–10 May 1969. New York: Bernard Danenberg Galleries.

Fletcher, Valerie. *Dreams and Nightmares, Utopian Visions in Modern Art.* Washington, D.C.: Smithsonian Institution Press, 1983.

Flint, Janet A. *Louis Lozowick: Drawings and Lithographs.* Exhibition, 12 September–23 November 1975. Washington, D.C.: National Collection of Fine Arts.

The Forum Exhibition of Modern American Painters. New York: Anderson Galleries, 1916.

Friedman, Martin. *The Precisionist View in American Art.* Minneapolis: Walker Art Center, 1960.

Gebhard, David. *Kem Weber: The Moderne in Southern California, 1920–1941.* Santa Barbara: University of California Art Galleries, 1969.

George Ault: Nocturnes. Introduction by John Baur. Exhibition, 7 December 1973–6 January 1974. New York: Whitney Museum of American Art.

Gleizes, Albert. "Art Européen—Art Américain." With a translation by Stephen Bourgeois. In *Annual Exhibition of Modern Art*. Exhibition, 3 May–24 May 1919. New York: Bourgeois Galleries.

Goodrich, Lloyd. *Max Weber: Retrospective Exhibition*. New York: Whitney Museum of American Art, 1949.

Griffith, Fuller. *The Lithographs of Childe Hassam*. Washington, D.C.: The Museum of History and Technolgoy, 1966.

Harvard University Fine Arts Library. *Guy C. Wiggins (1883–1962): American Impressionist*. Exhibition, 18 September–24 October 1970. Chicago: Campanile Galleries.

Hills, Patricia. *Turn-of-the-Century America*. New York: Whitney Museum of American Art, 1977.

Hulten, Pontus. *The Machine*. New York: Museum of Modern Art, 1968.

Inaugurating the New Wanamaker Building and a Tercentenary Pictorial Pageant of New York. New York, 1925.

John Marin: New York Drawings. Exhibition, 6 May–17 June 1978. New York: Marlborough Gallery, Inc.

John Marin: Watercolors, Oil Paintings, Etchings. Essays by Henry McBride, Marsden Hartley, and E.M. Benson. New York: Museum of Modern Art, 1936.

John Storrs (1885–1956): A Retrospective Exhibition of Sculpture. Exhibition, 13 November 1976–2 January 1977. Chicago: Museum of Contemporary Art.

Kraeft, June and Norman. *American Architectural Etchers: The Traditionalists (1900–1940)*. Exhibition at June 1 Gallery. Bethlehem, Connecticut, 1980.

Lieberman, William S., ed. *Art of the Twenties*. New York: Museum of Modern Art, 1979.

Louis Lozowick (1892–1973): Works in the Precisionist Manner. Exhibition, 16 February–15 March 1980. New York: Hirschl and Alder, Inc.

Louis Lozowick Lithographs. Introduction by Elke Solomon. Exhibition, 21 November 1972–1 January 1973. New York: Whitney Museum of American Art.

Machine Age Exposition Catalogue. New York: Little Review, 1927.

Man Ray. Introduction by Jules Langser. Los Angeles: Los Angeles County Museum of Art, 1966.

Marter, Joan M.; Tarbell, Roberta; Wechsler, Jeffrey. *Vanguard American Sculpture*. New Brunswick, New Jersey: Rutgers University Press, 1979.

Max Weber Memorial Exhibition. Exhibition, 19 January–18 February 1962. New York: The American Academy of Arts and Letters.

Max Weber Retrospective. Exhibition, 13 March–2 April 1930. New York: Museum of Modern Art, 1930.

Max Weber Retrospective Exhibition. Foreword by William H. Gerdts. Exhibition, 1 October–15 November 1959. Newark, New Jersey: The Newark Museum.

Max Weber: Sculpture, Drawings and Prints. Exhibition, 27 October–24 November 1979. New York: Forum Gallery.

Naef, Weston. *The Collection of Alfred Stieglitz: Fifty Pioneers of Modern Photography*. New York: Metropolitan Museum of Art, 1978.

National Collection of Fine Arts. *Charles Sheeler*. With essays by Martin Friedman, Bartlett Hayes, and Charles Millard. Washington, D.C.: Smithsonian Press, 1968.

Newhall, Nancy. *Paul Strand: Photographs, 1915–45*. New York: Museum of Modern Art, 1945.

O'Gorman, James F., ed. *Skyscraperism*. Exhibition, February–March 1979. Wellesley, Massachusetts: Wellesley College Museum.

Pennell, Elizabeth Robins. *Joseph Pennell*. Exhibition, 9 November 1926–2 January 1927. New York: Metropolitan Museum of Art.

Photography Rediscovered: American Photographs, 1900–1930. With an essay by David Travis and photographers' biographies by Anne Kennedy. New York: Whitney Museum of American Art, 1979.

Picturesque Chicago by Albert Fleury (checklist). Exhibition, 11 October–23 October 1900. Chicago: The Art Institute of Chicago.

Ralph Steiner: A Retrospective Exhibition. Organized by the Dartmouth College Museum and Galleries. Hanover, New Hampshire: Hopkins Center, 1979.

Robbins, Daniel. *Albert Gleizes (1881–1953)*. New York: Solomon R. Guggenheim Museum, 1964.

Robert Edmond Jones: Designs for the Theatre. Exhibition, 26 February–20 April 1958. New York: Whitney Museum of American Art.

The Rouge: The Image of Industry in the Art of Charles Sheeler and Diego Rivera. Foreword by Frederick J. Cummings. Preface by Mary Jane Jacobs and Linda Downs. Detroit: The Detroit Institute of Arts, 1978.

Rubin, William. *The Paintings of Gerald Murphy*. New York: The Museum of Modern Art, 1974.

Sawin, Martica. *Abraham Walkowitz, 1878–1965*. Salt Lake City, Utah: Utah Museum of Fine Arts, 1975.

Scott, David, and Bullard, E. John. *John Sloan, 1871–1951*. Washington, D.C.: National Gallery of Art, 1971.

Second Annual Exhibition of Paintings, Watercolors and Drawings of New York City (checklist). Exhibition, 23 April–15 May 1924. New York: Wanamaker Gallery of Modern Decorative Art.

Stefan Hirsch, 1899–1964: Retrospective Exhibition (checklist). Exhibition, 9 September–27 September 1964. Annandale-on-Hudson, New York: Bard College, 1964.

Stieglitz, Alfred. *Photographs at An American Place* (handwritten checklist by Stieglitz). Exhibition, 15 February–5 March 1932. Stieglitz Album in The Museum of Modern Art Library.

Tashjian, Dickran. *William Carlos Williams and the American Scene, 1920–1940*. New York: Whitney Museum of American Art, 1978.

Taylor, Joshua. *American as Art*. Washington, D.C.: The National Museum of American Art, 1976.

Tsujimoto, Karen. *The American Image: Precisionist Painting and Photography*. San Francisco: The San Francisco Museum of Modern Art, 1982.

Walkowitz. Exhibition, 30 December 1946–20 January 1947. New York: Egan Gallery.

Wilmerding, John, ed. *American Light: The Luminist Movement, 1850–1875*. Washington D.C.: National Gallery of Art, 1980.

Yeh, Susan Fillin. *The Precisionist Painters, 1916–1949*. Exhibition, 7 July–20 August 1976. Huntington, New York: Hecksher Museum.

Unpublished Sources

Papers, Theses, and Dissertations

Andersen, Stanley Peter. "American Ikon: Response to the Skyscraper, 1875–1934." Ph.D. dissertation, University of Minnestoa, 1960.

Black, Eugene R. "Robert Edmond Jones: Poetic Artist of the New Stagecraft." Ph.D. dissertation, University of Wisconsin, 1955.

Cox, Richard. "The New York Artist as a Social Critic, 1918–1933." Ph.D. dissertation, University of Wisconsin, 1973.

Docterman, Lillian. "The Stylistic Development of the Work of Charles Sheeler." Ph.D. dissertation, State University of Iowa, 1963.

Frackman, Noel. "John Storrs and the Origins of Art Deco." M.A. thesis, New York University, 1975.

Gibbs, Kenneth Turney. "Business Architectural Imagery: The Impact of Economic and Social Changes on Tall Office Buildings, 1870–1930." Ph.D. dissertation, Cornell University, 1976.

Greenough, Sarah E. "The Published Writings of Alfred Steiglitz." M.A. thesis, University of New Mexico, 1976.

Kies, Emily Bardock. "The City and the Machine: Urban and Industrial Illustration in America, 1880–1900." Ph.D. dissertation, Columbia University, 1971.

Lehman, Arnold. "The New York Skyscraper: A History of its Development, 1870–1939." Ph.D. dissertation, Yale University, 1974.

Milgrome, Abraham. "The Art of William Merritt Chase." Ph.D. dissertation, University of Pittsburgh, 1969.

Moak, Peter. "Cubism and the New World: The Influence of Cubism on American Painting, 1910–1920." Ph.D. dissertation, University of Pennsylvania, 1970.

North, Phylis Burkley. "Max Weber: The Early Paintings, 1905–1920." Ph.D. dissertation, University of Delaware, 1975.

Paynter, Edward Lloyd. "The Modern Sphinx: American Intellectuals and the Machine, 1910–1940." Ph.D. dissertation, University of California, Berkeley, 1971.

O'Dell, Kathy Rosalyn. "New York Night Imagery, 1900–1942." Seminar paper, University of California, Berkeley, and Stanford University, 1981.

Radde, Bruce. "Esthetic and Socio-Economic Factors of Skyscraper Design, 1880–1930." Ph.D. dissertation, University of California, Berkeley, 1975.

Ricciotti, Dominic. "The Urban Scene: Images of the City in American Painting, 1890–1930." Ph.D. dissertation, Indiana University, 1977.

Robbins, Daniel. "The Formation and Maturity of Albert Gleizes." Ph.D. dissertation, New York University, 1975.

Rosenblum, Naomi. "Paul Strand: The Early Years, 1910–1932." Ph.D. dissertation, City University of New York, 1978.

Roth, Moira. "Duchamp and America." Ph.D. dissertation, University of California, Berkeley, 1975.

Siegel, Priscilla. "Abraham Walkowitz: The Early Years of an Immigrant Artist." M.A. thesis, University of Deleware, 1976.

Silk, Gerald. "The Image of the Automobile in Modern Art." Ph.D. dissertation, University of Virginia, 1976.

Tarbell, Roberta Kupfian. "John Storrs and Max Weber: Early Life and Work." M.A. thesis, University of Delaware, 1968.

Yeh, Susan Fillin. "Charles Sheeler and the Machine Age." Ph.D. dissertation, City University of New York, 1981.

Zabel, Barbara Beth. "Louis Lozowick and Technological Optimism of the 1920's." Ph.D. dissertation, University of Virginia, 1978.

Zilczer, Judith. "The Aesthetic Struggle in America: Abstract Art and Theory in the Stieglitz Circle." Ph.D. dissertation, University of Delaware, 1975.

Zucker, Joel Stewart. "Ralph Steiner: Filmmaker and Still Photographer." Ph.D. dissertation, New York University, 1976.

Interviews

Sheeler, Charles. Bartlett Cowdrey. Interview, 9 December 1958. Washington, D.C., Archives of American Art, Charles Sheeler Papers.
Sheeler, Paul. Martin Friedman. Interview, 18 June 1959. Washington, D.C., Archives of American Art, Charles Sheeler Papers.
Strand, Paul. Milton Brown, New York. Interview, November 1971. Washington, D.C., Archives of American Art, Paul Strand Papers.
_____. Arnold Crane. Yvilenne, France. Interview, 1 October 1968. Washington, D.C., Archives of American Art, Paul Strand Papers.
Walkowitz, Abraham. Abram Lerner and Bartlett Cowdrey, New York. Interview, 8 December and 22 December 1958. Washington, D.C., Archives of American Art, Abraham Walkowitz Papers.
_____. Station W.N.Y.C., New York. Interview, 22 March 1944. Washington, D.C., Archives of American Art, Abraham Walkowitz Papers.

Specific Archival Material

Ault, Louise. *George Ault: A Biography*, n.d. Unpublished manuscript. Washington, D.C., The National Museum of American Art Library.
_____. Documentation written by Louise Ault for a collector, Mr. Bender, n.d. Washington, D.C., Archives of American Art, George Ault Papers, Reel D247.
Barker, Albert W. "A Painter of Modern Industrialism, The Notable Work of Colin Campbell Cooper," *Booklover's Magazine*. ca. 1905, pp. 327–30. Washington, D.C., The National Museum of American Art Library.
Craven, George M. *Charles Sheeler, A Self Inventory in the Machine Age* (undated manuscript). Washington, D.C., Archives of American Art, Charles Sheeler Papers, Reel NSH-1.
Stieglitz, Alfred. "The Hand Camera — Its Present Importance." *American Annual of Photography and Photographic Times Almanac for 1897*. New York, Museum of Modern Art Library.
_____. "Night Photography with the Introduction of Life." *American Annual of Photography and Photographic Times Almanac for 1898*. New York, Museum of Modern Art Library.
Walkowitz, Abraham. *A Portrait from the Objective to the Abstract* (pamphlet). 1937. Washington, D.C., The National Museum of American Art Library.
Weber, Max. "The New Humanity in Modern Art." *The Call Magazine*. 25 May 1919, pp. 2ff. Washington D.C., Archives of American Art, Max Weber Papers.
_____. "On the Brooklyn Bridge." 1912. Essay, 1 p. Washington, D.C., Archives of American Art, Max Weber Papers.

General Archival Sources

New Haven, Connecticut, Yale University, The Collection of American Literature, the Beinecke Rare Book and Manuscript Library, Alfred Stieglitz Archives, including exchange of letters between Stieglitz and Hart Crane, Alvin Langdon Coburn, Marius De Zayas, Marsden Hartley, Sadakichi Hartmann, Paul Haviland, John Marin, Mme. Picabia, Paul Rosenfeld, Edward Steichen, Gertrude Stein, Paul Strand, Karl Struss, Abraham Walkowitz, and Max Weber.
New York, Avery Library, Hugh Ferriss Papers.

New York, Museum of Modern Art Library, Files on Alfred Stieglitz, John Storrs, Max Weber, and Abraham Walkowitz.

New York, The New York Public Library, Astor, Lenox and Tilden Foundations, Rare Book and Manuscript Division, John Quinn Memorial Collection.

Rochester, New York, International Museum of Photography at the George Eastman House, Alvin Langdon Coburn Papers.

Washington, D.C., Library of Congress, Manuscript Division, The Pennell-Whistler Collection of the Papers of Joseph and Elizabeth Robins Pennell.

Washington, D.C., The National Museum of American Art, Archives of American Art, Papers of the following artists and institutions: American Academy of Arts and Letters, George Ault, Alvin Langdon Coburn, Childe Hassam, Louis Lozowick, John Marin, Miscellaneous Exhibition Catalogues, New York Public Library, Joseph Pennell, Charles Sheeler, John Storrs, Paul Strand, Abraham Walkowitz, Max Weber, and Whitney Museum.

Washington, D.C., The National Museum of American Art, Miscellaneous Files.

Other

Carpenter, John Alden. *Skyscrapers*, 1926. Recording with Meinhard von Zallinger, conductor. New York, American Recording Society.

Sheeler, Charles, and Strand, Paul. *Manhatta*, 1921. Film. With subtitles from the poetry of Walt Whitman. New York, Museum of Modern Art, Film Archives.

Skyscrapers. John Alden Carpenter orchestral score. New York: G. Schirmer Inc., 1926.

Index

Other DACAPO titles of interest